Cheryll –
May your adventures be
just as good!

Love,
Amy

James Joyce and Trieste

Recent Titles in
Contributions to the Study of World Literature

JAMES JOYCE AND TRIESTE

Peter Hartshorn

Foreword by Zack Bowen

Contributions to the Study of World Literature,
Number 86

GREENWOOD PRESS
Westport, Connecticut • London

Library of Congress Cataloging-in-Publication Data

Hartshorn, Peter, 1956–
    James Joyce and Trieste / Peter Hartshorn ; foreword by Zack
Bowen.
        p.   cm.—(Contributions to the study of world literature,
    ISSN 0738–9345 ; no. 86)
    Includes bibliographical references and index.
    ISBN 0–313–30252–9 (alk. paper)
    1. Joyce, James, 1882–1941—Homes and haunts—Italy—Trieste.
2. Joyce, James, 1882–1941—Knowledge—Italy—Trieste.   3. Irish—
Italy—Trieste—History—20th century.   4. Novelists, Irish—20th
century—Biography.   5. Trieste (Italy)—Civilization.   6. Trieste
(Italy)—Biography.   I. Title.   II. Series.
PR6019.09Z578   1997
823'.912—dc21
    [B]   97–9383

British Library Cataloguing in Publication Data is available.

Library of Congress Catalog Card Number: 97–9383
ISBN: 0–313–30252–9
ISSN: 0738–9345

First published in 1997

Greenwood Press, 88 Post Road West, Westport, CT 06881
An imprint of Greenwood Publishing Group, Inc.

Printed in the United States of America

The paper used in this book complies with the
Permanent Paper Standard issued by the National
Information Standards Organization (Z39.48–1984).

10 9 8 7 6 5 4 3 2

To Alfonso Mottola

Many of the things which had been complex before were now made simple. And it all boiled down to this: honesty, sincerity, no compromise with truth—those were the essentials of any art—and a writer, no matter what else he had, was just a hack without them.

Thomas Wolfe
You Can't Go Home Again

Contents

Photographs follow page 88.

Foreword

Peter Hartshorn provides the most readable and detailed account of James Joyce's Trieste years thus far. While he makes extensive use of already published materials and echoes the findings of Joyce biographers starting with Gorman and Ellmann, Hartshorn provides a historical, cultural background of Trieste that I have not found anywhere else and an enormously detailed account of the environment Joyce lived and worked in for ten of his most productive years as a writer.

This is a book that can be read with understanding and satisfaction by Joyceans and non-Joyceans alike, but Hartshorn took some risks in writing it. The introduction is a little disconcerting as it sets the stage with a dramatic, almost fictive-sounding account of Joyce's arrival in Trieste. But the first chapter, a colorful history of the city as an Austrian center of commerce with close ties and proximity to Italy, forms the political backdrop against which Joyce's life there is played out. A lot of this chapter might indeed be news to Joyceans, while the second chapter, with its contrasting account of Dublin, covers ground well known to the Joyce community but nevertheless necessary for the general reader in order to establish the attitudes Joyce carried with him to Trieste.

As the book builds step-by-step the life and times of Joyce in Trieste, the text becomes increasingly detailed in terms of both new information and the rearrangement of previously published material, especially the Joyce letters and Triestine historical documents newly translated for this book. With every succeeding page, the meticulous documentation of the account and the plausibility of the argument of Joyce's love/hate relationship with Trieste become more and more apparent. The book never strays from its ultimate purpose of informing what Joyce wrote. Everything is brought to bear on the literature. Nowhere are there any outlandish interpretive claims. Hartshorn handles the implications of Joyce's statements in an exceptionally open-minded way. Similarly, because he is so cautious about what to make of various people in Joyce's life and how they surfaced in Joyce's work, the biography is doubly convincing in its conclusions. For example, the author deals with the identification of Amalia Popper in *Giacomo Joyce* particularly well, stating the case for Popper fully and then pursuing all the other possibilities just as assiduously. His treatment of the obscene correspondence between Joyce and his wife is delicate yet manages to state the situation accurately and sufficiently for the purpose.

This eminently accessible book makes a singular contribution to Joyce scholarship and biographical interpretation.

Zack Bowen
University of Miami

Acknowledgments

When I started my research, I quickly realized that one major hurdle would be to absorb even a percentage of the Italian books, articles, and other material on Joyce and Trieste. So I am pleased to acknowledge the help I received in this endeavor from my father-in-law, Mr. Alfonso Mottola, and my wife, Cristina Hartshorn.

My research in Trieste was aided immensely by Mr. Mottola. A photographer and historian who has lived in Trieste for sixty years, Mr. Mottola tirelessly checked local archives in search of Joyce and offered insightful advice and analysis each step of the way. His spirited support and companionship was invaluable, and this project would have gone nowhere without it. Cristina had the unenviable role of translating the scores of books, articles, and letters sent by her father, a task she performed most effectively and with good cheer. Her help has been immeasurable.

I owe a large debt to others: Joseph Schork for his comments, support, and entertaining friendship; Joseph Cary, a fellow (and wiser) student of Trieste, for his enthusiastic assistance; Ira Nadel for giving the manuscript an early and perceptive reading; Zack Bowen for many encouraging words and for steering me in the right direction; Jim Stallings for a diligent reading (in a sickbed); and Stephen Brayton for his helpful insights on numerous points.

I also thank Robert Pack Browning, Robert Spoo, Carol Kealiher, and Corinna del Greco Lobner for additional help.

I thank the estate of James Joyce and Penguin USA for granting me permission to quote extensively from Joyce's letters and works, and Jeannette Joyce for permission to quote from the letters of Stanislaus Joyce.

At Greenwood Press, I thank Nina Pearlstein and Jason Azze for their guidance and editorial assistance, for which I was always grateful.

In Trieste, special thanks to Signora Ondina Ninino at the Museo di Storia ed Arte. Her patience and interest were always appreciated. The late Stelio Crise also gave generously of his time. Italo Svevo's daughter, the late Letizia Svevo Fonda

Savio, kindly answered my inquiries about Joyce and her parents and granted permission to quote from her father's letters.

I also express my gratitude to the following people: Dr. Claudio Bevilacqua, Dr. Grazia Bravar, On. Manlio Cecovini, Bruno Chersicla, Bruno Degrassi, the late Dr. Bianca Maria Favetta, Dr. Alberto Giammarini, Dragomir Elia Giorgi, Zora Koren, Luciano De Marchi Pirona, Nora Franca Poliaghi, Dr. Tino Sangiglio, Eddy Schleimer, the late Dr. Carlo Ulcigrai, Aldo and Xenia Venturini, Dr. Giorgio Voghera, and Marina Zennaro.

Sidney Huttner and Lori Curtis in the McFarland Library at the University of Tulsa and James Tyler in the Carl A. Kroch Library at Cornell University were most helpful.

Finally, I must acknowledge the youthful support of my children, Julia and Timothy, who regret only that Joyce did not write books with pictures in them.

Introduction

And trieste, ah trieste ate I my liver!

Finnegans Wake

Why is it I am destined to look so many times in my life with eyes of longing on Trieste?

letter from Joyce to Nora

The morning train passed along the cliffs high above the Adriatic Sea before descending toward the crowded harbor and finally pulling into the station. Among the people getting off was a young Irish couple, unmarried, completing the final leg of what had been a difficult and frustrating journey through much of Europe. Tired and nearly broke, the two made their way along the platform. No one met them; in fact, no one knew them. A rather desperate hope for employment—their most immediate worry—had drawn them across a continent to an entirely strange destination. But the man was not disheartened. If anything, he was emboldened by the bleak circumstances. He had suffered much in his life, yet he possessed an undeniable belief that not only success but fame awaited him.

The young traveller, a fledgling writer, was James Joyce. The city was Trieste, where Joyce would spend much of the next ten years with his companion, Nora Barnacle, in his obsessive quest to profoundly alter modern literature.

To Joyce, Trieste became a paradox. Often he was eager to abandon the city, but in later life he tended to reflect sentimentally upon his years there. Joyce's inconsistent views stem from the fact that, while he raised a young family and finally established himself as a writer in Trieste, he suffered terribly in the process.

That Joyce landed in Trieste at all was a surprise even to him. In the fall of 1904, at the age of twenty-two, he left Dublin for Switzerland in the mistaken belief that he had secured a teaching position in Zurich. He was sent on to Trieste where, excluding brief sojourns in Pola, Rome, and Dublin, he remained with his family until mid-1915. Following his wartime stay in neutral Zurich, Joyce returned to

Trieste for a period of eight months before moving in 1920 to France, where the publication of *Ulysses* secured for him the attention he sought, if not always the royalties.

What the Dublin Joyce knew about Trieste is unclear, but what he found there was a thriving port city, then under Austrian control, that reached the height of its prosperity during his stay. Located at the crossroads of Europe and the East and featuring a mosaic of cultures that created a dynamic and sometimes volatile political environment, Trieste was bustling with activity up to World War I. It was a city, however, in which entrepreneurs—not artists—made money, and Joyce quickly discovered the need to use his creative energy in both roles to survive. Joyce's lifestyle generally raised his ire more often than his income in Trieste.

The majority of his Triestine years were spent in literary obscurity—despite his ceaseless efforts for recognition—and poverty, much of which resulted more from his own irresponsibility than from meager wages. At the same time, Trieste was the place where Joyce and Nora settled and started a family after departing Ireland on an October night in 1904. In Trieste, both of their children were born, the family learned Italian and spoke the language at home, and Joyce achieved, far later and with much more anguish than he could have anticipated, a small measure of artistic fame. For Joyce, life in Trieste was an emotional and financial roller coaster that often severely tested his resourcefulness.

Joyce is most readily associated with the cities of his birth and his fame: Dublin and Paris. Yet, during the Triestine years, Joyce matured as a writer and completed substantial portions of *Dubliners*, *A Portrait of the Artist as a Young Man*, and *Ulysses*. Moreover, the city's effect on Joyce, as well as Joyce's impact on Trieste, have not been fully explored. This book brings Joyce and Trieste together, telling the story of the intriguing relationship between the man and the city.

James Joyce and Trieste

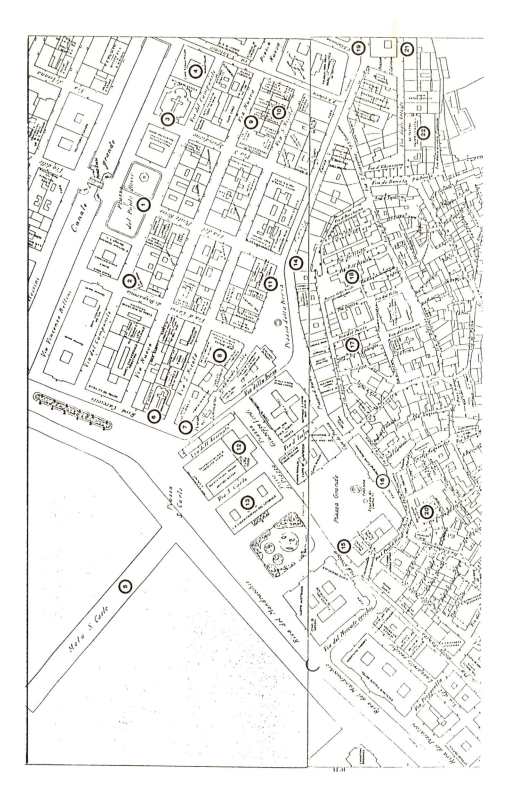

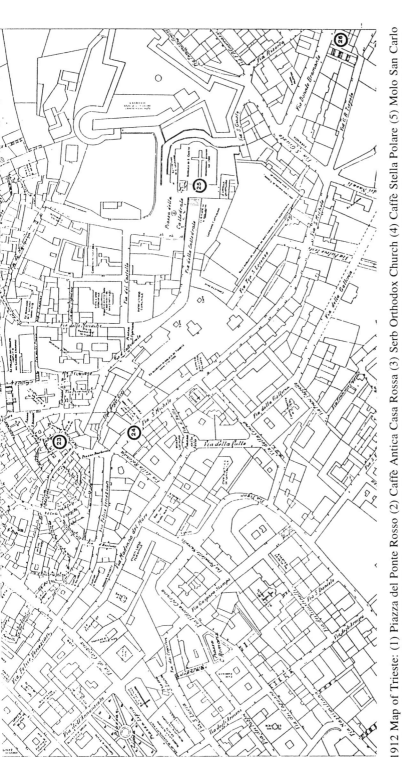

1912 Map of Trieste: (1) Piazza del Ponte Rosso (2) Caffè Antica Casa Rossa (3) Serb Orthodox Church (4) Caffè Stella Polare (5) Molo San Carlo (6) Greek Orthodox Church (7) Caffè Tommaseo (8) Restaurant Dreher (9) via Nuova 27 (10) via San Nicolò 30 and 32 (11) F.H. Schimpf's bookstore (12) Teatro Comunale Giuseppe Verdi (13) Palazzo della I.R. Luogotenenza (Austrian government headquarters) (14) *L'Indipendente* office (15) via Sanità 2 (16) Palazzo del Municipio (Trieste City Hall) (17) Trattoria Antica Marinella (18) Synagogue on via delle Scuole Israelitiche (19) via Santa Caterina 1 (20) Restaurant Bonavia (21) Synagogue on via del Monte (22) Teatro Filodrammatico (23) Arco di Riccardo (24) via San Michele (25) San Giusto (26) via Donato Bramante 4

1

Roman Roots

Trieste today stands as a somewhat forgotten city of Italy, tucked away along the country's extreme northeast Adriatic coast, just outside the border of Slovenia. Other than an occasional mention in the press because of its proximity to the recent war in the former Yugoslavia, Trieste receives little notice. It is not unusual, in fact, to find the expression "from Venice to Sicily" in references to the whole of Italy, as if the country exists only west of the Adriatic.

But Trieste was not always so neglected. For more than five hundred years, up to 1918, the city served as a key southern port in the Austrian Empire. Trieste's location made it an ideal facilitator of trade between the East, northern Africa, and the vast eastern European territory controlled by Austria, and it emerged as one of the economic strongholds of the empire. The city featured immense cultural diversity, with a mixture of people from Italian, German, Slav, Greek, and Albanian backgrounds, among many others.

When Joyce arrived, at the turn of the century, Trieste was at its economic peak. Yet, even then, many of its Italian citizens were clamoring for a return of the city to its mother country. Trieste's historical roots in the Italian culture extended far beyond its centuries under Austrian rule, all the way to pre-Roman days.

The founding date of Trieste is uncertain, but prior to the growth of the Roman Empire, it was a settlement largely influenced by the Veneti, who lived in the northern area of the peninsula and later founded Venice. Its original name, Tergeste, was derived from the Venetic words *terg* (market) and *este* (city).[1] The Romans formed a pact with the Veneti and took control of Tergeste, which grew in importance as the Romans built more roads in the area and commerce increased. (The Arco di Riccardo and a Roman theater, among other ruins, remain as examples of Trieste's Roman past.) Tergeste was overshadowed, however, by the major Roman port in the northern Adriatic, Aquileia, founded in 183 B.C. With the fall of Rome, barbarian attacks from the north on Aquileia and the outlying area caused business and trade to decline. Tergeste was thrust into a long, rather chaotic period of rule under numerous powers, including Charlemagne's Franks in the eighth century, when the city was given its present name.

Venice, which sought control of the Adriatic, was an ongoing threat to the city. Vastly weaker militarily, Trieste, in 1202, voluntarily submitted to Venetian domination. Trieste, though, kept an eye toward any alternative alliance that would be more favorable, the most obvious of which would be with Austria. But it was not until 1382 that Trieste and Austria could ally themselves, with Austria providing the city military protection as well as limited autonomy. Trieste finally was rid of its Adriatic rival and remained, with few brief exceptions, in the Austrian Empire until the end of World War I.

As one of Austria's few ports, Trieste had strategic relevance but did not begin to flourish commercially until the eighteenth century. Of particular significance was the forty-year reign (1740–1780) of Empress Maria Theresa. Her administrative, economic, and educational reforms turned Trieste into a thriving city with one of the world's most active ports.

The arrival of Napoleon's troops in 1797 temporarily disrupted Trieste's growth. But the nineteenth century would be highly profitable for the city. On one day in 1841, for example, fourteen ships from the United States alone were docked in Trieste.[2] The city's success was reflected along the waterfront, where monumental palaces were constructed to serve as headquarters for the successful insurance, shipping, and banking firms of the time.

The nationalist emotions stirred up during the Risorgimento in Italy deeply influenced Trieste. Both Venice and Milan had rebelled against Austrian rule in 1848, lending encouragement to the Italians in Trieste. The voices of Triestine irredentists, who demanded unification of the northeast territory of *Italia irredenta* (unredeemed Italy), especially Trieste, with the Italian state, were growing louder. Tacitly acknowledging the discontent while maintaining its grip on the city, Austria allowed some reform. In 1850, Trieste, now a city of fifty thousand, was classified as a provincial commune and was allowed to hold municipal elections, though the city's administrative head and police remained under Austrian supervision.

Trieste continued to flourish economically. Port traffic nearly doubled between 1860 and 1889, establishing Trieste as the leading Hapsburg port. A notable example of Trieste's significance was the large amount of Triestine capital and labor used to construct the Suez Canal in 1869.[3] Triestine financier Baron Pasquale Revoltella (who later established a school at which Joyce—most unhappily—taught English) invested heavily in the project, and the first vessel to pass through the canal was the Triestine ship *Primo*.

Of mounting concern to the Austrian authorities, though, were the Triestine irredentists, whose nationalist demands they found difficult to repress, particularly after the formation of the kingdom of Italy in 1861. While it was true that Trieste was a prosperous Austrian city with a rich ethnic mix, there was an undeniable groundswell of support, led by Italian intellectuals, for the idea that Trieste rightfully belonged under the aegis of Italy. The fact that a number of influential Jewish merchants and intellectuals, mindful of the anti-Semitism in Austria, found irredentism appealing helped the cause.

Irredentist pressure came not only from within Trieste but from Italy itself. Officially, the Italian government was not seeking the annexation of Trieste. But as early as 1845, some Risorgimento leaders had discussed the strategic benefits of extending the country's eastern frontier,[4] and in 1859, the Italian patriot Count di Cavour had stated his belief that Trieste one day would be part of Italy.[5] Developments in Trieste illustrated the controversy spawned by such views. In 1863, the Società di Ginnastica was formed to promote Italian culture, only to be followed by other organizations of Germans and Slavs—as well as Italians—in the nationalist rivalry.[6]

Perhaps most troubling to Austria was the rise of the irredentist press in Trieste. Publication of *L'Indipendente*, a pro-irredentist daily newspaper, began in 1877, and within a few months circulation had reached a respectable level of two thousand.[7] (The city's population was up to 130,000.) But the price of the paper was prohibitive, and irredentists sought a cheaper way of publicizing their cause. The result was a tabloid called *Il Piccolo*, founded in December 1881. Over the next three decades, its persistent support of irredentism would torment Vienna, with a little-known journalist—Joyce—playing a minor but curious role in the political wars. While never an irredentist, Joyce, through his connection to *Il Piccolo* and other nationalist institutions in Trieste, came to understand well the passion behind the movement.

Il Piccolo was the creation of a Jew named Teodoro Mayer, then only twenty-one. Mayer came from a poor background and had quit school to work to assist his family, but he was a devoted irredentist with boundless energy.[8] He had little money or help at the outset, so by necessity he put together and sold the newspaper at a tiny office at Piazza della Borsa 4. The first issue, dated December 29, 1881, was a mere two pages and sold only thirty-two copies. Mayer had seen the Austrians' harassment of *L'Indipendente* because of its open sympathy with irredentism, so he focused on general, not strictly political, news such as theater, which was quite popular in Trieste. He couched his pro-irredentist sentiments in very effective but subtle language that was less likely to arouse Austrian hostility. The Austrian government controlled the distribution sites of publications and was aware of Mayer's leanings. But because of the newspaper's sparse resources—Mayer had only two paid employees plus a reporter for the first year—the Austrians did not expect it to survive, and in January 1882 they granted *Il Piccolo* permission to be sold at tobacco stands. It was a decision they came to regret.

As the Austrians expected, the newspaper struggled initially. An evening edition, *Il Piccolo della Sera*, ceased publication after a few weeks, and Mayer concentrated on maintaining *Il Piccolo* as a morning journal. But 1882 would prove to be a turning point for both *Il Piccolo* and Trieste.

Irredentists already were annoyed over the state visit paid by Italy's King Umberto I to Austrian Emperor Francis Joseph in October 1881,[9] and their disappointment grew sharply when Italy joined Austria and Germany to form the Triple Alliance in 1882. From Italy's perspective, it was more practical at the moment to preserve good relations with Austria—even though nearly a million Italians were living under Austrian control—than to foment revolution for nationalist reasons in

Trieste. In addition, Trieste was Austria's major port, and a highly profitable one. Austria had no intention of losing it. Germany also favored stability in Trieste, as many of Trieste's most successful firms were German owned. Bismarck prized Trieste as "Germany's only port on the southern seas."[10]

The 1882 celebration of the five hundredth anniversary of Austrian rule in Trieste intensified the antagonism felt by both sides. To highlight the occasion, the Austrians organized a lavish international exhibition that opened in Trieste in August. Events spun out of control one day before the mid-September arrival of Francis Joseph when a young irredentist sympathizer from Trieste was discovered with two bombs on the Italian border. Wilhelm Oberdank, or the Italianized Guglielmo Oberdan, as he adamantly preferred, admitted his scheme of returning to Trieste to assassinate the emperor, and he was sentenced to death. Following his last defiant words of "Long live Italy! Long live free Trieste! Foreigners go home!" Oberdan was hanged in Trieste on December 20, 1882. He became an immediate martyr to the irredentists. Towns in Italy named streets and squares after him, Venice built a monument to him, and hymns and poems were dedicated to his memory.[11] In Trieste, Piazza Oberdan remains as a tribute to the fallen irredentist hero.

Much to the displeasure of the government, *Il Piccolo* shunned coverage of the extravagant exhibition but reported the Oberdan affair. Relations between the two sides deteriorated to the point that the Austrians began to sequester the paper routinely.[12] Such repression extended well beyond *Il Piccolo*: by 1885, Austria had prohibited the sale of 184 foreign journals, including 57 in Italian. Undaunted, Mayer gradually increased his paper's political content, despite the constant harassment it brought.[13] Concerned about Mayer's growing stature in Trieste, the Austrians tried and failed to deport him in 1885.[14]

The Austrians' actions only stiffened the opposition. *L'Indipendente* continued to publish, and Mayer resurrected *Il Piccolo della Sera* in 1886. Pressure also came from the Lega Nazionale, an organization begun in 1891 by one of Trieste's leading irredentists, Felice Venezian, to promote Italian culture in Trieste.[15]

An economic decline through the 1880s and the abolition of Trieste's *porto franco* (duty-free status) in 1891 increased anti-Austrian sentiment. The pendulum, though, was swinging both ways. Following the assassination of Empress Elisabeth of Austria by an Italian laborer in 1898, anti-Italian protests broke out in numerous places. In Trieste, spectators threw chairs and glasses at Italian musicians performing in an outdoor concert, and other rowdies stoned the offices of *Il Piccolo*.[16]

The political rhetoric grew more heated when socialists emerged as serious competitors to irredentists and to the growing number of Slav nationalists. The Partito Liberale Nazionale, the irredentist political party, was represented in the Vienna parliament by a young Triestine intellectual, Attilio Hortis. Hortis focused most of his attention on one overriding issue: unification with Italy. The socialists, themselves largely Italians, Slavs, and Austrians, offered a more universal agenda, including stances opposing militarism and supporting improved economic and social conditions for Triestine workers of all nationalities.[17] The socialist leader in Trieste, Valentino Pittoni, was a former irredentist who left largely because of the movement's uncompromising positions.[18] By the time of Joyce's arrival in 1904, the socialists were a legitimate party, further complicating an already labyrinthine political situation in Trieste.

Adding to the confusion were the mixed signals from Italy. Hardly eager to support the socialists or even Austria, its ally, the Italian government nevertheless maintained a neutral position toward the irredentists. In 1905 Foreign Minister Marquis di San Giuliano, seeking to reassure the Austrians, went so far as to state his belief that irredentism was gradually fading away,[19] a remark that must have struck the Austrians as black humor. Conversely, Ernesto Nathan, mayor of Rome and vice-president of the nationalist-leaning Dante Alighieri Society, called Trieste "a daughter of our common mother, Rome."[20] In 1910, an Italian general referred patriotically to the "hills bathed by the blood of our heroes, behind which are the unredeemed lands awaiting the hour of liberation."[21] Such posturing and hypocrisy on all sides inevitably led to more conflict and the ultimate disintegration of European order in 1914.

Irredentists were particularly concerned over the growing presence of the Slavs, mostly Slovenes from nearby towns but also including Serbs, Montenegrins, and Croats, who were drawn to Trieste by job opportunities.[22] Irredentists saw the potential for the group's political exploitation by the Austrian authorities, who clearly approved of the influx of Slavs as a counterbalance to irredentist pressure. The Austrians financed Slav schools and considered other measures favorable to Slavs.[23] Additional support for the Austrian position came from the Catholic Church: Catholic faith among Slavs often was strong in the surrounding countryside and, increasingly, in Trieste itself.[24] At the same time, the Italian Triestine middle class generally was not actively involved in church affairs, and a number of leading irredentists were not Catholic but Jewish. (In *A Farewell to Arms*, Hemingway noted another factor: an Italian officer commented derisively to a priest, "The Pope wants the Austrians to win the war. . . . He loves Franz Joseph. That's where the money comes from.")[25]

Still, for most Slavs, economic survival surpassed religion as a priority, so many were compelled to learn Italian in their effort to gain employment.[26] Inexorably, Slavs established themselves in Trieste. During Joyce's time, more than two hundred cultural and economic unions and clubs of Slovenes and Croats existed in the city.[27] Conflict with the Italians grew inevitable.

One obvious area of competition was education. Trieste could never pretend to rival the great Italian or Austrian cities as a center of culture, but learning was taken seriously by all sides. Slovenes at that time were debating whether to locate the first Slovene university in Trieste or Ljubljana.[28] Triestine irredentists had long advocated the establishment of an Italian university in Trieste, a move that Austria, naturally fearing any promotion of irredentism, rejected repeatedly.[29] Francis Joseph asserted to an Italian politician in 1904 that Trieste would never get an Italian university.[30]

In a conciliatory gesture, though, the Austrians did provide some law classes in Italian at the University of Innsbruck. In November 1904, a clash between German and Italian students erupted, and 137 students—all Italians—were arrested,[31] leading to a large irredentist demonstration in Trieste.[32] Even the Università Popolare, opened by irredentists in 1899 as an evening school for college students (and where Joyce later lectured), appeared to be a move designed mainly to counter the socialists' Circolo di Studi Sociali, which offered classes, a library, and public lectures.[33]

Critics of irredentism saw these actions as mere political ploys, with no sincere intention of addressing education problems. No faction, however, was truly above the fray. Triestine writer Scipio Slataper, himself of an Italian-Slav background, deeply regretted the bickering: "This great issue is simply being exploited in a game of party politics," he wrote.[34] As Joyce would quickly discover, political partisanship sharply divided Triestines.

2

The Dubliner

When Joyce arrived in 1904, Trieste contrasted economically and socially with Dublin. As a thriving seaport, Trieste saw its population swell from 145,000 to 230,000 between 1880 and 1910.[1] Many Dubliners dreamed of such prosperity, and their dreams were reflected daily along Dublin's piers. Hopeful emigrants, many bound for the United States, exchanged tearful goodbyes with family members. Despite the sad farewells, most of those leaving Dublin undoubtedly believed that whatever they found at the end of their journey would be a significant improvement over the conditions they had left, and the remaining family members could only envy them.

Catholic faith was strong in Dublin, but piety often was the only source of strength for the impoverished. Of the sixty thousand families in Dublin in 1904, nearly 40 percent of them lived in single rooms, with as many as ten to twelve people in a room.[2] One-third of the city's population consisted of unskilled laborers, hawkers, messengers, and other irregular workers, all of whom lived in poverty. Almost half of the deaths in Dublin occurred in charitable institutions, and the death rate of 23.3 per 1000 was high even compared to a rate of 16.1 in London, a city with its own large underclass.[3] A French newspaper referred to Dublin as the worst slum in Europe.[4]

The young Joyce, generally energetic, despaired occasionally over the bleak surroundings. Before leaving Dublin with Nora Barnacle, he confided to her that he saw no "naturalness or honesty" in Dublin life: "People live together in the same houses all their lives and at the end they are as far apart as ever."[5] Such conditions led to Joyce's later observation, "Italy . . . has two things to balance its miserable poverty and mismanagement: a lively intellectual movement and a good climate. Ireland is Italy without these two."[6]

Joyce and Nora certainly had known poverty in Ireland, although at the time of Joyce's birth in 1882, the Joyce family was living well enough. His father, John Stanislaus Joyce, held a sinecure in the Office of the Collector-General of Rates and Taxes in Dublin.[7] While he was already a man of "absolutely unreliable tem-per," as Joyce's younger brother Stanislaus recalled, John Joyce had not yet made home life unbearable.[8] Bozena Berta Delimata, the daughter of Joyce's sister Eileen, was told by her mother of many happy evenings in the Joyce house during which Joyce's mother, May, played the piano and his father and the children sang.[9]

In the 1890s, however, misfortune struck the family. John Joyce's bureaucratic position was eliminated, leaving him with a pension of one-third of his salary. The family began a nomadic existence, moving nine times in an eleven-year period mainly because John Joyce could not pay the rent,[10] a problem that also would plague James throughout the Trieste years. Each place was worse than the last, and the father's drinking and harassment of his family increased. Of greater conse-quence, illness set in. Joyce's brother George, the youngest in the family, died tragically of peritonitis in 1902 at the age of fourteen. The boy remained conscious and calm to his last moments, only saying to his mother, "I am very young to die."[11] Stanislaus wrote that their mother never recovered from the shock of George's death, and she passed away the following year.

The complexity of Joyce's nature can be seen in his relationship with his mother. During her sickness, he (and Stanislaus) refused to kneel in prayer as she lay dying in bed.[12] One of Joyce's best friends, J. F. Byrne, bristled at his action: "Joyce's attitude towards his mother affected me keenly. . . . I thought he was cal-lous, and did not hesitate to tell him so."[13] Yet, another close friend, Oliver St. John Gogarty (who later became a well-known writer and physician), remembered Joyce's deep attachment to his mother and his (Joyce's) description of how "he had seen her with her delicate fingers red from the lice she had killed on the bodies of his starving sisters."[14]

Family members themselves offered somewhat conflicting reports on mother and son. Eileen stated that James was their mother's favorite child; he "completely depended on her, not only for the usual sort of care, but even more for her moral support. He wanted her to believe that he would do well as a writer." During his mother's final illness, Joyce was the only one who could cheer her. "He used to sing for her, accompanying himself on the piano and leaving the doors open so that she could hear him. She liked that. It soothed her," Eileen recalled.[15] Another sister, May, believed that Joyce felt "remorse" toward their mother. "He hurt her badly by his way of life. She always was ambitious for him. She knew that he was very clever and probably would make a name in writing, but she was saddened by his falling away from the church," she said.[16]

Nora also had few comforts while growing up. She was born in 1884 in Galway, a city that knew great misery in the late nineteenth century. Most families lived in crowded tenements. Unemployment was high, and many of the jobs that existed were seasonal and temporary.[17] Hunger and disease were common plights.

Nora's father, Thomas Barnacle, worked as a baker. He was illiterate, with a weakness for alcohol,[18] and eventually was sent packing by his wife. Raised at various times by her mother, grandmother, and uncle, Nora lived a contented but poor life in Galway for twenty years.

By 1904, however, Nora was growing restless. A young, attractive woman of strong instincts, Nora saw little opportunity for independence or advancement in Galway. In early 1904, she boarded a train for Dublin, where she soon had her fateful meeting with Joyce on June 10 and their more famous first date on June 16, or Bloomsday.

Joyce and Nora did not flee Dublin only because they were tired of being poor. Joyce's irritation with his life in Ireland had been growing for several years before the Irish, as he put it, "drove me out of their hospitable bog."[19] His unhappiness had a variety of sources: his disgust with the current nationalistic focus of Irish literature, the oppressiveness of the Catholic Church, and his perceived lack of artistic freedom.

Literary activity in Dublin at that time was gaining world attention. William Butler Yeats had helped to establish the Abbey Theatre, and other recognized Dublin writers included Lady Gregory, J. M. Synge, George Russell, and Padraic Colum. Yet Joyce was not impressed. He had little interest in limiting himself to the myths and folktales on which other Irish writers, particularly Yeats and Lady Gregory, chose to focus. His goal was to present Dublin, the real Dublin as he knew it, to the world, and he rejected any traditional beliefs that interfered.

No better, Joyce thought, were Ireland's religious leaders. His personal struggle with Catholicism was nearly lifelong. Strongly influenced by his early Catholic education and his pious mother, Joyce as a child viewed the church as a benevolent protector and clearly was a "believer." His initial skepticism may have arisen from his disquieting recognition of, in his eyes, the unseemly politicization of religion in Ireland,[20] as well as the church's restrictive views on sexuality. His personal faith shaken, Joyce grew deeply bitter over the rigid hold of the Catholic Church on his country. He referred contemptuously to "the bloody nonsense that has been written about Ireland!—parish froth! I intend to lift it into the international sphere and get away from the parish pump."[21]

In a letter to Nora prior to their departure from Dublin, Joyce expressed the depth of his discontent with the church. He wrote,

My mind rejects the whole present social order and Christianity. . . . Six years ago I left the Catholic Church, hating it most fervently. I found it impossible for me to remain in it on account of the impulses of my nature. I made secret war upon it when I was a student and declined to accept the positions it offered me. By doing this I made myself a beggar but I retained my pride. Now I make open war upon it by what I write and say and do.[22]

Joyce remained consistent in these feelings throughout his life. Eugene Jolas, a close friend in Paris who later published segments of *Finnegans Wake* under the title "Work in Progress" in his literary magazine *transition*, recalled that Joyce's antireligious convictions were "unshakeable." Joyce's daughter, Lucia, showed an interest in Catholicism, to which Joyce responded, "Why should a young woman bother her head about such things? Buddha and Confucius and all the others were not able to understand anything about it. We know nothing, and never shall know anything."[23] Nora continued to respect Joyce's religious views following his death in 1941. When the possibility of having a Catholic service for him was raised, Nora replied, "I couldn't do that to him."[24]

Chief among the reasons why Joyce rejected religion was the supreme confidence he displayed in his own genius. He was afraid of failure "least of all," according to Frank Budgen, an artist Joyce befriended in Zurich during World War I. "His confidence in himself was as unbounded as it appeared to be," Budgen wrote.[25] Still, Joyce felt entirely misunderstood, a perception that hindered his relationships.

A number of influential Irish writers, including Russell and Yeats, recognized Joyce's ability and tried to assist his writing career, but Joyce possessed an arrogance that, despite his young age, allowed him to speak fearlessly. Even his first meeting with Yeats did not faze him. Yeats recalled that Joyce approached him in the street, saying that he had written some poems and that they had a common friend (Russell, who had spoken highly of Joyce to Yeats). Yeats agreed to meet Joyce to listen to his work, after which he offered praise and support. Joyce replied, "I really don't care whether you like what I'm doing or not. It won't make the least difference to me. Indeed I don't know why I'm reading to you."[26] Joyce then continued his assault, objecting to everything Yeats had written and asking him why he wasted his time on politics and folklore. He implied that Yeats had lost his creative inspiration. The discussion went on until Joyce got up to leave, stating his age and asking Yeats about his. Yeats told him, and Joyce replied with a sigh, "I thought as much. I have met you too late. You are too old." Yeats reported to friends, "Never have I seen so much pretension with so little to show for it."[27] Joyce later told Budgen that the conversation as reported was untrue.[28] Stanislaus conceded that James always denied the story, but he (Stanislaus) believed it to be substantially correct.[29]

Regardless, Yeats continued to help Joyce when possible. One example was his effort in 1915 to garner financial support for Joyce in wartime Zurich; an appreciative Joyce replied, "I cannot thank you enough for your kindness in taking so much trouble in the matter."[30] As years passed, Joyce showed respect for the Irish poet, often reciting Yeats's work from memory.[31] Their friendship lasted until Yeats's death in 1939. In his final homage, Joyce sent a funeral wreath and tribute to the grave.[32]

Yeats's close friend, Lady Gregory, did not fare as well with Joyce. To assist Joyce, she provided a letter introducing him to E. V. Longworth, the editor of the *Daily Express* of Dublin. Longworth agreed to hire Joyce as a book reviewer during his stay in Paris in 1902-03. In return, Joyce initially sent her a letter of gratitude but later used a review entitled "The Soul of Ireland" to attack one of her folklore books.[33] He included the incident in *Ulysses*, describing her as "that old hake Gregory."[34] Naturally stung by the criticism, Lady Gregory nevertheless maintained her perspective, writing in 1920 that although she disliked his fiction, she retained "a profound respect" for him and his work.[35]

But it was Joyce's impetuous nature that caused him to air grievances, to seek revenge, and, ultimately, to escape enemies who did not exist. Joyce, in fact, made an impressive group of friends in Dublin precisely because of his own positive characteristics. He had a keen and curious mind, a sharp sense of humor, a love of literature, music, and history, and a gift for conversation that, somewhat unfortunately for Joyce, thrived mainly in small settings. Yet, Joyce often felt that his Dublin friends did not understand or support him—even as they were lending him money or taking an active interest in his writing—and he would accuse them accordingly.

Such behavior strained relationships and painted Joyce as an eccentric. Critic Leon Edel commented, "He had loyal, devoted friends, but . . . friends existed to be used. . . . He is very concrete, very demanding, utterly egocentric."[36] More than once, Joyce acknowledged his own deliberate complicity in these clashes. He wrote to Stanislaus in May 1905 that it was "a youthfully exaggerated feeling of this maldisposition of affairs which urged me to pounce upon the falsehood in their attitude towards me as an excuse for escape."[37] In Dublin, Joyce confided to Nora, "There is something also a little devilish in me that makes me delight in breaking down people's ideas of me and proving that I am really selfish, proud, cunning and regardless of others."[38] Joyce seemed to enjoy playing the role of victim, and to the extent that he could position his exile in this light, he did.

Joyce's impatience with Ireland was reflected in the statements of his fictional (but highly autobiographical) characters. In *A Portrait of the Artist as a Young Man*, Stephen Dedalus observed, "Ireland is the old sow that eats her farrow."[39] Joyce's exasperation probably was best expressed through Stephen Dedalus's comment, "When the soul of a man is born in this country there are nets flung at it to hold it back from flight. You talk to me of nationality, language, religion. I shall try to fly by those nets."[40] Joyce had little reason or intent to remain in his native land.

How curious Joyce was about the response of his friends to his departure is somewhat vague. At times he appeared to be unconcerned over how others viewed him. When Byrne and he were discussing the accuracy of a biography on Joyce years later, Joyce exclaimed, "Ah, sure I don't care what they write."[41] Byrne stated, "At no time since I knew him, and that was from the time he was 11 years old, did Joyce care what the vast majority of people said or wrote about him."[42]

Joyce, however, already had left Ireland once—for Paris—and he may have thought of his next move abroad as a short trip designed to have maximum impact on his friends and on literary Ireland. He told Nora a week before their departure, "It amuses me to think of the effect the news of it will cause in my circle."[43] It is obvious from his letters to Stanislaus that Joyce was acutely conscious of how his "circle" viewed his status, and he gave strict instructions to his brother regarding what information about him should be circulated. At the same time, Joyce followed closely the Dublin scene. Padraic Colum, a friend of Joyce, asserted that "there is no doubt that Joyce looked forward to a return to Ireland with Nora when he would be recognized and honored."[44] Jocular predictions by friends that Joyce might return as a beggar or a drunk surely fueled his desire to succeed.[45]

Joyce, though, did not hate Ireland, even as he endlessly criticized it. In truth, he was devoted to his country in the sense that his life's work provides a portrait of Ireland and its people that has never been equaled. Joyce himself once called Dublin his "first city of the world."[46] However, Joyce held Ireland to unfair standards. Ireland had great writers, for example, but Joyce was largely unimpressed. He also studied Irish history in detail, an indication of his determination to understand his native land, yet his observations regarding the Irish tended to lament missed opportunities rather than to note accomplishments. Still, he believed that Ireland must be presented to the world. Not surprisingly, he saw himself as uniquely able to carry out this mission, which became the focus of his work. Joyce was Ireland's greatest publicist, if not its most supportive.

Nora's reasons for agreeing to leave Ireland with Joyce are not difficult to understand. While Joyce had made no marital commitment to her, Nora had few strong ties to Ireland. She had already left Galway behind, and she had been in Dublin less than one year. Moreover, like Joyce, she had an adventurous spirit, so a trip abroad—and a chance to escape the poverty of Ireland—must have seemed enticing. Joyce did not minimize the uncertain future they would face. He told her that she would be sharing a "hazardous life" with him,[47] and he asked her several times if she were sure of her decision. Nora was undeterred.

Joyce's attachment to Nora underscored his ambiguous feelings toward women. While his affection for Nora was sincere, Joyce to that point had found much of his contact with women only in Dublin's brothels. "He considered sexual contact a necessary physical fulfillment and made no apologies for it," Stanislaus observed.[48]

At the same time, Stanislaus noted that Joyce "longed to copulate with a soul,"[49] a desire satisfied in his relationship with Nora. She was "the most beautiful and simple soul in the world" to Joyce, and he opened his heart to Nora as he had never done with another woman.[50] He told her, "I never could speak to the girls I used to meet at houses. Their false manners checked me at once. Then you came to me."[51]

The mutual attraction was not only emotional but physical. Nora had an alluring appearance, accented by her seductively thick, red-brown hair. Joyce also cut a rather striking figure; his former University College classmate Constantine Curran described him as "tall, slim, and elegant; [he had] an erect and loose carriage, an up-tilted, long, narrow head, with a chin that jutted out arrogantly; firm, tight shut mouth, blue eyes that for all their myopic look could glare suddenly or stare with indignant wonder; a high forehead that bulged under stiff-standing hair."[52] Their need for one another was the underpinning that bound them together for the next four decades.

3

Exile

Joyce was twenty-two and Nora twenty when they saw Trieste for the first time. They arrived in the Adriatic seaport on October 20, 1904, although Trieste had hardly been in their plans when they departed Dublin nearly two weeks earlier. In September Joyce had written to the Berlitz School in London seeking a European position and was informed that a job awaited him in Zurich. After borrowing money from numerous friends, including Lady Gregory and George Russell, he had only enough to reach Paris.[1]

Nevertheless, he left Dublin's North Wall, a quay along the Liffey River, on the night of October 8. Stanislaus and John Joyce came to see Joyce off, but only Stanislaus knew of Nora, who had boarded separately. The subterfuge met immediate misfortune when Nora was spotted by a friend of Joyce's father, who quickly suspected her purpose on the boat. By the time he reported the news to Joyce's father, however, the boat had departed. John Joyce initially was stunned when told of Nora's presence, but after he learned that her last name was Barnacle, he replied in good humor, "She'll never leave him."[2]

Joyce and Nora disembarked at Liverpool and boarded a train for London, where Joyce planned to visit influential critic and poet Arthur Symons, whom he had met through Yeats in 1902.[3] Symons had agreed to help Joyce find a publisher for *Chamber Music*, Joyce's first volume of poetry, which Symons called remarkably good.[4] A small loan was probably on Joyce's mind more than his poetry, but Symons, unfortunately, was not home.[5] During the visit, Joyce left Nora alone in a park for what would be the first of several such waits during the long journey, a pattern that did little to reassure her. Nearly broke, they continued on to Paris, where Joyce sought help from old Paris friends while Nora again waited in a park. He was able to secure enough money to finish the journey to Zurich, where they arrived on the morning of October 11.[6]

Joyce's relief quickly vanished when he visited the Berlitz School that same morning and discovered that his position did not exist. Herr Malacrida, the school's director, knew nothing of Joyce and had no vacancy. Shocked, Joyce appealed to Berlitz headquarters in Vienna but received only a statement of innocence from the director.

Luckily for Joyce, Malacrida sympathized with him and offered to help. After a week of anxious waiting, Joyce learned through Malacrida that a Berlitz teaching post was available in the Austrian city of Trieste.[7] So Joyce and Nora headed by train for Trieste, only to disembark mistakenly in Ljubljana, where they had to spend the night in a park.[8] Finally, on October 20, they arrived in the city that would be their home for most of the next eleven years. Joyce left Nora to sit on another park bench, this one in the Piazza della Stazione across from the busy Trieste train station, an important stop along the Orient Express. He set out to take care of their immediate business; instead, he landed in jail.

From the train station Joyce walked about a mile along the waterfront to Piazza Grande (now Piazza Unità). A squadron of twelve British ships was docked in Trieste,[9] and Joyce entered a conversation with three English sailors in a pub. They were scheduled to depart for Venice that day, and they may have been indulging in a final toast when their carousing grew out of control and led to their arrest. Playing the role of good samaritan, Joyce tried to act as an intermediary for the sailors, who spoke no Italian; in fact, some English-speaking policemen had been hired specifically to avert problems with the sailors.[10] The police asked Joyce to accompany them as an interpreter to the via San Nicolò station, a few blocks away, but in the ensuing confusion all four were jailed.

Stunned, Joyce demanded a meeting with the British consul, Harry Lionel Churchill,[11] who was not impressed by Joyce's story, suspecting that he had deserted his ship, and provided little sympathy. Churchill ultimately secured his release, but Joyce, contemptuous of the British (he once stated, "An Irish safety pin is more important to me than an English epic"),[12] never forgot the arrogance of the Englishman. Joyce finally returned to the park to get Nora, and the two left and walked back down via della Stazione to the centerpiece of the harbor, the Canale grande.[13]

For a change, luck was with Joyce, and he was able to find a room in the Piazza del Ponte Rosso, alongside the canal in the heart of the city.[14] From there, Joyce and Nora could easily view the bustling activity of the *venderigole*, women sellers who came daily from the villages around Trieste to the hectic outdoor fish markets and vegetable and fruit stalls crowded along the canal. The area left an impression on both newcomers. With his eye for detail, Joyce later wrote in *Giacomo Joyce*, "The Sellers offer on their altars the first fruits: green flecked lemons, jewelled cherries, shameful peaches with torn leaves."[15] During a stay in Locarno, Switzerland, in 1917, Nora recalled vividly the old days near the canal: "Yesterday was market day and it was quite lively to hear the men calling out the prices and making as much noise as they could just like in Triest they are just like Italians lively and dirty and disorderly."[16]

Adding to the chaotic environment were the numerous carts and carriages pulled by oxen, donkeys, or horses that remained the typical mode of transportation, as automobiles and an electric tram had become available only recently in Trieste. The *macigno* (stone) that covered the streets often broke apart under the heavy traffic, filling the air with dust.[17] Perhaps most annoying to Joyce was the frequent barking of the dogs that were used to guard the many ships docked in the canal.[18] From his apartment window, Joyce no doubt quickly grasped that commerce was the essence of the city.

Joyce had barely recovered from his skirmish with the police when misfortune struck again. Upon inquiring about employment at the nearby Berlitz School at via San Nicolò 32, he was informed by the assistant director, Giuseppe Bertelli, that no position was open. Joyce, though, was a survivor. He always had a unique way of evading what seemed to be inevitable crises. "I never knew anyone with such a gift for getting people to do things for him," his later friend Stuart Gilbert observed.[19] Describing his resourcefulness to Stanislaus in Dublin, Joyce reported: "When I was told to leave I spent days looking for a post as English correspondent in a commercial house. We had a terrible time for some days, I of course borrowing *in Trieste* right left and centre. I succeeded however in getting one tuition and could have done well in private lessons if I had had money to keep me alive."[20]

Forced to scramble for lodgings, Joyce and Nora changed their address at least four times over a ten-day period in Trieste.[21] This was a particularly distressing time for Nora: she had been moving constantly with Joyce since their departure from Dublin, and she now found herself virtually penniless in an Austrian city where most people spoke Italian, a language totally foreign to her. To Joyce, however, such turmoil was barely a distraction, and his ability to write under unusually stressful conditions would prove invaluable over the next decade in Trieste. In Zurich he had finished the twelfth chapter of his autobiographical novel *Stephen Hero*, which he had started in Dublin, and he began a story, "Christmas Eve," that was later completed under the title "Clay."[22]

The employment situation improved when Joyce met the director of the Berlitz School, Almidano Artifoni, whose name he would appropriate for *Ulysses*. Eying naval officers as potential students, Artifoni recently had established a new Berlitz School in Pola, site of a major Austrian port 150 miles south of Trieste along the Istrian coast. (Pola, renamed Pula, is now a Croatian port.) Sympathetic to Joyce's plight, Artifoni offered him a teaching position at the Pola school. The only problem was Joyce's marital status: after Joyce admitted that he was single and travelling with a young woman, Artifoni recommended that he sign all papers as if he and Nora were married.[23] So, after barely a chance to see more than the busy waterfront, the two departed Trieste in late October 1904 on the SS *Graf Wurmbrand*, headed for Pola.[24]

Their arrival was noteworthy due to their threadbare appearance and Joyce's remarkable self-assurance. Alessandro Francini-Bruni, Joyce's friend and fellow teacher (of Italian) in Pola,[25] had a gift for caricature that found a perfect subject in the enigmatic Irishman:

Ragged and tattered as a beggar, he dragged along nonchalantly a hyena of a suitcase that had lost its fur but not its vice of laughing immoderately at the distress of its owner and master. From every rent in it things hung dangling in the breeze, but he did not trouble himself to tuck them in. On the contrary, he dragged it behind him with absolute poise, hobbling along as if it were the most natural thing in the world.[26]

While Trieste and Pola were significant Austrian ports, they differed sharply in purpose. Pola's excellent harbor had convinced the Austrians in 1863 to build their largest naval arsenal and dockyard there, and it was still the most prominent Austrian military port when Joyce arrived.[27] Although smaller than Trieste, Pola was similar to its northern neighbor in being a city of numerous languages. German was the city's official language, but in fact Italian was the most popular. In 1900, nineteen thousand of Pola's twenty-five thousand citizens were Italian,[28] and the population in the surrounding villages was largely Croatian.[29] The Berlitz School itself offered courses in German, Italian, English, Croatian, and even Japanese,[30] so Joyce found himself in another linguistic melting pot along the Adriatic. Not surprisingly, the majority of his students were Austrian naval officers,[31] and his teaching position provided him with a relatively livable wage of two pounds for sixteen hours of work.[32]

In his early letters home, Joyce did not complain about his new teaching assignment. But Francini's cynical description of the Berlitz system and its students portrays the truly dreary job that lay ahead of Joyce. Francini wrote, "Such a school must be as much like a zoo as possible; that is, the teacher has to behave like a bloody monkey. The students are vain and dull apes of every imaginable kind: coquettish women, cashiers about to abscond, single girls with no hope of ever being otherwise, officers as ignorant as donkeys, jobless waiters, ship's officers ready to embark, and more."[33]

Regardless, Joyce and Nora finally were established, and initially they were content enough in Pola. The Francinis, who also were recent arrivals in the city, became their best friends. Francini and his wife, Clotilde, had eloped from Florence, which helped to solidify the relationship between the couples, although Nora and Clotilde were unable to speak a common language at first.[34] Entertainment was a major part of their lives. Joyce and Nora frequently invited the Francinis to dinner, after which they often enjoyed singing. Joyce had been an accomplished singer in Ireland—Constantine Curran called music an "abiding passion" for him.[35] In Pola and Trieste, Joyce would pass many lively nights of singing and drinking with his colleague.

Joyce himself was a language student in Pola, having made "good progress," he thought, in German lessons.[36] The German exercises in his Italian workbook attest to his diligence. But Italian drew more of his attention. Joyce had studied Italian in school, and the writing of Dante and Gabriele D'Annunzio influenced him significantly.[37] He was particularly intrigued by Francini's Italian. Francini had grown up in Siena and spoke the Tuscan dialect, considered the purest form of Italian, and Joyce was eager to learn from him. (Clotilde was teaching Nora.)[38] They agreed to exchange lessons in Tuscan Italian and Dublin English. Joyce's Italian, which Francini referred to as "a crippled Italian full of ulcers,"[39] contrasted sharply with the heavy slang spoken in Pola and Trieste and must have amused people in both cities. Joyce was not nearly as diligent in giving English lessons to Francini, who stated, "Joyce grabbed but did not give."[40]

The first few weeks in Pola provided some much-needed rest and stability for Joyce and Nora, but their chronic inability to budget wisely left them needlessly poor. Daily, Joyce wore the same suit and Nora the same dress.[41] When the winter months arrived, even Joyce, who was accustomed to spartan living conditions, conceded that the stoveless apartment was a serious problem. He was forced to do his writing in cafes. To Stanislaus, he referred to himself as a "somewhat grave" person: "I drink little or nothing, smoke vastly, sing rarely,"[42] a characterization most unusual for Joyce regardless of the circumstances. His impoverishment in Pola would follow him to Trieste and Rome.

Nora also grew uncomfortable. She had cut herself off almost entirely from Ireland, sending home only one brief postcard since leaving. As time passed, she had less to keep her occupied in Pola. Of Joyce's writing she knew or cared little. In December 1904, Joyce wrote to Stanislaus, "I read Nora Chap XI [of *Stephen Hero*] which she thought remarkable but she cares nothing for my art."[43] Six weeks later, he again complained to his brother, "Nora, of course, doesn't care a rambling damn about art. . . . When she saw me copy Epiphanies into my novel she asked would all that paper be wasted. . . . She wants me to hurry up the novel and get rich and go to live in Paris."[44] Emphasizing that the couple had a strong relationship, Joyce's sister Eileen nevertheless noted that in the Trieste years, Nora "was always at him to teach more and spend less time at the silly writing, so as to earn more money."[45]

Nora's intellect has often been questioned. Yet, as Arthur Power pointed out, "Those who took Mrs. Joyce for a fool made a great mistake. For she was extremely shrewd, judged character in a flash, and was firm in her judgments."[46] Budgen concurred, seeing her as a "stately presence" with "absolute independence." "Her judgements of men and things were swift and forthright and proceeded from a scale of values entirely personal, unimitated, unmodified," he wrote.[47] Although her progress was slow, Nora in fact was studying Italian and French in Pola.[48] While she was not a literary type, Nora uniquely complemented Joyce.

Both soon grew weary of Pola. Joyce felt stranded there, cut off from the mainstream of Europe and surrounded by a culture he little respected. He understood that, as an exile, he could hardly pronounce any measure of success to the Dublin literati from, as he saw it, such a backwater. Life in Pola was becoming an embarrassment. In a letter to his Aunt Josephine, who had been very close to Joyce's mother and who took an active interest in all of the Joyce children,[49] Joyce scorned Pola: "I am trying to move on to Italy as soon as possible as I hate this Catholic country with its hundred races and thousand languages. . . . Pola is a back-of-God-speed place—a naval Siberia—37 men o' war in the harbour, swarming with faded uniforms. Istria is a long boring place wedged into the Adriatic peopled by ignorant Slavs who wear little red caps and colossal breeches."[50]

Things grew more complicated when Nora became pregnant. Aware of his ignorance on the matter, Joyce asked Stanislaus to study "midwifery and embryology" and to inform him of what he learned.[51] The cold apartment was unhealthy for a pregnant woman, so in December Joyce sought a new living space. His only comment at this time on impending fatherhood was his assertion that "my child . . . will of course not be baptized but will be registered in my name."[52] Viewing the plight of his friends, Francini invited them to stay on the second floor of his house at via

Medolino 7, where they moved in January 1905, remaining until they left Pola in March.[53]

In the first few months of the new year, Joyce continued to teach but focused mainly on his writing, finishing chapter 17 of his novel and working on the stunningly realistic short stories that would form *Dubliners*. The stories revealed Joyce's keen understanding of the misery endured by many in Dublin. To Grant Richards, a young English publisher, he stated that his objective in the stories was "to write a chapter of the moral history of my country and I chose Dublin for the scene because that city seemed to me the centre of paralysis."[54] He explained to Constantine Curran, "I call the series *Dubliners* to betray the soul of that hemiplegia or paralysis which many consider a city."[55]

Curran, though, found Joyce unfair in his judgements, seeing "little validity" in them. In his memoir he reflected,

They were quite divorced from the Ireland I knew; they were contrary to my own experience and based on trivial or imagined occurrences. Yeats had already in 1899 written of the intellectual excitement which followed the lull in political life after the Parnell split and of premonitions of things about to happen. When Joyce was writing in 1903-04 these things were in fact happening and all sorts of converging lives were carrying from disparate, newly tapped sources unsuspected energies which in that very decade founded a new school in literature and in the next established a new State. Nothing seemed to me more ' inept than to qualify the focus of this activity as a hemiplegia or paralysis, however much one might quarrel with its exuberances or fanaticisms. That Joyce thought fit to call it so is the measure of his ardour and youthful impatience.[56]

But, as Curran acknowledged, Joyce was "his own lawgiver," and his judgement—particularly on Ireland—was not subject to appeal.

Joyce maintained regular contact with Ireland, chiefly in the form of letters to Stanislaus. He frequently sent chapters of *Stephen Hero* for Stanislaus's review, which he expected to be extensive.[57] Particularly important to Joyce was news of Ireland. Just after reaching Trieste, he asked Stanislaus to "send on at once a long and documented letter containing all the news as it is nearly a month since I left Ireland and I have had none yet."[58] From Pola he wrote, "Tell me about my literary friends—the theater &c."[59] (He later considered asking his Aunt Josephine for a wall map of Dublin, commenting, "I suppose I am becoming something of a maniac.")[60] Stanislaus largely accommodated his brother in these requests, although never as promptly as the eager Joyce would have liked. He corresponded occasionally with his father, but he did not allude to Nora in his writing, assuming that his father still was ignorant of her.[61]

Despite the difficulty of their situation, Joyce and Nora remained devoted to one another. Joyce reprimanded Stanislaus for his poor opinion of Nora, admitting that while Nora had an "untrained" mind, "her disposition, as I see it, is much nobler than my own, and her love also is greater than mine for her. I admire her and I love her and I trust her."[62] Certainly love was paramount in the relationship; Joyce had no intention of being compromised in any way. He asserted, "I want to avoid as far as is humanly possible any such apparition in our lives as that abominable spectre which Aunt Josephine calls 'mutual tolerance.' "[63]

But neither Joyce nor Nora loved Pola, and as winter closed in 1905, they were ready to go. The circumstances of their departure remain vague. Francini claimed that Joyce was expelled from Pola in March as an "undesirable alien" by the Austrian authorities.[64] But scholar Ivo Vidan indicated that there is no evidence of such an eviction. He cited a letter dated April 13, 1905, in which the Austrian Ministry of Interior informed the Ministry of War that two Italians responsible for anti-Austrian agitation in Pola were under surveillance.[65] It seems unlikely that Joyce, only a local teacher and not even an Italian, would be expelled before two known troublemakers. A possible factor, according to Stanislaus, was that the school was far less than punctual in paying his brother.[66] Joyce, who in February had expressed to Stanislaus his wish "to get to Italy by summer,"[67] simply noted that he had been "transferred" to the Berlitz School in Trieste.[68]

In what became a pattern for Joyce, he looked at Trieste as a kind of safe haven, a place in which he would always be accepted even after having deserted it repeatedly. For various reasons, Joyce was destined to depart Trieste no less than seven times over sixteen years (and considered but rejected additional chances to go) for extended stays elsewhere. Yet in each case he made his way back before finally leaving Trieste permanently for Paris in 1920. At this early juncture in Joyce's exile, Trieste was the obvious alternative to Pola, but the Austrian city—particularly when Nora remained there—exerted a remarkable pull on Joyce over a long period. So it was that on a Sunday morning in early March 1905, Joyce and Nora left Pola, heading north for Trieste.

Joyce had changed visibly during his stay in Pola. He had put on weight (a stark contrast to earlier days in Dublin and Paris in which he went without food and appeared markedly thin),[69] grown a moustache, and bought both a new suit and a pince-nez for his already weak eyes.[70] His interest in his own appearance had increased noticeably, an indication of his emerging sense of identity as a more sophisticated man of Europe. In his work, the maturing Joyce would thrust the provincialism of Ireland in its face as part of his indictment of his native land.

4

A Triestine

In contrast to Pola, the cosmopolitan atmosphere of Trieste aroused more of Joyce's curiosity, which at times focused intently on his immediate surroundings. Carola Giedion-Welcker, later a friend of Joyce in Zurich, observed, "Joyce had a deep interest in towns . . . and in their design and history. They appeared to him as collective individuals, history turned into shape and space, large reservoirs of life. . . . Even if only passing through he always tried to penetrate into their special 'nature' and into the secret laws of their complex substance, and to listen to their current and eternal heartbeat."[1] Through many walks along the streets and evenings in the pubs, Joyce would come to understand well the heartbeat of Trieste, even while his own heart—and mind—rarely left Dublin.

Nora and he moved into a room on the third floor at Piazza del Ponte Rosso 3, the same square facing the main canal where they initially had stayed the previous October. Her pregnancy quickly became an obstacle. Only a month after their arrival, their landlord served notice that she did not want a baby in the building. Although adept at overcoming crises, Joyce faced a serious challenge when he realized, after being turned out of two more apartments, that most landlords in Trieste shared the same attitude about infants.[2]

Hardly unaccustomed to such pressure, Joyce responded effectively. He explained to Stanislaus: "I conceived the daring plan of living in the house next the school [Berlitz] and astonishing the landlady [Mrs. Canarutto] by the glamour of that wonderful establishment." He conceded, "This ruse has succeeded so far but we are still in danger of being put out." Artifoni, who had no children, viewed Joyce's antics and found him to be "stark mad."[3] The apartment, at via San Nicolò 30, was well situated for Joyce, as it was near downtown Trieste and just four blocks from the waterfront.

Joyce enjoyed the constant activity of the area, familiar to him from his first stop in Trieste. In his walks along the waterfront he would have seen vessels from around the world filling the harbor, with their sailors and crewmen, speaking numerous languages, crowding into the little shops and markets that lined the canal. On days with fewer ships docked, Joyce also would have been struck by the contrast between the canal and the piers. The incessant commotion of the canal area, bisecting the business district, was just yards away from the silent contemplation of Triestines and foreigners walking or sitting along the fingerlike stone piers, the most popular of which was Molo San Carlo, jutting into the harbor. They looked with wonder at the Adriatic melting into the distant horizon, the city behind them. On occasion, the young Joyce was one of them.

He at times entertained himself by visiting the nearby Orthodox churches—"moping in and out of the Greek churches"—as a colleague observed, according to Joyce.[4] (The observation was slightly inaccurate. There were two Orthodox churches near Joyce's apartment: the Greek-Oriental church [San Nicolò dei Greci] on Riva Carciotti, and the Serbian church on via S. Spiridione.)[5] Joyce particularly favored the San Nicolò dei Greci. The church, the Palazzo Carciotti, and the Teatro Verdi, all part of Trieste's impressive waterfront area, were designed in neoclassical style by Triestine architect Matteo Pertsh at the turn of the nineteenth century.[6] It is unlikely, though, that Joyce took particular note of the city's varied architecture, a subject that generally did not capture his interest. Joyce remembered buildings mainly for their associations with certain people or events rather than for their architectural style.[7]

What did interest him about the church was its ceremony. He described to Stanislaus his cynical fascination with the religious service:

The Greek mass is strange. The altar is not visible but at times the priest opens the gates and shows himself. He opens and shuts them about six times. For the Gospel he comes out of a side gate and comes down into the chapel and reads out of a book. For the elevation he does the same. At the end when he has blessed the people he shuts the gates: a boy comes running down the side of the chapel with a large tray full of little lumps of bread. The priest comes after him and distributes the lumps to scrambling believers. Damn droll![8]

But the church services and the music intrigued Joyce, and attending Easter ceremonies each year was among his favorite activities in Trieste.[9]

Joyce took a special delight not only in church music but in opera, which probably was the most popular art form in Trieste, reaching its peak each year during the winter season. Aware of Trieste's enthusiasm, companies touring Vienna, Venice, and Milan often stopped there for performances.

By far the most prominent Triestine theater—and one that Joyce attended frequently—was the Teatro Comunale Giuseppe Verdi, just a block from his via San Nicolò apartment. Teatro Verdi embodied the paradox of the irredentist spirit and the German influence that uniquely marked Triestine culture. In 1843, *Nabucco* became the first Verdi opera to be staged at the theater, then named Teatro Grande; the emotion and patriotic themes that distinguished the work of Verdi quickly established his popularity among Triestines, who would shout "Viva Verdi!" during performances to display their allegiance to Italy. Two Verdi operas, *Il Corsaro* (1848) and *Stiffelio* (1850), premiered, albeit unsuccessfully, in Trieste. In fact, only Milan's La Scala featured his work to the extent of Teatro Grande in the mid-1800s, inspiring Verdi to dedicate two operas to Trieste. Following Verdi's death on January 27, 1901, the theater embraced his name as its own.[10] Teatro Verdi also staged productions of older Italian composers such as Vivaldi, Frescobaldi, and Monteverdi, as well as more modern works by Puccini, Mascagni, and Antonio Smareglia, a Triestine, another indication of the nationalist sentiment that often found expression through the Verdi.[11]

Yet, alongside the Italians in the musical esteem of Triestines was Richard Wagner, whose works regularly packed the theater. Additional Teatro Verdi performances of note in the early 1900s included Strauss's *Salomé* (which Joyce reviewed for *Il Piccolo della Sera*), Mussorgsky's *Boris Godunov* and concerts of Beethoven, Brahms, Debussy, Mahler, and Sibelius. The musical scene received serious coverage in both the socialist newspaper, *Il Lavoratore*, and *Il Piccolo*, and Joyce, who particularly loved the work of Verdi, most likely was an avid reader of the reviews.

Opera never ceased to absorb Joyce. French surrealist writer Philippe Soupault recalled that "only children are as passionately attentive as Joyce was. He was always the first to applaud and to shout 'encore' after the great arias."[12] Joyce had long been taken by Italian opera in particular. Curran recalled that in Joyce's Dublin one rarely heard such opera, but Italian composers Donizetti, Bellini, and Rossini, among others, remained popular with the older generation, including Joyce's father.[13] John Joyce had an unbounded enthusiasm for the Italians that Joyce eagerly absorbed, and in the Trieste years Joyce's familiarity with Italian opera grew impressively, the music of Verdi always being his favorite.

A major reason for Joyce's delight, according to Jacques Mercanton, later a friend of Joyce in Paris, was the artistic integrity that pervaded both the Italian music and Joyce's writing. Mercanton accurately observed, "It was not only the brilliance and the virtuosity of the singing that attracted him to Rossini, Verdi, and to other Italians. . . . It was the truthfulness and the purity of his own soul. He recognized in them the 'sincerity' which is the secret behind all of the secrets of his own art, and which he valued so highly."[14]

Along with Joyce, Nora enjoyed the performances, and she later told Eugene Jolas's wife, Maria, of her frequent trips to the opera. Jolas was impressed by "the number of operas and the words from them—Italian words, of course—that she remembered. . . . Nora would sing, and I would say, 'What's that from,' and she would give me some name I had never heard before."[15] Stanislaus agreed, admitting that Nora recalled arias more accurately than he did.[16]

While Joyce's enthusiasm for opera in Trieste was first rate, his seating at times assuredly was not. In *Giacomo Joyce* he describes vividly the rather malodorous atmosphere of the *loggione*, or top gallery seats, in a Triestine opera house, possibly the Filodrammatico, noted for its less than ideal ambience and located nearby several Joyce apartments. He wrote, "The sodden walls ooze a steamy damp. A symphony of smells fuses the mass of huddled human forms: sour reek of armpits, nozzled oranges, melting breast ointments, mastick water, the breath of suppers of sulphurous garlic, foul phosphorescent farts, opoponax, the frank sweat of marriageable and married womankind, the soapy stink of men."[17]

Trieste cannot be seen, however, as an artistic or cultural paradise for Joyce. It was true that opera and theater performances were well attended in the city, but the heart and soul of its citizenry clearly lay in its economic prosperity. Writer Jan Morris captured this sense: "All the robustness . . . went to the making of money, and the Trieste style is essentially a glorification of commercial opportunity: a plump and optimistic style, whose banks and office blocks express as devout a faith in the comforting power of Cash as did the great Victorian railway stations in the fructifying force of steam."[18]

Others agreed. During his tour of duty as French consul in Trieste, Stendhal complained, "I am living among peasants who only recognize one religion, that of money." Charles Yriarte, a French visitor in the 1870s, was not impressed by the custom of many Triestines of heading to the exchange each evening at precisely 8:00 to learn what ships had been reported.[19] (Trieste's shipping activity gave them good reason to be curious, particularly in Joyce's time: in 1910, for example, halfway through Joyce's stay in Trieste, nearly twelve thousand vessels docked in the harbor.)[20] Joyce himself noted the bustling port in a letter to Stanislaus: "In the canal here the boats are lined along the quays. They are the same old galley-looking affairs which were in use during the MiddleAge. The men row the row-boats from the standing posture. Inside the great bosom of the prow every sailing ship has an image of some saviour, Saint Nicholas or the Madonna or Jesus walking on the waters."[21]

Italian Triestine intellectuals lamented the paucity of culture around them, particularly in comparison to the great heritage of artistic expression found in Italian cities.[22] Slataper noted that although many Triestines looked sentimentally to Florence and Rome as models of Italian culture (especially since Trieste had no university around which an artistic movement could develop), they owed their comfortable lifestyles to the efficiency of the Austrian regime, which in Trieste emphasized commerce, not art. He referred to Trieste as a city with a lot of masons but few architects.[23] A Triestine poet commented that to be born in Trieste meant to be born fifty years behind the times culturally.[24] People seemed to view their appearances at theater events either as brief pleasurable respites from their main affairs of the day or as merely fashionable behavior. Slataper regretted the situation: "The history of Trieste is ice cold without an effort for idealism, without a need for art, without affection for the spirit. It was chained to the need to earn."[25] Joyce certainly shared the Triestines' designs on earning money, but he hoped to do so through his art, an odd notion in Trieste.

With little money to get started, Joyce and Nora again unwittingly gained attention due to their attire. Joyce complained to Stanislaus that another teacher had commented to him, "Eccentric people have very little taste," advising him to "stick to grey. Doesn't matter what kind—always looks gentlemanly."[26] (Ironically, during his first desperate days in Trieste, Joyce had seriously considered opening an agency for Foxford tweeds.)[27] Nora, according to Joyce, was treated no more respectfully: she was always "nudged at and sniggered at" by Triestines viewing her "short four crown skirt and hair done over the ears,"[28] increasing her discomfort in

Trieste.

Proper clothes, with a heavy emphasis on formal fashion, were a staple of Triestine culture; Triestines proudly displayed their latest dress in their evening and Sunday strolls along the piers. Joyce noted that "the Trieste people are great 'stylists' in dress, often starving themselves in order to be able to flaunt good dresses."[29] Critic Corinna del Greco Lobner described the Triestine women as "stiffly elegant in the ample gowns gathered behind in a culisson, a bustle, after the Viennese fashion, wearing huge hats lavishly decorated with ostrich plumage and colorful silk ribbons." Men were no less prominent, sporting black bowler hats, ties "viciously stabbed by jeweled pins," and walking sticks crowned by an ivory, silver, or gold handle.[30] Prior to Stanislaus's arrival in Trieste later in 1905, Joyce not surprisingly admonished him in three letters to come well dressed.

A subject that Joyce could better appreciate was politics, which in Trieste grew more heated each year, particularly on the Italian side. *Il Piccolo* pushed harder for Italian control of the city, and Teatro Verdi often was a forum for vociferous irredentist protest.[31] The extent to which the city was Italianized can be seen in the names of the streets and plazas. In the downtown area alone, the names included Gioacchino Rossini, Giuseppe Verdi, Vincenzo Bellini, Niccolò Machiavelli, and Giosuè Carducci.[32] Joyce, who was well versed in Irish history and followed Irish politics closely,[33] recognized the political similarity between Trieste and Dublin, the most obvious element of which was the fact that both had been "occupied" cities for centuries. He spoke of this parallel with his Italian friends.[34]

Joyce supported Irish independence, but he was not optimistic that Ireland would have the ability to free itself from England's grip, viewing its nationalist movement as just "a noise in the street," according to Padraic Colum.[35] Joyce told Djuna Barnes in Paris, "The Irish are people who will never have leaders, for at the great moment they always desert them. They have produced one skeleton—Parnell—never a man."[36] He concluded a 1907 speech to a Triestine audience:

It is well past time for Ireland to have done once and for all with failure. . . . Ireland has already had enough equivocations and misunderstandings. If she wants to put on the play that we have waited for so long, this time let it be whole, and complete, and definitive. But our advice to the Irish producers is the same as that our fathers gave them not so long ago—hurry up! I am sure that I, at least, will never see that curtain go up, because I will have already gone home on the last train.[37]

Joyce, however, did not equate Ireland with Austria. Triestine politics were largely peripheral to his gaze. Probably intrigued by the ubiquitous irredentist activity in Trieste, Joyce initially displayed an interest in Italian history, particularly in the works of the historian and journalist Guglielmo Ferrero, whose columns appeared in *Il Piccolo della Sera*.[38] Trieste's chances for independence, though, were not of serious concern to Joyce: he was not a supporter of irredentism. Triestine writer Silvio Benco observed, "He could not suffer in the same way over Trieste's own dogged effort towards national freedom."[39] Moreover, Stanislaus wrote, Joyce believed that "fanned nationalisms . . . were to blame for wars and world troubles."[40] Clearly the irredentists, who were fanning their Italian nationalist propaganda around Trieste as much as possible, had little to offer Joyce, and he never embraced them.

Morally and politically, he saw himself as a "socialistic artist,"[41] and Trieste presented Joyce with numerous opportunities to discuss socialism, which had become a genuine political force there by Joyce's years. In Città Vecchia, the city's old quarter marked by numerous cafes and apartments squeezed among narrow winding roads, and in the bars (particularly the Antica Casa Rossa) near the waterfront, Joyce enjoyed drinking and discussing socialism with dockworkers. Stanislaus recalled that the young Joyce's political leanings also had been "towards socialism" in Dublin, where he attended meetings of socialist groups in "backrooms."[42]

Joyce's socialist stance stemmed partly from his fear of the church gaining political control. In a long letter to Stanislaus, he wrote: "But can you not see plainly . . . that a deferment of the emancipation of the proletariat, a reaction to clericalism or aristocracy or bourgeoisism would mean a revulsion to tyrannies of all kinds. . . . For my part I believe that to establish the church in full power again in Europe would mean a renewal of the Inquisition."[43] The immediate importance of socialism to Joyce, though, was much more personal: the possibility that such a system of government might provide a subsidy to "starving artists" like Joyce, who continually depended upon others for financial support.

Yet, he was very sensitive to criticism on this issue. To the charge that he was promoting socialism simply out of self-interest, he responded, "This is not quite true. . . . If I made a fortune it is by no means certain that I would keep it. What I wish to do is to secure a competence on which I can rely, and why I expect to have this is because I cannot believe that any State requires my energy for the work I am at present engaged in."[44]

He extended his socialist views to his relationship with Nora. Discussing his unwillingness to marry her, he asked Stanislaus, "But why should I have brought Nora to a priest or a lawyer to make her swear her life to me?"[45] Nora hardly shared Joyce's principled stand regarding marriage. She told Byrne in 1927 that her unmarried status was the "only . . . fly in the amber of my happiness."[46]

For the moment, however, socialism was doing nothing to pay Joyce's bills, leaving Berlitz as his major source of income. He complained to Stanislaus of the "dullness" in his life[47] and of the "intolerable duties" at Berlitz.[48] Joyce often referred sarcastically to the school as "Berlicche," an expression used jokingly in Trieste in reference to devilish or clownish behavior. Adults would sometimes shake the tips of recalcitrant children's noses and say, "berlicche, berlicche."[49] The unabashed Joyce saw no reason to respect the school or its students, who annoyed him. "Some day I shall clout my pupils about the head, I fear, and stalk out," he wrote to Stanislaus.[50] Joyce gave this description of an encounter with a student: "While I was reading [a letter from Stanislaus] in the school, one of my pupils passed through, a vulgar little Hungarian, saying flatly, 'Good morning, sar' to which I replied with intention 'The divil bite your bottom.' Honestly it is awful!"[51] His classes consisted mainly of "noblemen and signori and editors and rich people,"[52] the only Triestines likely to have any interest in English; at the time, Italian,

German, the Slavic languages, and even French were more commonly used than English in Trieste. But, despite his complaints, his classes did not have more than eight students, and he earned a reasonable weekly wage of forty-five crowns.[53]

Student reaction to Joyce as a teacher was mixed. Some found it easy to believe that Joyce took little pleasure in his duties. One student, Stanko Pastrovic, recalled that Joyce was "not very keen" on teaching.[54] Another student had fond memories of Joyce but learned very little English. "My mother kept wondering if it wouldn't be a good idea to find me another teacher," she recalled.[55]

But among others, most notably some of the school's wealthy pupils, Joyce was a teacher in demand. In particular, Count Francesco Sordina, a rich merchant, praised Joyce's teaching and encouraged friends to enroll in his classes.[56] It seems likely that Sordina and others appreciated Joyce not so much because he was an effective English teacher—at times, he clearly was not—but more because he was such an entertaining character, often eccentric or outlandish in his behavior and his comments. In Trieste, where decorum was important and where teachers (later including Stanislaus) generally saw themselves as serious and high-minded individuals, Joyce was a breath of fresh air to some students.

Artifoni naturally was glad of the school's sudden surge in popularity. But he was well aware of Joyce's constant problems with money. Joyce was the first in line each Saturday to pick up the weekly pay,[57] and Artifoni himself served at times as a benefactor to Joyce. He feared that his prize teacher might consider establishing his own school or at least seeking a higher salary elsewhere. Joyce lamented—with some exaggeration—to Stanislaus, "The slightest disapproval on the part of my genteel pupils would be sufficient to obtain for me dismissal and with my 'immorality' belled about the town I should find it next to impossible to get anything to do here." He decried the restrictions, calling Artifoni's control over him a "reign of terror."[58] Joyce and Artifoni, in fact, remained on reasonably good terms for the moment.

Joyce, however, was never at a loss for devising moneymaking schemes, one of which involved his fine tenor voice that he hoped eventually would enable him to sing professionally. The Triestines' enthusiasm for music, well understood by Joyce, surely encouraged such hopes. Clotilde Francini, who had performed on the operatic stage before her marriage, persistently urged Joyce to take lessons; she was convinced that his voice could be his meal ticket.[59]

In late May 1905, Joyce acted. "I am going to the conservatory about my voice," he informed Stanislaus.[60] Two weeks later, he announced, "I am now definitely studying for the theatre."[61] His teacher was the Triestine operatic composer Giuseppe Sinico, whose opera *Marinella*—written more than fifty years earlier—contains an aria, "Inno di San Giusto," which is well known in Trieste.[62] (The aria was particularly meaningful to the irredentists because it depicts the people of Trieste defending the city against attack from Venice and raising the Trieste flag over the San Giusto church.)[63] Sinico told him that his voice had a "very beautiful timbre."[64] Soon, though, the lessons were discontinued, probably for lack of reimbursement. It was not the last time that an unlikely Joyce plan for additional income would fail.

Perhaps bitter about his tough start in Pola and Trieste, as well as his failure to impress his fellow Dubliners after more than seven months in exile, Joyce decided to publish his scandalous broadside, "The Holy Office." Written the previous year, the work was a vicious attack on the Irish literary movement, particularly the works of Yeats, Synge, Colum, and other well-known writers. Joyce had one hundred copies of "The Holy Office" printed in Trieste on May 23, 1905, and, through Stanislaus, distributed fifty to friends and writers in Ireland.[65] He did have the grace not to provide copies to Yeats or Lady Gregory, whose earlier help obviously had been conveniently "forgotten." His position as an exile, removed from daily contact with Ireland, only increased his desire to reveal the truth about the Irish as he saw it. It is the subject of nearly all of his fiction.

Bored in Trieste, Joyce urged Stanislaus in May to write more often, complaining, "You know the martyrdom my life is here and its dullness."[66] As summer arrived, life for Joyce and Nora had become so strained that Joyce asked Stanislaus in early July to come to Trieste "by hook or crook" to discuss a "very serious matter."[67] Stanislaus was unable to make the expensive trip, so Joyce confided his problems by letter. Trieste presented difficulties for Joyce and, more particularly, Nora. Joyce declared, "Trieste is the rudest place I have ever been in. It is hardly possible to exaggerate the incivility of the people. The girls and women are so rude to Nora that she is afraid to go out in the street."[68] He endured with humiliation a Triestine girl's "sneering" at his "impoverished country."[69] Compounding the problem was the fact that Nora could speak only "about 30 words" of the Triestine dialect (she later became fluent in Italian,[70] although Joyce for the moment admitted defeat in teaching her French),[71] so Joyce accompanied her on nearly every shopping trip.

But the main burdens were Nora's exhausting pregnancy, her trouble in adjusting to the unsettled lifestyle Joyce had set for them, and their ongoing financial woes. Often crying, Nora suffered terribly in the summer heat and rarely cooked anymore. To cover the dining bills, Joyce borrowed continuously. As Nora's condition worsened, Joyce observed, "She seems to me to be in danger of falling into a melancholy mood which would certainly injure her health very much." Nora herself admitted that she could not endure such a lifestyle much longer.

Her behavior perplexed Joyce. He confessed to Stanislaus that he knew very little about women, asking him to consult Aunt Josephine for her assessment of the situation. Joyce's conclusion was that Nora was "really very helpless and unable to cope with any kind of difficulties," and he could not see any prospect of happiness for her in Trieste. "This present absurd life is no longer possible for either of us. . . . The very degrading and unsatisfactory nature of my exile angers me and I do not see why I should continue to drag it out," he wrote. Joyce did not address the issue of his own substantial drinking, which only increased Nora's discomfort.

His solution to their dilemma was sincere but impractical. Not surprisingly, and not for the last time, Joyce contemplated leaving Trieste. He suggested to Stanislaus that they save as much money as possible up to Easter, 1906, so that Joyce's family and Stanislaus could "take a small cottage outside Dublin in the suburbs, furnish it and pay the rent for a half-year in advance." Even Joyce suspected that his answer to the Trieste problem would not come to pass. "I have proposed so many things which are now considered follies of mine and done so few of them that I am beginning to think it is not right for me to expect people to help me out in my notions," he admitted to his brother. Life in Pola and Trieste had taken a toll on him: he conceded to Stanislaus, "It is possible that my idea is really a terrible one but my mind's eye is so distracted after nine months of my present life that I am unable to see things with my former precision." The move to Dublin was soon forgotten after the birth of Giorgio.

Neither Joyce nor Nora was prepared for the arrival of the child. Despite the fact that Nora had been "laid up with neuralgia" and "dropping down with weakness" a week earlier,[72] the moment of the actual birth on July 27 took them by surprise, as they had anticipated that the event would occur at the end of August. When Joyce returned that afternoon from a cafe, he found Nora in great distress. He had no idea it was labor pain but sought help from Mrs. Canarutto when it persisted. A midwife arrived, and the landlady assisted her while Joyce went for Dr. Gilberto Senigaglia, one of his pupils. The doctor visited Nora immediately and helped with the birth, later telling Joyce that Nora was "very brave and hardly uttered a cry." At 9:00 in the evening, Mrs. Canarutto emerged from the room and announced, "Xe un bel maschio, Signore."[73] (It's a fine boy, sir.) The child later was named Giorgio, after Joyce's deceased brother.[74] Joyce informed the Dublin family of the event with a three-word telegram: "Son born Jim."[75]

Fulfilling his earlier pledge, Joyce did not have the child baptized. Stanislaus sided with Joyce on the issue of religious indoctrination, writing of the birth of Giorgio, "It is not a small thing either that one human being is born, to whom the churches can lay no claim, whose commonsense will not be worried by the necessity of taking seriously the fable of Jesus of Nazareth."[76] Others in the family disagreed, though; seven years later, two of Joyce's sisters arranged for Giorgio's baptism without Joyce's knowledge at the home of his Aunt Josephine in Dublin.[77]

5

Another Joyce in Trieste

Joyce and Nora were happy to be parents. "The most important thing that can happen to a man is the birth of a child," he later told his sister Eve.[1] According to Stanislaus, Joyce "believed in fatherhood and considered it a form of cowardice, 'too great a fear of fate,' not to have children."[2] Indeed, fatherhood seemed to spark Joyce's creativity. He had finished chapter 24 of *Stephen Hero* by early June,[3] and, for *Dubliners*, completed "The Boarding House" (inspired by a conversation with a Berlitz colleague),[4] "Counterparts," "Ivy Day in the Committee Room," "An Encounter," "A Mother," and "Araby" by mid-October.[5] He organized the stories to represent four stages of life in Ireland: " 'The Sisters,' 'An Encounter' and another story ['Araby'] which are stories of my childhood: 'The Boarding House,' 'After the Race' and 'Eveline,' which are stories of adolescence: 'The Clay,' 'Counterparts,' and 'A Painful Case' which are stories of mature life: 'Ivy Day in the Committee Room,' 'A Mother' and the last story of the book ['Grace'] which are stories of public life in Dublin."[6]

Joyce was pleased with his progress and expressed to Stanislaus his conviction of the book's importance: "When you remember that Dublin has been a capital for thousands of years, that it is the 'second' city of the British Empire, that it is nearly three times as big as Venice it seems strange that no artist has given it to the world."[7] Yet Joyce maintained his low opinion of the rest of contemporary Irish literature, which he considered to be "ill-written, morally obtuse formless caricature."[8] Reviewers hardly rated better in his mind: after Joyce submitted his story "Clay" to a magazine, "the cursedly stupid ape that conducts that journal neither acknowledged it nor sent it back," he wrote to Stanislaus. "Am I an imbecile or are these people imbeciles? That journalist that wrote so superiorly about Tolstoy [in a review] is (thank the devil) dead and, I hope, damned," he went on.[9]

Another irritant to Joyce was the Trieste climate. He complained to Stanislaus about the extreme summer heat in which he had to teach and to write: "Tomorrow . . . in this torrid weather I have to give eight lessons during which I must keep continually on the alert and interested. Many of the frigidities of "The Boarding-House" and "Counterparts" were written while the sweat streamed down my face on to the handkerchief which protected my collar."[10] In late September, Joyce sarcastically told Stanislaus of his gratitude for the end of summer: "I went out yesterday for a walk in a big wood outside Trieste. The damned monotonous summer was over and the rain and soft air made me think of the beautiful (I am serious) climate of Ireland. I hate a damn silly sun that makes men into butter."[11] In fact, he referred to the winter, with its opera and carnival events, as the "best season" in Trieste.[12]

Obviously, Joyce did not consider himself settled in any sense. In September 1905, he expressed his intentions to Stanislaus: "If I once convince myself that this kind of life is suicidal to my soul, I will make everything and everybody stand out of my way as I did before now. However I am doing what I can to live without causing unhappiness to the few people for whom I have affection."[13] Joyce was more succinct in a letter a few days later: "For the love of the Lord Christ change my curse-o'-God state of affairs."[14]

A change for which Joyce had long been hoping finally took place in late October: Stanislaus left Dublin for Trieste to live with him. Joyce had introduced the possibility of the brothers living together in a letter to his father in November 1904,[15] and the following September he informed Stanislaus that Artifoni would hold a teaching position for him.[16]

For Stanislaus, the decision to leave Dublin was not reached easily. He was closer to his six sisters and his brother Charlie than was Joyce, who had been away for long periods at school, in Paris, and in Austria. Joyce's comment to Nora, "My brothers and sisters are nothing to me. One brother alone [Stanislaus] is capable of understanding me," six weeks before they departed Dublin was an overstatement, but in truth he was not as involved as Stanislaus in family affairs.[17]

Stanislaus worried that a move to Trieste would force him to abandon his siblings to a father who by then was passing much of his time in the pubs. While Joyce admired the strong Irish character of his father and shared his love of music and Dublin lore,[18] Stanislaus despised him. "My antipathy to him seemed to have been born with me," he wrote.[19] Stanislaus described his father as "shallow without love" and "domineering and quarrelsome."[20] He believed that his father was a "crazy drunkard" who "hastened Mother's death [in 1903]." On the latter point, Joyce agreed. He wrote to Nora that his mother had been "slowly killed" by, among other causes, his father's ill-treatment of her.[21]

Furthermore, Stanislaus charged that their father had "no love or care" for his children. John Joyce regularly called his children bastards, and often attempted to strike his daughters with a poker, plate, cup, or pan. Feeling almost like a prisoner, Stanislaus complained that one of the sons always had to be home to protect the girls. His account of one of his father's outbursts is appalling: "Ye dirty pissabed, ye bloody-looking crooked-eyed son of a bitch. Ye ugly bloody corner-boy, you've a mouth like a bloody nigger. Ye black-looking mulatto. You were black the day you were born, ye bitch. Ye bloody, gummy, toothless bitch."[22] Atonement for such acts was rare. Stanislaus bitterly noted that one of his father's favorite maxims was,

"Never apologize."[23]

John Joyce saw the situation in quite a different light. In a 1907 letter to James, he stated,

Perhaps in years to come, long after my release from this world, you may learn to feel some of the pangs I have endured, and then you will appreciate the feelings of a Father who loved his children and had high ambitions for them, and spared no money when he could afford it, to educate and make them what they should be, but who when adversity came and he could no longer gratify all those wants, was despised disrespected, jeered at, scoffed at and set at defiance. . . . I pray God, you may be spared such ingratitude.[24]

Constantine Curran, familiar with all parties, concluded that while John Joyce had become "a legendary character, the legend hardly outruns the facts."[25]

Stanislaus not only was uncomfortable leaving his siblings alone with his father, but he also understood that such a tight living arrangement with his brother's family in Trieste would be far from ideal. His character was quite contrary to Joyce's. Stanislaus valued order, privacy, and personal responsibility. He once wrote, "Reflection is my predominate habit."[26] (Eileen Joyce bluntly described him as "too Prussian."[27] Curiously, though, she wrote more often to Stanislaus than to Joyce when she later lived in Udine, near Trieste.) Like Joyce, Stanislaus was quick to judge others, often harshly, but was more withdrawn. While Joyce confronted the world with his criticism, Stanislaus chose to dwell privately on such thoughts, particularly as a young man.

What would be worse for Joyce and Nora was his self-righteousness. Stanislaus's attempts at sensitivity frequently ended in futile moral lectures, the most common topic being Joyce's drinking. Stanislaus was only a casual drinker, and it disturbed him a great deal to be fighting a continuous battle to keep Joyce out of the bars. As a result, he saw himself time after time as an innocent victim, which only increased his isolation.

Yet, in important ways, they needed to be near each other, an indication of which was the sizable volume of letters that had passed between them in the preceding year. Joyce respected Stanislaus's opinion of his writing and sent him his manuscripts for review. "Your criticism of my novel is always interesting," he wrote to Stanislaus in February, also noting his intention to dedicate *Dubliners* to him.[28] Their common interests extended beyond literature. Joyce told Stanislaus that "in most essential things you share my opinions."[29]

Stanislaus's views, while not always in agreement with those of Joyce, were expressed with equal verve, and Joyce obviously appreciated this quality. He wrote wittily to Nora before they left Dublin, "I must tell you about my nice brother, Stannie. He is sitting at the table ½-dressed reading a book and talking softly to himself 'Curse this fellow'—the writer of the book—'Who in the devil's name said this book was good' 'The stupid fuzzy-headed fool!' 'I wonder are the English the stupidest race on God's earth' 'Curse this English fool' etc etc."[30] Above all, Joyce required someone with whom to discuss his writing and someone who would lend some stability, especially financial, to the family.

In turn, Stanislaus greatly admired his brother as an artist. Intelligent and well

read, Stanislaus shared Joyce's intense interest in literature; he described their earlier conversations in Dublin as "interminable,"[31] and now insisted that Joyce continue the dialogue from Trieste. Joyce noted in a July letter, "I am writing to you
fully as you wish me to do."[32] Stanislaus believed that James had more literary
talent than anyone in Ireland except Yeats.[33] To remain active in Joyce's literary
career and to escape the misery of Dublin were enticing prospects to Stanislaus, for
his father was insufferable and his job options bleak. Finally, after much ado,
Stanislaus left Dublin on October 24, 1905, never to return.

The relationship between Joyce and Stanislaus, particularly in the Trieste years,
has been controversial, with critics questioning the validity of Stanislaus's account
of Joyce and his family during that time. It is true that Stanislaus was not the most
objective observer. He sometimes did exaggerate the extent of Joyce's poverty and
of his own efforts to "rescue" Joyce, as he claimed.

But his words cannot be ignored. Stanislaus went to Trieste only after repeated
urgings from his brother: he was not an unwelcome guest. Teaching at the Berlitz
and often living with Joyce, Stanislaus spent more time with him than anyone except Nora, and Joyce confided in him regularly. Stanislaus also was among the very
few, unfortunately, who left a written record of Joyce's Trieste years. It was a time
of turbulence for both brothers, but as often as they disagreed, they reconciled, a
pattern that continued for the rest of their lives. Joyce never cut him off. So while it
is regrettable that more documentation on Joyce in Trieste is not available, the accounts left by Stanislaus should not be easily cast aside. He, after all, was there.

Joyce's success at convincing Stanislaus to come to Trieste was not duplicated
in his effort to persuade publishers to bring out his work. In July, publisher William
Heinemann declined to print *Chamber Music*.[34] Undaunted, Joyce mailed a copy of
Dubliners to Heinemann two months later, only to suffer the same fate.[35] Grant
Richards, the English publisher to whom Joyce had submitted *Chamber Music* in
August,[36] also rejected the poems, citing their lack of commercial appeal.[37] It was
actually the second time that Richards had received *Chamber Music*. In a scenario
that typified the misfortune Joyce's work would meet continuously over the next
decade, Richards admitted that the first manuscript had been packed up mistakenly
with some furniture and stored in a warehouse.[38]

Still, Joyce pressed on. He again wrote to Richards on October 15 and offered
Dubliners to him. Although he scorned convention and always insisted on writing
with an honesty and clarity that practically guaranteed the objections of publishers,
Joyce nonetheless was acutely aware of the mass-appeal factor: "It is possible that
you would consider it to be of a commercial nature," he wrote hopefully.[39] On December 3, Joyce did submit the stories to Richards.[40]

He had finished *Chamber Music* and *Dubliners* (he later added three stories)
and written twenty-four chapters of *Stephen Hero*, yet none of his work was close
to publication. His teaching position was bearable for the present, but he certainly
had no illusions about the importance of his job. To Joyce, the Triestine students
were "cursed, stupid snobs."[41] Additional stress came from his ongoing financial
problems, his new responsibilities as a father, and his effort to maintain a stable
relationship with Nora. The arrival of his brother was a welcome relief.

Stanislaus reached Trieste after a difficult trip of several days by ship and rail from Dublin. He moved into a room next to Joyce and began teaching at the Berlitz School the following day, earning a weekly sum of forty crowns that he turned over to Joyce for household expenses. Problems surfaced quickly, though. Nora did not warm immediately to Stanislaus, giving most of her attention to the baby and speaking in Italian to Joyce.[42] Stanislaus attempted to fit in by sharing his money and, in some cases, his clothes with his brother, but Joyce did little to amend his self-indulgent ways, undoubtedly irritated by Stanislaus's stern approach to family life. As the relationship among the three deteriorated, both Stanislaus and Joyce wrote to Aunt Josephine to plead their cases. Stanislaus complained that Joyce and Nora mistreated him as well as each other.[43]

A major cause of the discord was Joyce's drinking. He had been an occasional drinker until their mother's death in 1903, after which he began to drink "riotously," according to Stanislaus.[44] In September 1904, Stanislaus vividly depicted both his brother's drunken behavior and his own antipathy: "I hate to see Jim limp and pale, with shadows under his watery eyes, loose wet lips, and dank hair. I hate to see him sitting on the edge of a table grinning at his own state. It gets on my nerves to be near him then. Or to see him sucking in his cheeks and his lips, and swallowing spittle in his mouth."[45]

Joyce told Stanislaus, "The first thing I look for in a city is the cafe."[46] No doubt his words rang true in Trieste. The cheap hangouts in Città Vecchia, where lively conversations—and venereal diseases—were commonplace,[47] attracted Joyce. Francini, who had moved with Clotilde to Trieste, was familiar with Joyce's routine:

He embraced the holy oil with passion. He knew by heart all the little holes in the wall around town and could locate them even by feel. The great problem came when he had to get out and find the bowel that would lead him from the blind gut of the old part of town to the main street. Then he would grope along with his hands, trying to chase the fog away from before his eyes, and, if he managed to find the main street, he would run down it until he reached the corner. Here he would prop himself against the wall and wait for some Samaritan to come and collect him.[48]

Often, the Samaritan turned out to be Francini, who would carry Joyce over his shoulder back to the apartment. At times, Joyce was brought in while merrily singing the Triestine drinking song, "Ancora un litro di quel bon, Che no go la ciave del porton" (Another liter of the good stuff, Because I've lost the key to my door).[49]

Nora had equally little sympathy for Joyce's habit. He once wrote pleadingly to her,

[One] night I came home to your bed from the café and I began to tell you of all I hoped to do, and to write, in the future and of those boundless ambitions which are really the leading forces in my life. You would not listen to me. It was very late I know and of course you were tired out after the day. But a man whose brain is on fire with hope and trust in himself *must* tell someone of what he feels. Whom should I tell but you?[50]

Francini himself was hardly temperate, which encouraged the friendship. When Francini and Joyce later shared an apartment in Trieste, there were festive evenings in which Francini would get into Giorgio's carriage and squeal and cry like a baby while Joyce pushed him around. As the wine flowed freely, Joyce would sing Gregorian chants and Francini would grab Joyce and kiss him.[51] Budgen also saw this lighter side of Joyce's character, describing it as "a self-forgetting, impish humor expressed in fantastic antics and drolleries, songs, and dances."[52] To Nora's embarrassment, Joyce at times was not shy about publicly displaying his eccentric behavior: as the two strolled along the waterfront, Joyce would suddenly break into a solo dance, in full view of passers-by.[53]

Yet even Francini conceded what many others came to realize: that Joyce, in the main, was a person of dignity. "Joyce is a great gentleman, a born gentleman. He stinks of the gentleman a mile away, even when he is stinking drunk," he wrote.[54] Maria Jolas presented Joyce with more diplomacy: "He was an extraordinarily dignified man even under circumstances when a lot of people lose their dignity."[55] Another friend recalled once telling a dirty joke to Joyce, who reacted with obvious discomfort and stated that he did not use such words in conversation.[56] Joyce was unequivocal on this point; he told Nora, "As you know, dearest, I never use obscene phrases in speaking. You have never heard me, have you, utter an unfit word before others. When men tell in my presence . . . filthy or lecherous stories, I hardly smile."[57]

Such anecdotes are contradicted somewhat by Stanislaus's recollection of a younger Joyce recounting sexual exploits in Dublin, but he clearly shunned vulgarity in conversation as he grew older. Joyce generally had yet to introduce obscenity in his writing, either, although *Ulysses* and his highly personal letters to Nora in 1909 (unpublished until 1975) would firmly establish his reputation in that regard. Why he was more comfortable with such words emerging from his pen rather than his mouth is unclear.

After a year abroad, the increasing strain between Joyce and Nora was a serious concern for him, and he contemplated leaving her. On December 4, 1905, he sent a pessimistic letter to Aunt Josephine in which he informed her that "the present relations between Nora and myself are about to suffer some alteration." He admitted that he was difficult to live with and that he shared the blame for the decline of the relationship, but he asserted, "I have no intention of changing." With disappointment he wrote that Nora "does not seem to make much difference between me and the rest of the men she has known." He concluded, "I am a little weary of making allowances for people."[58]

For her part, Nora was hardly intimidated by Joyce. Aunt Josephine observed that Nora "knew just how to deal with Jim."[59] Despite their life on the brink of poverty, Nora did not hesitate to coax—or simply take—money from Joyce, especially for clothes, and she had domesticated him to the point of peeling vegetables.[60] Maria Jolas commented years later that Joyce "was married to the only kind of woman who could possibly have done for him."[61] Joyce himself conceded that Nora was in no way deceived by any of his posturing. He once asked her, "You proud little ignorant saucy dear warm-hearted girl how is it that I cannot impress you with my magnificent poses as I do other people? You see through me, you cunning little blue-eyed rogue, and smile to yourself knowing that I am an imposter and still you love me."[62] But as 1905 closed, it was far from clear what destiny awaited the couple in Trieste.

Money continued to be in short supply for Joyce, so in January 1906, he accepted Francini's offer to share living quarters and expenses with Joyce's family. All moved into an apartment in late February at via Giovanni Boccaccio 1, a residential area near the harbor on the northern side of the city. Joyce and Nora were happy to be reunited with the Francinis. They resumed their old ways, in particular dining out frequently, a favorite spot being the Restaurant Bonavia near the waterfront.[63]

Joyce maintained his Italian lessons with Francini, and he now had the challenge of mastering the peculiar Triestine dialect of Italian with its odd mixture of, among others, German, Greek, and Slav expressions and words. (Alois Skrivanich, a Croat and a private pupil of Joyce, helped him with some lessons.)[64] His task was complicated by the Triestines' tendency to distort on purpose their own words,[65] a practice that surely intrigued Joyce, eager to explore new complexities in language.

Joyce had first heard Triestine slang from the German poet Theodor Däubler, whom he had met during his earlier stay in Paris. The relationship became memorable after a mutual acquaintance informed Joyce that Däubler was contemplating a duel with him over some perceived insult. Däubler never approached him on the matter; Joyce, aware of his limitations, told Stanislaus that he would have left Paris on the first train if trouble appeared likely.[66] Däubler's speech probably interested Joyce—if at all—only because of his keen ear for linguistic diversity, as he had no hint at that time that he would ever be in Trieste.

In the Berlitz classroom, Joyce's teaching remained an irritation. But he never reformed his eccentric character for the sake of propriety, continuing to entertain his students with outrageous anecdotes or digressions. His polemics were recorded by Francini:

The tax collector is an idiot who is always annoying me. He has filled my desk with little sheets marked "Warning," "Warning," "Warning." I told him that if he didn't stop it, I would send him to be f . . . ound out by that swindler, his master. Today the swindler is the government in Vienna. Tomorrow it could be the one in Rome. But whether in Vienna or Rome or London, to me governments are all the same, pirates.[67]

The Dubliner spends his time ceaselessly babbling in bars, pubs, and whorehouses, never tiring of the concoction which he is served and which always is made up of the same ingredients: whiskey and Home Rule. And in the evenings when he can't stand it any longer, swollen with poison like a toad, he feels his way out the door, and guided by an instinct for stability seeks out the sides of buildings, then makes his way home, rubbing his behind along all the walls and corners. He goes "arsing along," as we say in English. There you have the Dubliner.[68]

Joyce's income from teaching remained critical, however, as the start of the new year brought little hope for financial reward from his writing. *Chamber Music* had been rejected by several publishers and Joyce had written nearly one thousand pages of *Stephen Hero* with still no idea as to who might want it. Moreover, teaching and parental responsibilities dominated his time. He informed Richards, "It is quite impossible for me in present circumstances to think the rest of the book [*Stephen Hero*], much less to write it."[69]

Finally, on February 17, good news arrived from Richards, who thought highly of *Dubliners* and agreed to publish it, although he anticipated that sales for a book of Irish short stories would be low.[70] Joyce finished another story, "Two Gallants," and sent it on February 22 to Richards, who passed it along to the printer without reading it. As the printer had the right to do under English law, he refused to print this story, and others, because of what he considered to be objectionable material for which he could be prosecuted. Consequently, Richards informed Joyce on April 23 that he must remove passages of sexual innuendo and obscenity from his work.[71]

In his response, Joyce did not mince words with Richards: "Your printer's opinion of [*Dubliners*] does not interest me in the least."[72] On May 5, he sent a long, impassioned letter to Richards defending the artistic integrity of his writing. For the printer, Joyce's disgust was obvious: "O one-eyed printer! Why has he descended with his blue pencil, full of the Holy Ghost, upon these passages and allowed his companions to set up in type reports of divorce cases, and ragging cases and cases of criminal assault."[73]

Joyce's protest was useless. Richards would not risk lawsuits against the printer or himself. He sided firmly with the printer. The use of the word *bloody* in "Grace" particularly irritated the printer, and Joyce then further weakened his case by indicating that the word also appeared in other stories, to which Richards naturally extended his disapproval.

The issue to Joyce was not just one of money or pride, but of principle. The art itself was the thing of value, and Richards's reasoning puzzled him: "I cannot understand what has been admired in the book at all if these passages have been condemned. What would remain of the book if I had to efface everything which might give offence? The title, perhaps?"[74] The nature of Joyce's lonely crusade was revolutionary. "I believe that in composing my chapter of moral history in exactly the way I have composed it I have taken the first step towards the spiritual liberation of my country," he wrote Richards.[75] Joyce concluded, "I have very little intention of prostituting whatever talent I may have to the public,"[76] a sentiment of his that never wavered.

The two debated throughout the spring of 1906 until Joyce grudgingly agreed to make revisions. On July 9, he submitted the *Dubliners* manuscript with changes to Richards in the hope that this would allow publication of the stories.[77] Unfortunately for Joyce, it was a forlorn hope.

His troubles with Nora also persisted. Stanislaus kept Aunt Josephine informed of the circumstances, and in June she sent a lengthy letter to him in which she expressed her serious concern over the problems. She excused Joyce's drinking, stating that he probably was simply trying to forget the hard Dublin years with his family, and assigned much of the blame to Nora's immaturity.[78] Undoubtedly Nora was somewhat less than responsible at times, but she had legitimate reasons—one certainly being Joyce's drinking—for feeling such discomfort in Trieste. She had been away from Ireland for nearly two years but, with Joyce, had barely improved her lot. Her plight was obvious: home every night with her infant son, unable to make friends easily in a city whose people spoke such difficult Italian (if they spoke Italian at all), bound completely by the ongoing misfortunes of Joyce, and harassed by Stanislaus's judgemental comments, Nora must have wondered how life in Trieste could ever be pleasant for her. Joyce, distraught over his writing but determined to succeed abroad, easily could have overlooked Nora at times as he grappled with his own weighty problems.

Adding to the dilemma were troubles at the Berlitz School. Earlier in the spring, Bertelli had taken money from the school and disappeared. As a result, Artifoni told the Joyces that he could not afford to keep both of them through the summer. Stanislaus, while he saw Trieste as a snobbish city with too many bars,[79] was in no mood to relocate again.

Conversely, Joyce was restless. In a February 28, 1906, letter to Richards describing his life, Joyce had written, "I hope these details will not bore you as much as they bore me."[80] Sensing an opportune moment for a fresh beginning, Joyce considered moving to Marseilles, Genoa, or Rome.[81] He checked employment advertisements in the *Tribuna* of Rome and in May found a bank, Nast-Kolb and Schumacher, in need of a correspondence clerk fluent in English and Italian. Joyce immediately sent several references, including one from a Berlitz pupil, Roberto Prezioso, who was the editor of *Il Piccolo della Sera*. By mid-June 1906, he had secured a two-month trial employment to begin on August 1 at a salary equivalent to $62 per month.[82]

Prior to departing for Rome, Joyce paid a few debts and left the rest, including Francini's rent on the via Boccaccio apartment and some furniture payments, to his brother. But Joyce was looking ahead, not back. With his plans firm, he brought his family to the train station, and soon they were on their way south to the Adriatic port of Fiume, away—again—from Trieste.

6

Italian Interlude

It was not out of any great desire to see the Eternal City that Joyce moved to Rome. His main wish was that fewer hours of work and an increased salary at the bank would reduce the financial strain on his family and allow him to finish *Stephen Hero*, his ever-growing novel that he hoped to complete within eighteen months at most.[1] As was often the case, though, Joyce's plans encountered problems.

The family arrived in Rome on July 31, 1906, and moved into a house on via Frattina. Quickly, though, Joyce's patience with banking expired. He had anticipated that the work would be "easy and mechanical,"[2] but was discouraged to learn that his hours were "damn long," extending from 8:30 to 7:30, with a two-hour lunch break.[3] Trying to set aside time and energy for writing was futile. Joyce also was underwhelmed by what culture Rome had to offer. He thought the size of St. Peter's Cathedral disappointingly small and the music "nothing much," and he compared the neighborhood of the Colosseum to "an old cemetery with broke columns of temples and slabs."[4] Even the Tiber River frightened him.[5]

Joyce used Stanislaus to tend to affairs in Trieste. In an August 7 letter, Joyce directed Stanislaus to pay the baker, lie to the tailors (creditors of his) regarding Joyce's address, ignore the rent owed to Francini until he inquired about it (and then refuse to pay it), and find out if his furniture had been sold.[6] Several days later, Joyce told Stanislaus to pay no more debts without consulting him and asked him to send more money, offering—with unwarranted optimism—to reimburse the money at the end of the month. Of more interest to Joyce was news from Trieste and Dublin. He relied on Stanislaus to supply copies of *Il Piccolo della Sera*,[7] while Aunt Josephine sent him the Irish papers.[8]

Roman life eventually began to take on a certain regularity, albeit an uncomfortable one, for Joyce and Nora. Work in the correspondence department was boring. Joyce wrote between two hundred and two hundred and fifty letters daily, sometimes staying beyond his official departure time.[9] While his work was tedious, he displayed a certain conscientiousness in his new endeavor, keeping an extensive notebook on banking practices. His long hours away each day left Nora in near isolation with the baby at home. To pass time, Nora began taking Giorgio to the cinema to watch popular romantic films that allowed her to escape momentarily from the drudgery of her home life.

Predictably, Joyce and Nora found themselves spending more money than they had, and the bank's system of monthly salary payments only made things worse. Their dining habits, as in Trieste, contributed largely to the problem. They enjoyed eating out. Arthur Power described dining as "a serious and carefully chosen ritual" for Joyce, one that he developed largely in Trieste and Rome. Later in Paris, according to Power, it constituted his only form of relaxation.[10]

As much as Joyce despised Rome, he loved its food. "There is literally no end to our appetites. I don't believe I ever was in better health. . . . I stand fascinated before the windows of grocers' shops," he wrote.[11] Nora was getting "much healthier," Joyce noted, with her typical dinner including roast beef, two *polpette* (meatballs), a tomato stuffed with rice, part of a salad, and a half-liter of wine.[12] Joyce was equally enthusiastic: he reported to Stanislaus (three days after another demand for money) that one night he and Nora had finished an entire roast chicken and a plate of ham, bread, and wine for dinner, and "went to bed hungry."[13]

By the end of August, Joyce was on the verge of destitution and pleaded to Stanislaus, "If you cannot do something at once to help me over this month I do not see how I can live." He explained, "I don't wish to 'sponge' on you but only to ask you to try and help me over this month."[14] Stanislaus replied that he had no extra money and in fact was living on ham and bread. Money, though, had a way of finding Joyce at critical moments. A private student agreed to pay Joyce in advance for English lessons,[15] and in early September, Stanislaus did forward some money, temporarily stabilizing the financial situation. Yet, Joyce's evening lessons, given from 8:00 to 9:00, made his workload even more burdensome and left Nora alone with the baby for the day and evening hours.

Despite his stormy correspondence with his brother, Joyce again sought Stanislaus's presence, encouraging him to move to Rome.[16] While such requests were motivated in part by his constant need for money, Joyce sincerely missed their lively discussions on literature, the family, and other matters. He often asked that Stanislaus write to him regarding his (Joyce's) work, as well as other literature, urging him to compose long letters.[17] It remained a difficult relationship between two strong-willed men, but not one truly in danger of imminent collapse.

Joyce certainly was not finding many new friends in Rome. The main concern of Romans, according to Joyce, was "the condition . . . broken, swollen etc of their *coglioni* [testicles] and their chief pastime and joke [is] the breaking of wind rereward."[18] Three months later, Joyce gave an equally graphic assessment of his fellow workers: "When I enter the bank in the morning, I wait for someone to announce something about either his cazzo [penis], culo [ass], or coglioni."[19] On December 7, he announced to Stanislaus, "I am damnably sick of Italy, Italian, and Italians, outrageously, illogically sick."[20]

Adding to Joyce's unhappiness in Rome was his complete lack of progress on *Dubliners*. Letters from Joyce to Richards went unanswered ("not a word from the cursed son of a bitch in London," Joyce told Stanislaus),[21] and while Joyce contin-ued to read before work each morning, his discouragement and anger prevented any further writing. He complained to Stanislaus,

My leisure time is of little use to me. . . . You cannot imagine I want to continue writing at present. I have written quite enough and before I do any more in that line I must see some reason why—I am not a literary Jesus Christ. However, I hope that Mr. Grant Rich-ards shall perhaps also hope within a very few years to be able to see his way to make some communication to me regarding the unfortunately delayed MS which he admires so profoundly.[22]

As the end of each month neared and money became scarce, Joyce's overtures to Stanislaus became routine. Yet each crisis passed. Joyce amazingly was able to function in such chaos. Stanislaus simply perservered. While he was not overjoyed to hear Joyce's constant pleas, he felt lonely in Trieste, at one point considering a return to Dublin.[23] For this reason, Stanislaus looked forward each day to his brother's letters and did not abandon him.[24]

Joyce might have endured everything had his primary purpose for going to Rome—to forward his writing career—been realized. But to the contrary, Joyce encountered only endless problems with Grant Richards, who eventually rejected *Dubliners*. Sacrificed in the chaos was Joyce's writing. He described the dilemma succinctly to his brother: "No pen, no ink, no table, no room, no time, no quiet, no inclination."[25] Each day was a struggle. On Christmas, they were reduced to eating "paste" (pastries) in an effort to ration their money to last the month.[26] It was hardly the life Joyce had envisioned six months earlier.

Slowly, though, Joyce's luck began to turn during the first few weeks of 1907. He was pleased to learn that Nora would have a second child. With parental pride, he wrote to Stanislaus, "Certainly Georgie is the most successful thing connected with me. But he's only a small part mine. I think he rather likes me, however."[27]

Further good news arrived in a letter from Arthur Symons regarding *Chamber Music*, which Joyce had submitted to English publisher Elkin Mathews. With great pleasure, he wrote that Mathews had decided to print the poems, and Symons promised to do all that he could to promote them.[28] The publication contract reached Joyce in January, the terms of which stipulated that he would receive roy-alties only after the sale of three hundred copies. The news was disappointing, but Joyce accepted Mathews's offer. A practical problem for him was finding the time to correct the proofs, so for the moment he assigned the responsibility to Stanislaus, who had fewer burdens in Trieste.[29] Joyce's decision was not surprising, as he had never developed the personal attachment to the poems that he did to *Dubliners*. Yet, he recognized their importance in portraying his more youthful thoughts: "It is a young man's book. I felt like that," he told Stanislaus.[30]

Of most significance were the ideas for stories that were taking shape in Joyce's mind. In September 1906, Joyce had briefly mentioned to Stanislaus an addition to *Dubliners* that concerned Alfred H. Hunter,[31] an Irishman married to an unfaithful wife and known to both Stanislaus and Joyce.[32] The story was to be called "Ulysses," although it remained in an imaginary state for months; Joyce informed

Stanislaus on February 6 that the story had progressed no further than its title. He also had inspirations for other stories, the most important being "The Dead."[33] That two major works steeped in history—*Ulysses* and "The Dead"—had their origins in Rome demonstrates that Joyce, who showed no hesitation in mocking the rich past of the city, was himself not immune to the influence of such history.

Still, Joyce's voluminous correspondence from Rome with Stanislaus reveals the degree to which Joyce's thoughts overall were focused not on Rome or Trieste but Dublin. He commented extensively on acquaintances and developments there, pronouncing Yeats a "tiresome idiot" and the Abbey Theatre "ruined" following the controversy that arose over performances of Synge's *The Playboy of the Western World* in January 1907. "This whole affair has upset me. I feel like a man in a house who hears a row in the street and voices he knows shouting but can't get out to see what the hell is going on. It has put me off the story I was 'going to write'— to wit, *The Dead*," he wrote to Stanislaus.[34]

By contrast, Joyce's infrequent references to Trieste were brief and of marginal importance. He wondered, for example, why Artifoni could not provide loans more often to Stanislaus, and he recalled the political instability in Trieste by wryly noting to his brother, "It is pleasant to reflect that in the event of rupture between Italy and Austria I have my office in the Austrian Consulate."[35] The letters between the brothers were postmarked Rome and Trieste, but their contents were almost strictly Irish.

In fact, Joyce in Rome experienced a remarkable but short-lived thaw in his bitterness toward Dublin, admitting to Stanislaus, "I have not reproduced its [Dublin's] ingenuous insularity and its hospitality. The latter 'virtue' so far as I can see does not exist elsewhere in Europe."[36] An underlying motivation for his change of heart, according to critic Robert Spoo, was that Joyce's "bitter experiences on the Continent had shown him that there were worse microcosms than Dublin to which a writer might consecrate his art."[37] To Joyce, Rome was the most distasteful of these microcosms, with Trieste at times not far behind.

It had become painfully clear to Joyce that he was merely a sojourner in Rome. Restless, he again looked to Trieste. He abruptly telegrammed Stanislaus on February 14 that he had given his notice at the bank and would be returning to Trieste.[38] Two days later, he told Stanislaus that he had "not put pen to paper" in Rome and wanted to regain his old teaching position in Trieste, which Artifoni had told him, probably out of politeness, would be held for him.[39] Joyce's words took Stanislaus and Artifoni by surprise. Scrambling for a solution, Stanislaus told Artifoni that he would accept a salary reduction if Artifoni would take Joyce back. While sympathetic, Artifoni explained that the Berlitz School was in debt and with the school year nearly finished, he simply could not put another teacher on the payroll. Both felt that Joyce was better off remaining in Rome.[40]

Joyce, though, had other thoughts. He recalled how Trieste, in contrast with Rome, was a more agreeable city. Its people were approachable and its scenic coastal beauty, viewed from atop its numerous hills or along the waterfront, invited contemplation, something Joyce needed but rarely could afford in Rome. He wrote of Trieste almost with sentimental fondness: "I would like to be in Trieste again not for the sake of the school but because I should sometimes have opportunity of meeting somebody who shared to a certain extent, my temperament. . . . I am a fish out of water. I would like to go back to Trieste because I remember some nights walking along the streets in the summer and thinking over some of the phrases in my stories."[41] Of course, the stories focused on Dublin, not Trieste, but Joyce simply could not see Dublin as clearly from Rome.

The impending move gave Joyce pause for thought regarding his future. In Trieste, Joyce had declared to Stanislaus, "The delusion which will never leave me is that I am an artist by temperament."[42] But he was still a starving artist. He recognized that the time had come for him "to become a writer or a patient Cousins," and that to continue on his present path would certainly result in his "mental extinction."[43] Joyce needed a reasonably agreeable job, a livable wage, and, most of all, a place where he could write. Trieste, he knew, could meet his needs. Joyce and his family headed back in March 1907.

7

Joyce as Journalist

Joyce and his family had left Italy, but hardly their problems, behind. They arrived in Trieste on March 7 with a total of one lira after Joyce, drunk, had been robbed of two hundred crowns just before departing Rome.[1]

From Rome, Joyce had indicated to Stanislaus that he planned to teach privately in Trieste, an idea Stanislaus rejected as wishful thinking. But Joyce was undeterred, preferring to leave what Stanislaus and Artifoni saw as a stable job in Rome for a very uncertain life back in Austria. Nearly destitute, Joyce probably had every expectation that, once again, his brother and others would sustain his family while he quickly devised another scheme for survival.

Meanwhile, Joyce was glad to be rid of Rome and back with friends and family in Trieste. Despite his experience in Rome, Joyce's element clearly was the city. "He was an urban type," wrote Budgen. "Cities with their streets, people and the noises of people, cafes and the conversations of cafes; these things were what he wanted when he went out of his door."[2]

In Trieste, Joyce found these things. He once again could enjoy operas at Teatro Verdi, attend Orthodox church services, and take long walks, often with Stanislaus. Joyce's "sedentary" life in Rome had displeased him: "I was always accustomed to walking a good deal," he lamented to Stanislaus.[3]

The brothers walked along the piers and, on more adventurous days, out to the seaside castle of Miramare. The castle had been built for Emperor Francis Joseph's brother, the ill-fated Archduke Ferdinand Joseph Maximilian, and his wife, Carlotta. They resided briefly at Miramare before leaving Austria on a bizarre mission to Mexico, which had a tragic and absurd end in 1867. Installed by France as the Mexican emperor, Maximilian was soon captured and executed by Benito Juarez's forces. Carlotta, driven insane by the disastrous turn of events, left Mexico and lived another fifty pathetic years in Europe. The royal couple's destiny left a compelling mystique about Miramare, but it was mainly the castle's panoramic view of the harbor that attracted not only the Joyces but nearly everyone else in Trieste.

James and Stanislaus probably did not blend in with the crowd, though. Both were easily recognizable in Trieste by their unusual gait. Stanislaus's nickname was *omo salta* (the man on springs).[4]

Stanislaus and Joyce also ventured up to the Carso hills around the city, a popular retreat for many Triestines. For centuries a stony, barren land buffeted by the gusts of the *bora* (a winter wind), the Carso landscape was altered dramatically shortly before Joyce's arrival in Trieste. A huge reforestation project transformed the region into an appealing site for Triestines to use for picnics or hikes, or, in some cases, to settle in. The Carso's numerous caves also attracted many local explorers.[5] Scipio Slataper's major work, *Il mio Carso* (My Carso), expresses the sentiment felt by Triestines toward the rugged but scenic hills. Triestine writer Silvio Benco, who would come to know Joyce well, had a particular fondness for walking among the hills, and frequently did so with another young writer, Giani Stuparich.[6] Although Joyce did not visit the Carso as much as Stanislaus did, he was well aware of the Triestines' attachment to it.

Back in the city, a favorite spot of Joyce's was Schimpff's Bookshop in Piazza della Borsa. Schimpff's was the most well-known bookstore in Trieste. It was founded in 1849 by a German, Federico Schimpff. The shop was a popular place for browsing and had very liberal policies, functioning almost as a library. Giani Stuparich recalled that customers could borrow books with ease,[7] and it is likely that Joyce, often broke, took advantage of such an opportunity.

Joyce's immediate concerns, however, were more basic: he needed a place to live and a job. With help, he soon resolved both problems. While Joyce was in Rome, Stanislaus had moved from Francini's house to via San Nicolò 32, the former address of the Berlitz School, which had relocated across the street.[8] Upon Joyce's return, Stanislaus took a cheaper apartment on via delle Beccherie, allowing Joyce's family to have the via San Nicolò apartment. Still broke, however, the unpredictable Joyce, having just brought his family from Rome, promptly applied for a correspondent's job in Sicily.

Reason set in on March 9 when Joyce and Artifoni agreed that Joyce could teach part time at Berlitz for fifteen crowns a week, with the understanding that Joyce would solicit his former pupils to attend the school.[9] No sooner had he settled his employment crisis than he again, for unknown reasons, uprooted his family and moved to via Nuova 45, four blocks away, where Stanislaus joined them on March 15.[10] Almost in spite of himself, Joyce had landed on his feet in Trieste.

For Joyce, teaching had always been simply a means to an end: namely, earning money. His real ambition was to write, and one of his students, Roberto Prezioso, offered to help. Prezioso's responsibilities as the editor of *Il Piccolo della Sera* were increasing, mainly due to Teodoro Mayer's frequent trips to Rome to garner support for Triestine irredentists.[11] He already had hired Francini,[12] and now it was time to help Joyce.

When he heard Joyce complaining about the ignorance in Europe regarding the plight of Ireland,[13] Prezioso saw the advantage of publicizing a comparison of the foreign dominance that existed in both Ireland and Trieste. He recognized that the paper had to remain at least somewhat guarded in its pro-irredentist sympathies:

later in the year, *L'Indipendente* would be banned temporarily by the Austrians for devoting an issue to the memory of Oberdan.[14] Still, he understood that Joyce's perspective might prove useful to the irredentist cause, and in March 1907 he discussed the matter with Joyce. Prezioso sweetened the deal by offering Joyce a higher pay rate based on two factors: Joyce was writing in a foreign language, and he desperately needed the money.[15]

Although not an irredentist, Joyce easily could see the benefits of accepting. He knew that Trieste's newspapers enjoyed significant popularity. In 1907 alone, twelve newspapers began publishing (followed by twenty-nine more the next year),[16] with the well-established *Il Piccolo della Sera* among the city's leading papers. Joyce not only could display his knowledge of Irish politics and his proficiency in Italian to a large audience, but, more importantly, he also could improve his financial lot.

He began writing immediately, producing three articles. "Il fenianismo" (Fenianism) appeared in the March 22 issue, "Home rule maggiorenne" (Home rule comes of age) on May 19, and "L'Irlanda alla sbarra" (Ireland at the bar) on September 16. Probably to the surprise of Prezioso, the first two were remarkable as much for their criticism of the Irish as for any blame assessed to foreigners, while the third was a genuine assault on England. None of the articles overtly compared conditions in Dublin and Trieste. In fact, Joyce never referred to Trieste. But all showed the great extent to which Joyce had studied and considered the evolution of Irish politics.

Joyce's work for *Il Piccolo della Sera* afforded him the chance to meet and work closely with Silvio Benco, a noted journalist, novelist, and literary critic. Determined to be a writer, Benco had joined the staff of *L'Indipendente* as a teenager in 1890 before moving to *Il Piccolo* in 1903.[17] A soft-spoken but gifted intellectual and a strong irredentist, he was considered the leading journalist in Trieste.

At the request of Prezioso, Benco reviewed the Italian in Joyce's articles. Joyce asked that the revisions be done in his presence, probably, Benco believed, out of a simple desire to improve his language skills. Benco found the writing to be "a bit hard and cautious," but quite precise. The collaboration was short lived. Benco understood that Joyce's work in Italian needed little editing, and when he suggested a word change, a disagreement ensued that left Joyce—with his dictionary—the victor.[18] Joyce, however, did not hold a grudge, and their relationship was unharmed. "He always treated me as a friend," Benco wrote,[19] although his daughter Aurelia noted that the introspective Benco "was not really close to Joyce or anyone else."[20]

Pleased by his efforts for the newspaper, Joyce told Stanislaus, "I think I must have a talent for journalism."[21] Others were equally impressed with Joyce's ability. Francini suggested that he speak at the Università Popolare. The timing was appropriate: the 1907 political campaign in Trieste had become highly charged, with posters and graffiti covering the city. Socialists and irredentists were particularly competitive, and the Università naturally supported the latter. Attilio Tamaro, a student of Joyce and later a leading irredentist author, asked Joyce to present a series of lectures on Ireland at the Università.[22] The school regularly presented speakers, but in Scipio Slataper's opinion, most gave rather boring addresses that received only polite applause.[23] Tamaro's hope was that Joyce's words, showing Triestines that they were part of a larger cause, would inspire further support for the irredentists.

Concerned less about the politics of the situation than the chance for additional exposure and income, Joyce again accepted the offer. He later decided to give only a single speech, entitled "Irlanda, isola dei santi e dei savi" (Ireland, island of saints and sages) focusing on the former greatness of Ireland that had all but disappeared following the institution of British control, a result irredentists were eager to publicize.

The speech, for which Joyce received twenty crowns, was given on April 27, 1907, and the attendance of 139 was excellent,[24] partially due to the presence of numerous Berlitz students, all of whom had been given tickets by Artifoni. Reflecting his ongoing poverty, Joyce wore a broadcloth jacket borrowed from Artifoni and an overcoat on loan from Stanislaus. Using a prepared text, Joyce spoke deliberately, especially for a largely Italian audience, yet was received warmly by the gathering and with acclaim by his peers. Artifoni was happy because of the positive impression Joyce, as a Berlitz representative, had created for the school, and Prezioso complimented Joyce on his mastery of Italian.[25]

Joyce was satisfied by the response. Nora, on the other hand, had a very different view of the night. Watching the fashionably dressed Triestines enter the hall, Nora, in her simple attire and without a hat, felt too ashamed to join them. Instead, she took Giorgio to the movies, while Joyce and Stanislaus enjoyed the evening's success over drinks at the Stella Polare.[26]

Joyce's articles for *Il Piccolo della Sera* and his speech gave him his first public exposure as a writer in Trieste. Still, despite the best hopes of Prezioso and Tamaro, Joyce's words had limited effect. Most Italian irredentists, already grappling with the Austrian authorities, Slav nationalists, and socialists (including other Italians), could not have been seriously interested in the plight of the Irish, any more than Joyce was concerned over the irredentists' situation. From the perspective of Prezioso and Tamaro, Joyce's words gave an international flavor to the irredentist cause. But there is no indication that irredentists, as much as some of them respected Joyce's intellect, were influenced by him. The fact is that the socialists pulled off a startling victory over the irredentists in the May 14 election just two weeks after Joyce's speech, which had received generous coverage in *Il Piccolo*. It is also worth noting that while violent demonstrations marred the election, Joyce, in conversations with Stanislaus, continued to focus on Irish politics, even as cafe windows were being smashed just blocks away.[27]

Joyce's modest success in Trieste continued with the publication of *Chamber Music* in early May. The title had been suggested by Stanislaus based on "the passionless love themes and studious grace of the songs."[28] Joyce "composed them in his head first, during his wanderings about Dublin, and then wrote them out without corrections, often in odd places," such as post offices or "the snug of some pub," according to Stanislaus.[29]

Joyce, though, had serious reservations about the quality of the poems, believing that they were weak and not even honest in their expressions of love. Filled with doubt a month earlier, he had told Stanislaus one evening that he would cable Mathews to cancel publication. Stanislaus, mindful of Joyce's previous disappointments with publishers, insisted that Joyce leave the decision to Mathews. The brothers spent most of the night pacing about the Piazza delle Poste before Stanislaus could convince Joyce to let the matter stand, and the poems were published.[30]

As he had promised, Arthur Symons wrote the first review of *Chamber Music*—four years after Joyce initially had asked him for help in locating a publisher—in the *Nation*. He called the work "pure poetry."[31] Otherwise, the poems generally were ignored. Even in Ireland, only three reviews appeared. An indication of Joyce's own discomfort with the poems is that he apparently told almost no one in Trieste that the book had been published, despite the favorable, albeit limited, publicity he had received just weeks earlier for his articles and speech. Of more importance to Joyce, a scant 127 copies had been sold by July 24, far short of the 300 sales needed to realize a profit.[32] Nevertheless, it was ironic that Joyce, who did not think of himself as a poet and in fact had devoted thousands of hours to his stories and his novel, would find his first published volume to be one of poetry.

Over the summer, an interesting turn of events gave Joyce reason, finally, to look favorably upon *Chamber Music*. Geoffrey Molyneux Palmer, an English organist and composer, wrote to Joyce through Elkin Mathews and offered to put the poems to music. Joyce was enthusiastic over the idea and gave his consent.[33] By July 1909, Palmer had written music for eight of the poems, and Joyce was pleased with the results.[34] (He maintained a polite and respectful correspondence with Palmer, prompting him to comment in a 1911 letter to the composer regarding *Dubliners*, "I don't think you will recognise me in it at a first glance as it is somewhat bitter and sordid.")[35]

In mid-May, poor health beset Joyce. Plagued by a fever and painful, bloodshot eyes, Joyce was confined to bed with what Dr. Senigaglia called rheumatic fever, a diagnosis that has come under question by modern physicians. Dr. J. B. Lyons of Dublin finds it to be "almost certainly incorrect," stating that "the combination of acute rheumatic symptoms with iritis suggests today either Reiter's syndrome or sarcoidosis, neither of which could have been diagnosed in 1907."[36] Dr. Oscar Oblath examined Joyce's eyes, but Joyce made treatment difficult by insisting on reading, and several weeks passed before he could resume teaching.

The timing of Joyce's illness could not have been worse. Nora was due to give birth, and Stanislaus was in no position to pay such expenses. Artifoni recognized the plight of the Joyce brothers, and he assured Stanislaus that Berlitz would cover Joyce's medical bills, a seemingly foolish gesture given the school's financial predicament. Taking Artifoni at his word, Stanislaus borrowed a large sum of money from the school with the naive expectation that the debt would be excused. In fact, Artifoni temporarily leased the school, leaving Stanislaus accountable for repayment. Then Stanislaus was hit with an eviction notice by his landlord before finding refuge again with the Francinis in mid-June.[37]

Joyce, still at via Nuova, also considered another move, with ample reasons to do so. The summer heat had arrived, and he was soon to have the responsibility of

another child. His teaching still bored him. His finances were in shambles. *Dubliners* was going nowhere—in fact, he considered translating his stories into French
because he did not think they would be published in English.[38] Groping for any
improvement, he wrote in early July to the South Africa Colonisation Society for a
job. Undoubtedly to the benefit of his family, Joyce learned that no opening existed. Unfazed, he next looked back to Rome, applying for a secretary's position
with the Society for the Prevention of Cruelty to Animals.[39]

Meanwhile, Nora was having her own misadventures during pregnancy. Although she felt sick, she refused to let Dr. Senigaglia examine her until Joyce
agreed to buy her new clothes, which he eventually did.[40] On July 12, the doctor
recommended that Nora enter the hospital, mentioning that they would need to
show a marriage certificate. To Senigaglia's amazement, Joyce pointedly stated
that none existed; Stanislaus then suggested that Joyce at least get Nora a ring for
the sake of appearance, an idea that surely pleased her but not Joyce.[41]

Finally, on July 26, 1907, just one day before Giorgio's birthday, Nora gave
birth to Anna Lucia in the pauper ward. The baby was "almost born on the street,"
she later told the Francinis.[42] A midwife told Joyce that the baptism would take
place on July 28, a plan that he quickly squelched.[43] Sadly, Lucia, as she was
called, did not enter the world unblemished: she was born with a cast in her left
eye.[44] Her self-consciousness over this defect, combined with severe emotional
problems that led to her being institutionalized, later caused Lucia to be a source of
constant anxiety and difficulty for Joyce and Nora. As a teenager, Giorgio would
write poignantly to Lucia,

> Amid roses without thorns
> May your life pass
> And there be no end
> To your happiness.[45]

In Lucia's tragic case, though, it was a forlorn wish.

Curiously, Joyce seemed to have taken Artifoni's previous advice—to present
himself as a married man—to heart. When completing the paperwork regarding
Lucia's birth, Joyce indicated that Nora and he had been married in Dublin on May
5, 1907,[46] an obvious impossibility since both were in Trieste at the time. Joyce and
Nora did refer to each other as husband and wife in various letters, but they were
not legally married until July 4, 1931, at the Kensington Registry Office in London
where, coincidentally, the equally controversial D. H. Lawrence had married Frieda
Weekley seventeen years earlier.[47]

When she left the hospital on August 5, Nora received a charitable gift of twenty
crowns, but that did little to relieve the family's financial strain. Stanislaus stayed
with them for two weeks to help out, particularly with the lively Giorgio, but Nora
still faced day after day of hard work with two children while the family's debt
grew steadily. Matters worsened when Joyce was given one week's notice to vacate
the via Nuova apartment. Stanislaus and he searched diligently, only to hear the
familiar objection to children. On August 18, Joyce and his family moved to an

apartment at via Santa Caterina 1, still downtown but five blocks removed from the waterfront. Two weeks later, Stanislaus left the Francinis to rejoin Joyce.

Complicating the matter further, Joyce, unhappy that Artifoni had leased the Berlitz School, quit his job. He chose to offer private lessons at ten crowns each. Although he had been a popular instructor at Berlitz, Joyce was humbled somewhat when he found himself teaching just two or three lessons a week,[48] leaving Stanislaus as the only regularly employed member of the household.

Another chance to depart Trieste presented itself in the form of a letter (containing a one-pound gift) from Gogarty in Vienna, where he was taking a course in surgery. He invited Joyce for a visit, the intent being that Gogarty would help him to find a job as a German instructor. Quite cynical of Gogarty's bourgeois lifestyle, Joyce—with some prodding from Stanislaus, who harbored an old dislike for Gogarty—decided against uprooting his family again for an uncertain future.[49]

Joyce pondered what he already had written and what new ideas were worth pursuing. Virtually unemployed, with no lessons until 5:30, Joyce now had time to write, which he eagerly did. By September 20, he had finished "The Dead" (part of which he had dictated to Stanislaus while still sick in bed),[50] and begun to reshape *Stephen Hero*, soon to be retitled *A Portrait of the Artist as a Young Man*, into a novel consisting of five extensive chapters. The first three of these he completed by early April 1908.[51]

His effort to revive *Dubliners* turned to Elkin Mathews, to whom Joyce sent the stories in September.[52] In his review, Mathews's reader offered a depressingly familiar critique: the literary talent was there, but the content was appalling. He commented,

Most of these stories treat of very lower-middle class Dublin life. They are never enlivening, and often sordid and even disgusting. There is a faded, musty odour about them: the scenes are in gloomy back streets, in houses with dust-stained fan-lights and windows, in rooms with battered prints on the walls and only a coal of fire in the grate, in the bars of Public Houses. Most of the characters are too fond of drink, and nearly all are physically repulsive. It is a dismal and depressing world, this. The writing is smooth-flowing, and the stories often subtly and skilfully evolved. The dialogue is easy and natural. The last 20 pages of "The Dead" finds the author at his best.[53]

Mathews rejected the stories.[54]

"Ulysses" also was becoming more focused in Joyce's mind. The character of Ulysses had fascinated Joyce since childhood.[55] As he later explained to a Zurich friend, Joyce believed that the "most beautiful, all-embracing theme is that of the Odyssey. It is greater, more human than that of *Hamlet*, *Don Quixote*, Dante, *Faust*."[56] Stanislaus noted that Joyce was planning to expand his work to create a "Dublin 'Peer Gynt.' "[57] Undoubtedly Joyce's own odyssey through Zurich, Pola, Rome, and Trieste, exposing him to several cultures and languages, contributed to his affinity for the story.

Conversation between the two brothers frequently centered not on fiction but on drama. In the summer, Joyce had mentioned to Stanislaus a possible topic for a play, which may have contributed to the development of his later—and only—play,

Exiles.[58] He retained a strong interest in (if rare approval of) Irish literature, particularly in the dramas of J. M. Synge. In March 1908, Joyce enlisted the help of his friend Nicolò Vidacovich, a Triestine lawyer and man of letters, in translating Synge's *Riders to the Sea* into Italian. The text's use of Tuscan[59] reflects the success of Joyce's earlier Italian lessons with Francini. Following Synge's premature death in 1909, though, his heirs did not consent to the work.[60] The translation finally was published more than twenty years later, in the September-October 1929 issue of *Solaria*. (Joyce and Vidacovich also attempted a translation of "Ivy Day in the Committee Room." The result, unfortunately, was "a dismal failure," Joyce conceded to Yeats.)[61]

Joyce's hunger for theater activity was well nourished in Trieste. In addition to the Verdi, theaters included the Politeama Rossetti, which held five thousand people,[62] the Armonia, the Filodrammatico, and the Fenice.[63] The Verdi featured performers such as Eleonora Duse, Emma Grammatica, Ermete Zacconi, and Ermete Novelli in plays by D'Annunzio, Ibsen, and Benelli.[64]

Sometimes using free tickets provided to him by Francini (courtesy of *Il Piccolo della Sera*), Joyce attended the theater with an enthusiasm bordering on addiction. Over a two-week period in October 1908, for example, Joyce went to at least seven performances of *La Boheme*.[65] Earlier in the year, he watched Eleonora Duse in *Rosmersholm* and Ermete Zacconi in *Ghosts*. Zacconi astonished Joyce: "Compared with such an actor we who are not Italians should hide our faces. No other country has anything like it. The Italians have an enormous genius for the stage. Definitely they are the greatest actors in the theater of life," he exclaimed to Francini.[66] Joyce's emotion carried into the theater itself, and Triestine theatergoers were accustomed to his outbursts. Somewhat less excited was Nora, home with the children and unable to go out as much. She complained at times over how often Joyce and Stanislaus went to operas. Joyce was not unsympathetic to her position, but he did not alter his nightlife.[67]

8

Schmitz-Svevo

Although Joyce had been away from Ireland for nearly three years, he still lacked a literary soulmate abroad. In Trieste, Joyce had not found replacements for Byrne, Curran, and the other intellectuals who had provided the Dublin Joyce with such a stimulating environment, even if, in his assessment of Ireland, he chose to minimize their influence on him. Stanislaus had a sincere interest in and respect for Joyce's work, but their personal feuds placed a certain restraint on their relationship. Among Triestines, Francini was a good friend and enjoyable drinking companion, and others, including Benco, would move closer to Joyce over time. Yet, his literary mission in Trieste had been a solitary one until he discovered that a private student, Ettore Schmitz, was a kindred spirit. Joyce did not make a practice of confiding in Triestines regarding his writing, but the artistic sensitivity of Schmitz, who used the authorial pseudonym Italo Svevo, signaled to Joyce that here was an exception. The relationship would prove to be significant for both writers, especially Svevo.

Svevo was born in Trieste a generation before Joyce, on December 19, 1861. His father, Francesco, a Jew of German-Italian parentage, was a moderately successful glassware merchant, and the Schmitz family lived in a comfortable home at via dell'Acquedotto 16. Svevo attended a public elementary school for Jews in Trieste before his father, proud of his German heritage, sent the boy off to a commercial academy in Germany in 1874 to learn German in preparation for what was assumed would be a business career.[1] Svevo did very well academically and socially at the school and stayed there until he was seventeen, when he returned to Trieste.

Although he had been well trained for a life in commerce, Svevo found himself to be more curious about philosophy and literature, particularly drama, than business, and secretly hoped he could become a writer. To delay his expected entry into the working world, Svevo convinced his father to allow him to enroll in the Scuola Superiore di Commercio Fondazione Revoltella, founded in 1877 with money bequeathed by Baron Pasquale Revoltella. While there, Svevo developed a sympathy for the irredentist cause.[2]

But, for reasons that are not entirely clear, he changed course in 1880 and accepted a position as a clerk at the Banca Viennese Union. Though a diligent and punctual employee, Svevo despised the tedium and overall boredom that filled his days at the bank. His mind increasingly turned to literature and to his writing.[3] Articles and reviews written by Svevo (often under the pseudonym E. Samigli) were published in the literary columns of *L'Indipendente*, where he later met Benco.[4] He also worked some evenings for *Il Piccolo*, reading foreign newspapers.[5] Svevo's months at the bank, however, dragged into years, with no change in his attitude toward his job and little hope for recognition as a writer. His life had settled into a hectic and unsatisfying routine: days at the bank, evenings walking along the busy Corso, reading in the library or pausing in a cafe, and nights at the newspaper.[6]

The premature death of his brother Elio, in whom he had often confided his private literary dreams, left Svevo even more disillusioned. He was taken by a melancholy that, to various extents, remained forever with him. Turning greater attention to his writing, he focused mainly on his novel, *Una vita* (A Life), that vividly depicted the monotonous daily routine of a bank clerk. After more than two years of work, though, Svevo was not optimistic:

With all the enormous ambition I once had, not to have found anyone, *anyone at all*, to take an interest in what I'm thinking or doing; to spend my time having to take an interest in other people's doings as the only way of getting a little attention for my own. Two years ago exactly I began that novel which was to have been God knows what; and in fact it's a disgusting mess and will choke me in the end. My real strength always lay in hoping, and the worst of it is, I'm even losing my talent for that.[7]

Fortunately for Svevo's morale, one of his best friends was the energetic Triestine painter Umberto Veruda, a successful, widely travelled artist eight years younger than Svevo. Veruda's confidence contrasted sharply with the introspection of Svevo. He was known mainly for his portraits, probably the most famous of which is one of Svevo's later wife, Livia, that eventually was given by Svevo to Joyce. When Veruda completed a portrait of Svevo and his sister Ortensia in 1893, the dedication read, "Ettore Schmitz, more brother than friend."[8] Svevo's closeness to the painter provided him emotional stability during a very difficult period. Following Veruda's untimely death in 1904, Svevo quietly cared for Veruda's blind father and organized a Veruda exhibit in a pavilion along the Canal grande.[9]

In 1892, the same year his father died, Svevo published *Una vita* at his own expense, using for the first time the name "Italo Svevo" (Italian Swabian), which reflected Svevo's own origins as well as the hybrid government that ruled Trieste.[10] To cover the cost, he took a part-time teaching position at the Scuola Revoltella.[11] Critical response was lukewarm and minimal. Most of the Italian press, save for a few local reviewers, simply ignored it.[12] A major problem was Svevo's inability to write in "literary" Italian. Italians insisted that serious literature be written in pure, almost lyrical Italian, a standard impossible for Svevo to reach. Having received a German education (his favorite writer was Schopenhauer), yet practiced in the Triestine dialect, Svevo produced a kind of tortured Italian that was scorned by Italian critics and the reading public. (Joyce himself was very aware of this linguistic peculiarity: in *Giacomo Joyce*, he referred to the "boneless Viennese Italian" of a Triestine student.)[13] One critic stated that Svevo's use of local idioms remained vague even to Triestine readers.[14]

Moreover, in the eyes of many Italian Triestines, the status of Trieste as an Italian city cut off from Italy only increased their desire for distinguished Italian writing that would promote the visibility of Italian culture in the city. Italian critic and poet Eugenio Montale described this phenomenon: "More than any other Italian city Trieste has felt the need to assert the tie that binds it to Italian culture.... And for this reason perhaps the denomination 'Triestine writer' seems to have acquired a special meaning: the meaning of a writer tightly linked to the life, the habits, and the difficult destiny of his city."[15] In fact, Svevo was very much a local writer, drawing his characters and settings from his native city. But his prose, particularly with its German flavor, was anathema to Italian readers. Svevo seemed like an amateur, and his writing was treated accordingly. *Una vita* was soon out of print.

In December 1895, two months after his mother's death, Svevo became engaged to Livia Veneziani, a Catholic thirteen years younger and whose mother was a first cousin of Svevo. Livia's parents, Gioacchino and Olga, owned a very successful company that manufactured an anticorrosive paint for the keels of ships. The family lived in Chiarbola, a Trieste suburb, near the main factory. In addition to the Trieste plant, the company had facilities in Italy, France, and England. Livia's parents expressed concern over the relatively low social status of Svevo before eventually relenting, and the two, Jewish and Catholic, were joined in a civil ceremony in July 1896. Following his baptism as a Catholic a year later, Svevo married Livia at the San Giacomo church in Trieste.

Svevo and Livia settled into an enjoyable life at the spacious and elegant Villa Veneziani. Livia quickly became pregnant, and their only child, Letizia, was born in September 1897. Svevo, who was contributing money to his brother Adolpho to operate the Schmitz family business, worried about his ability to support his wife and daughter in a comfortable manner at least somewhat independent of his wealthy in-laws. To this end, he continued to teach evenings at the Scuola Revoltella until 1901.[16]

More discouraging to Svevo was the futility of his literary efforts. His second novel, *Senilità*, was published at his own expense at the end of 1898. It was reviewed largely unfavorably by six journals,[17] and was generally ignored by the public. Benco later observed, "*Senilità* was one of those unfortunate books that, once printed, don't succeed in losing their virginity."[18] Svevo still felt a desire to write, but he was deeply embittered by the silence that met his work.[19] The disappointing realization that he was writing mainly for himself caused him, reluctantly, to abandon his dream. He later told Stanislaus, "I could only come to the conclusion that I was not a writer."[20] When he accepted a position in the Veneziani company in May 1899, his literary career seemed over.

Success did come to Svevo as a businessman. By the end of 1900, he was supervising the Murano, Italy, plant, which supplied the Italian navy. As years passed, Svevo settled comfortably into the lifestyle of a wealthy man.

Svevo could speak Italian, German, and French, but his need to speak a fourth language—English—became evident when the company decided to build a plant in Charlton, England. He would be spending one or two months each year overseeing the work at Charlton,[21] and his English had not improved sufficiently for such an assignment. So he sought an English tutor, and in January 1908 he found Joyce.

As the instructor of Count Sordina, Prezioso, and later the sons of Prince Konrad von Hohenlohe,[22] the Austrian ruler of the city, Joyce became rather well known in academic circles in Trieste. His reputation certainly was not lost on Artifoni. In a bizarre move designed to capitalize on Joyce's popularity, Artifoni actually had offered to sell the Berlitz to him in April 1907. His rationale was that Joyce and Stanislaus were friendly with so many wealthy Triestines that the brothers would have little trouble raising the money. Joyce, almost penniless, briefly considered the proposal before declining.[23]

Joyce not only needed more private students, but, by this time, wished to find someone like Svevo with whom he could seriously discuss his work.[24] Through the early Trieste years, almost no one there thought of Joyce as a writer of fiction, for he had written only the articles for *Il Piccolo della Sera* as far as most people knew. As late as 1912, the newspaper referred to him as a "thinker, man of culture, and freelance writer."[25] His face, of course, was recognizable to many Triestines who had been his students, but as Benco noted, that gave him only "the fame of an English teacher."[26]

Such fame was good enough for Svevo. During their lessons, Joyce covered an array of topics. To Svevo's satisfaction, the pair often focused on literature, and Joyce discovered that Svevo indeed was curious about his writing.[27] He displayed his respect for the Svevos by reading *Chamber Music* and his *Dubliners* stories to Livia and Svevo at the house in Chiarbola, where the lessons for both initially took place twice each week. (Eileen Joyce later taught Letizia at the Svevo home.)[28]

How much of the English reading the Svevos understood is questionable, but the event clearly captivated them. Livia was so moved upon hearing "The Dead" that she gathered some flowers from the garden and presented them to Joyce, which Stanislaus recalled as possibly the first sign of appreciation toward Joyce from a "common" reader.[29] Svevo, sensing a mutual yearning for recognition, confided to Joyce that he had written two novels years earlier with no critical or popular success, and he offered him the books for his comments. Joyce delighted and probably shocked Svevo by responding favorably.

Unlike the Italian critics, Joyce found Svevo's use of local names and dialect intriguing; not one to bestow praise easily, Joyce asked Svevo, "Do you know that you are a neglected writer? There are passages in *Senilità* that even Anatole France could not have improved." (Joyce and Stanislaus had attended a lecture on Anatole France in early 1908,[30] possibly explaining why Joyce had France in mind.) The encouragement inspired Svevo, and his old dream of being a writer, long dormant, was revived. Hearing his teacher recite lines of his writing from memory, Svevo could not restrain his enthusiasm in discussing his literary ambitions with Joyce.[31] Accompanying Joyce all the way back to his apartment, Svevo was, as Joyce told

Stanislaus, quite *commosso*[32] (deeply moved).

Regardless of Joyce's opinion, Trieste, hardly renowned for its appreciation of literature, was not prepared to receive Svevo as a literary talent. But Svevo was not alone. The energetic voices of a younger generation of Triestine writers, including Umberto Saba, Guido Voghera, Virgilio Giotti, Scipio Slataper, and Carlo and Giani Stuparich, found it little easier to gain local recognition. Consequently, most temporarily left Trieste and headed for Florence, the city of "pure" Italian, to improve their writing and to establish a name for themselves. Svevo himself regretted never having made the pilgrimage there to "cleanse" his Italian of its Triestine influence. The younger writers were associated prior to World War I with the important Florentine journal *La Voce*, which provided a forum for a wide range of intellectual discussion.

Their works (excepting Saba's) at times were politically charged, but not simply in support of nationalism.[33] Ignoring the heavy propaganda of the time, they portrayed political and social truths as they saw them. The young writers revealed their love of Italy as well as a sympathy for the humanistic features of socialism, a stance that naturally disturbed the irredentists. Indeed, one of the founders of *La Voce*, Giuseppe Prezzolini, used its pages to urge Triestine Italians to better appreciate Slav culture,[34] recognizing that Slavs now constituted nearly 25 percent of Trieste's population of 220,000. While Slataper and Carlo Stuparich fought and died for Italy in the war, the Triestine writers had never been in the irredentist camp as consistently as other Triestine intellectuals, such as Benco. Yet, Trieste was (or would be) the focus of much of their work, even as they were unable, like Svevo, to engage the literary imaginations of Triestines. Ironically, the city now looks back with nostalgia at this creative period, with numerous statues, parks, and streets honoring these Triestine writers, including Joyce.

Unfazed by the tepid reading public, Joyce undertook a campaign to promote Svevo, but his effort fell flat. When he mentioned Svevo's name to Vidacovich, the lawyer "pursed his lips, half-closed his eyes, and shook his head slowly and sadly." Joyce's own students, many of whom had received higher education and were well-read,[35] were nearly incredulous when he informed them that Svevo was the only Italian writer who interested him. "Ma dai, professore" (Come off it, professor), they responded.

No one in Trieste, according to Triestine scholar Niny Rocco-Bergera, was interested in Svevo the writer: "not . . . his family and relatives, not the group of young Triestine writers who were making their way in Florence in connection with the *Voce Review*, not his friends at the coffee-house, not the young journalists of the Editorial Office of the *Indipendente*, not the group of big shots and irredentists led by Felice Venezian, not the intellectual group of the pretty and handsome friends of Signorina Livia."[36]

It was not surprising, given the differences in their characters, that Joyce invested more energy in promoting Svevo than did Svevo himself. Joyce was a young, eccentric, brash man of action who, for all of his complaining, was generally an optimist willing to take the initiative. Joyce once asked Svevo to describe his teacher, and his account shows the extent of Joyce's determination: "When I see him walking on the streets I always think that he is enjoying a leisure a full leisure. Nobody is awaiting him and he does not want to reach an aim or to meet anybody. No! He walks in order to be left to himself. He does also not walk for health. He walks because he is not stopped by anything."[37]

Svevo, influenced by the death of his brother and the failure of his novels, was more skeptical, at times melancholy, expecting less of the world. Perhaps he was touched by what Triestines call *smara*, a sense of unease brought on by the frigid *bora* that whips through the city each winter.[38] A friendly and humble man, his humor often was directed inward, such as the times he referred to himself as a "submarine painter."[39] Svevo did not possess the biting, sometimes vicious, wit of Joyce. His financial success also placed him in a completely separate stratum of Triestine society, far above Joyce. At least partly because of this, as well as their age difference, Joyce and Svevo maintained a formal relationship. They addressed each other by their surnames, and Svevo once referred to Joyce as "my teacher and friend."[40] Joyce always acted in a gentlemanly manner with the Svevos,[41] in contrast with his more animated behavior with Francini.

According to Mary Kirn, later a maid in the Joyce household, Svevo's business-like demeanor created a certain distance between the two. Svevo, who took some lessons at Joyce's apartment, always arrived punctually, and this sense of propriety never changed.[42] Their friendship existed largely because of their literary interests. Still, even as he approached middle age, Svevo could remember his younger days as a bank clerk and a struggling writer, so he appreciated Joyce's plight. Proud of Joyce's Trieste connection, Svevo later wrote, "We Triestines have a right to regard him with deep affection as if he belonged in a certain sense to us."[43] Joyce, of course, belonged to no one. But, feeling rejected by Dublin, he would have taken some private satisfaction from Svevo's words.

9

Of Bloom and Politics

While Joyce's poverty in Trieste went on unabated, he was not oblivious to the family's needs. In the spring of 1908, he bought furniture and other items for the apartment (where he had to give lessons), as well as clothes for Nora and the children. Yet, with a touch of Joycean absurdity, the apartment had no clock. In fact, it had not had one for months, frequently causing Stanislaus, and presumably Joyce, to be late for lessons. The brothers thought they were in luck when a clock store opened across the street, only to see the clock in the front window break on the second day, remaining stuck at 8:00.[1]

To keep creditors at bay and food on the table, Joyce turned his mind away from teaching to other potential sources of income. His imagination, unfortunately, was more successful at creating employment ideas than in producing cash. Joyce's schemes demonstrated that he was open to almost any possibility. In June 1908, he considered selling Irish tweeds; in July, training his voice or applying for a civil-service appointment; and in August, seeking a teaching position in Florence. None of the plans materialized, although Joyce later did take voice lessons from Romeo Bartoli, a Triestine voice instructor who had studied English with him.[2]

The need for additional money became somewhat less urgent when Nora suffered a miscarriage in early August, although Stanislaus claimed in September that he rescued his brother six times from starvation.[3] It was clear that they could barely cover the expenses or handle the responsibility of their present family. Nora never again became pregnant.

From Stanislaus's point of view, another factor that complicated family matters was the emotional isolation he felt. Often alone with his thoughts in Trieste, Stanislaus yearned for attention and appreciation, particularly from a woman. But his deepening introspection, combined with his frequently dour demeanor, dashed most such hopes. Almost inevitably, Stanislaus found himself increasingly attracted to Nora through the summer and autumn of 1908.[4]

There is no indication that Stanislaus ever acted on his impulses toward Nora, and she evidently was unaware of them—one can easily imagine her laughing heartily had she known. Had Joyce known, on the other hand, the issue would have been far less humorous. While his relationship with Nora was strained at times, Joyce would not have tolerated a rival. Even the subject of Nora's previous boy-friends disturbed him and would cause a personal crisis the following year in Dub-lin. In this instance, he apparently knew nothing. But Stanislaus's fixation on Nora—and the guilt caused by such thoughts—further hampered his own often clumsy efforts to solidify the family.

The ongoing battle of wills—Stanislaus preaching endlessly to Joyce and Nora about their spending, and Joyce alternately cursing and comforting Stanislaus—could not last. After an argument with Joyce over money, Stanislaus moved to an apartment at via Nuova 27.[5] As usual, though, the hostility was short lived. Joyce and Stanislaus went the next day to look for an apartment for Joyce's family, and Stanislaus continued to eat meals with them. In March 1909, Joyce and his wander-ing family were on the move again, to an apartment at via Vincenzo Scussa 8, across from the city's public garden.

Following his burst of writing the previous spring, Joyce fell into another crea-tive swoon. Months passed and he wrote little. The manuscript of A Portrait lay unfinished at three chapters, and the stories of Dubliners languished in publishing oblivion. Relief ultimately came from Svevo. Given an assignment by Joyce to assess the completed chapters of A Portrait, he responded with a letter on February 8 indicating that he was impressed by the second and third chapters, particularly the sermons in the latter. Svevo observed, "I have read them with a very strong feeling and I know in my own little town a lot of people who would be certainly stroke by the same feeling."[6]

Encouraged by Svevo's words, Joyce focused his attention on A Portrait and his other work. He sent a letter on February 13, 1909, to Geoffrey Molyneux Palmer, expressing his admiration for the music the composer had written to accompany his poems. On the same day, Joyce wrote to Mathews regarding the Dublin publishing firm Maunsel, to whom Joyce ultimately submitted Dubliners in April.[7] He also resumed his work for Il Piccolo della Sera. Strauss's Salomé, based on Oscar Wilde's play, was being performed in Trieste, and Joyce wrote an article entitled "Oscar Wilde: Il poeta di 'Salomé' " (Oscar Wilde: The poet of "Salomé") that appeared on March 24.

As the conversations between Joyce and Svevo intensified, one of the topics discussed most frequently was Leopold Bloom, in particular his character as a Jew and the essence of Jewish culture. They talked about Bloom "from all angles," according to Stanislaus.[8] Trieste lent itself in an obvious way to such inquiry. Al-though an Austrian city, it exhibited a tolerance of Jews that contrasted with the anti-Semitism found in much of the Hapsburg empire. (The emergence in 1897 of Austria's most anti-Semitic political group, the Christian Social Party, came only seven years prior to Joyce's arrival in Trieste.)[9] Italy was far more accepting of Jews, as evidenced, for example, by the rise of Sidney Sonnino, a Jew who served terms as the country's prime minister and foreign minister.

Trieste favored the Italian disposition. Thus, it was not surprising that in 1912 the Tempio israelitico, Europe's largest synagogue (seating fifteen hundred people),[10] was opened in Trieste on via della Crociera,[11] near the public garden, or that Jewish-Christian marriages, while not common, generally were accepted by Triestine society.[12] At the turn of the century, a number of Trieste's leading businessmen, including Giuseppe Lazzaro Morpurgo, head of the large insurance firm Assicurazioni Generali,[13] were Jews, many of whom had come to Trieste from foreign lands. Stanislaus was amazed at how many businesses were closed on Jewish holidays; he estimated that one-third of the larger firms in Trieste were owned by Jews.[14]

As a melting pot, Trieste certainly offered a relatively appealing environment to a wanderer and exile like Joyce. Sir Richard Burton, British consul in Trieste in the late nineteenth century, and his wife, Isabel, saw the "enlightened and hospitable Hebrews" as their best friends. Lady Burton observed, "It is the Jews who lead society here."[15] While small, comprising only 4 percent of the population in 1910,[16] the Jewish community played a significant role in the city's prosperity.

Joyce had a lively curiosity about Jews, with whom he could identify as a homeless, persecuted individual. Budgen observed that while Jews at times irritated Joyce, he respected them. "I sometimes think," he told Budgen, "that it was a heroic sacrifice on their part when they refused to accept the Christian revelation. Look at them. They are better husbands than we are, better fathers, and better sons."[17] He often used Svevo as a source of information about Jews. Svevo once commented to Stanislaus, "Tell me something about Irishmen—something intimate, something not generally known. You know, your brother has been asking me so many questions about Jews that I want to get even with him."[18] Joyce also had a number of Jews as students, including Ciro Glass, a young Italian-Zionist leader, and Moses Dlugacz, the son and grandson of rabbis and himself an ordained rabbi. Both students undoubtedly conversed enthusiastically with Joyce on Jewish affairs.[19] Another student, Oscar Schwarz, later gave Joyce Hebrew lessons.[20]

Joyce had additional opportunities to develop his own intimacy with Jewish culture in Trieste. Across the street from Joyce's apartment was a Jewish quarter on via del Monte, which Triestine poet Umberto Saba called "the street of our sacred affection."[21] The quarter included a temple where Joyce attended at least one service; he told Stanislaus of his surprise at seeing so many of his own students there.[22] Nearby were a cemetery, a school, and a hospital. Also in the vicinity of several Joyce apartments were an older temple and a Jewish school on via delle Scuole Israelitiche.

There is no record that Joyce ever had any connection with the impressive new Tempio israelitico,[23] but given his interest in Jews, the attention he paid to Triestine newspapers, and his habit of walking about the city, Joyce surely knew something of the temple and may have visited it. The building, in fact, was a five-minute walk from an evening school where Joyce later taught. His infatuation with a Jewish girl, who became the subject of *Giacomo Joyce*, confirms that Joyce was acutely conscious of the Jewish element in Trieste.

As Thomas F. Staley and other critics have pointed out, Joyce used Svevo's words as well as his personality to form much of the character of Leopold Bloom.

Among other similarities, Svevo resembled Bloom physically; was older than Joyce (as Bloom was older than Stephen Dedalus); had recent ancestral roots, like Bloom, in Hungary; and shared closely his character. Stanislaus concluded, "It may not be too far-fetched to see in the person of Bloom Svevo's maturer, objective, peaceable temper reacting upon the younger writer's more fiery mettle."[24] When questioned as to why Bloom was the son of a Hungarian, Joyce replied, "Because he was."[25] Teodoro Mayer, also a Jew of Hungarian descent (and for whose newspaper Joyce was writing), probably contributed further to Joyce's creation of Bloom. The name Leopold may have come from that of another Triestine Jew, Leopoldo Popper, the father of a Joyce student named Amalia, while Bloom came from a family of the same name known to Joyce in Ireland.[26] Joyce had ample Jewish subjects from whom to draw upon in Trieste, and he borrowed liberally, with the focus on Svevo.

Tragically, Trieste's Jews later were spared none of the horrors of World War II. San Sabba, on the southern edge of Trieste, became the Nazi's only extermination camp in Italy, and a nephew and a niece of Svevo would perish there.[27] Joyce almost seemed to anticipate the suffering of the Jews with his description of a Jewish cemetery in *Giacomo Joyce*: "Corpses of Jews lie about me rotting in the mould of their holy field. Here is the tomb of her people, black stone, silence without hope."[28] Today, only about seven hundred Jews, many of them elderly, remain in Trieste.[29]

Literature was a passionate interest for both Svevo and Joyce, and they enjoyed discussing it during their walks together in Trieste.[30] But another issue—politics—had dwindled in importance to them. It is noteworthy that as nationalist sentiment in Trieste—from three sides, no less—peaked just before World War I, Svevo and Joyce found the political situation less than compelling. How much the two discussed politics and may have influenced each other is unknown, but it seems likely that their positions changed independently. Svevo, middle aged, was settled in a comfortable lifestyle befitting his wealthy status. Joyce, as an Irishman, remained largely detached from the local propaganda that swirled around him. Regardless, the political stances of both writers were clearly transformed during the prewar years.

Svevo's early support for irredentism is evident. As a young man, he had worked devotedly for *L'Indipendente*, at one point volunteering his time after the entire editorial board was arrested for treason.[31] He also had supported the pro-irredentist Lega Nazionale and Società Ginnastica and later was under suspicion by Austrian authorities during World War I, sometimes being awakened and questioned during the night.[32]

But Svevo distinguished art from politics, and the former was the stronger calling. Remarkably, Svevo's novels, set in Trieste and written in a turbulent political climate by a man personally involved in the clamor for change, rarely refer to the turmoil. Such a posture surely contributed to the cool reception accorded his work, especially among irredentists.

Svevo had little reason to agitate for reform. His business responsibilities—and income—had increased substantially, and his life had become stable and somewhat placid. There simply were no compelling reasons for him to take to the streets in protest. Triestine writer Lina Galli observed, "The political struggle was for him contingent, temporary, and did not touch deeply the human essence."[33]

Other Triestine irredentists, many of whom, like Svevo, belonged to the comfortable bourgeois class, have been similarly portrayed. Critics suggested that, given the extent to which the Austrian regime tolerated the city's Italian presence, the irredentists often exaggerated their grievances. A friend of Svevo's described this phenomenon of the "typical" irredentist, using Svevo as a model: "He would have voted Liberal; he would have given a modest contribution to the Lega Nazionale; he would have felt a certain combative fervour in his box at the Teatro Comunale during *I Puritani* or Verdi's 'Va pensiero sull'ali dorate'; and would have done his best to feel himself oppressed by Austria."[34]

In fact, criticism of the irredentists had increased markedly in recent years. Irredentist hostility toward the socialists, opposition to voting rights for Slavs,[35] and a general appearance of insensitivity all weakened the party. Irredentist leader Felice Venezian was one of the worst offenders. He once casually remarked, "We will give our superfluous wealth to the poor."[36] The irredentists were stunned by the socialist victory in the 1907 election and by the death of Venezian the following year. Still, tacit support for the irredentist movement clearly did exist among many of Trieste's Italians.[37] By 1911, for example, the Lega Nazionale, with forty thousand members, had opened 210 schools in Trieste.[38] On the waterfront, Caffè Tommaseo remained a popular meeting place for irredentists. Svevo's contribution to irredentism was more than tacit, but he was hardly going to lead the revolution.

Joyce's enthusiasm for politics similarly wavered. During his first years in Trieste, he certainly held political, albeit somewhat conflicting, views. He expressed support for Irish separatist Arthur Griffith and Sinn Féin to the extent of admitting, "If the Irish [Sinn Féin] programme did not insist on the Irish language I suppose I could call myself a nationalist. As it is, I am content to recognise myself an exile."[39] Griffith had been instrumental in starting the *United Irishman*, a separatist weekly for which Yeats, Gogarty, Russell, Colum, and Moore had written.[40] In both Dublin and Trieste, Joyce faithfully read the publication, which featured articles on history, politics, and the arts. At the same time, he enjoyed the passionate socialist discussions that marked his Triestine cafe life. A socialist leader Joyce respected was Arturo Labriola, who later became a correspondent for *Il Lavoratore*, the socialist newspaper in Trieste.[41] In Joyce's words, Labriola wished to "hasten *directly* the emergence of the proletariat. And to do this he would include in his ranks Catholics and Jews, liberals and conservatives."[42]

But, as critic Harry Levin noted, Joyce cannot be identified easily with any movement,[43] particularly in Trieste. The power struggles there between the socialists and the irredentists captured little of his attention. An avowed but hardly active socialist, he did not involve himself with Triestine socialists; there is no evidence, for instance, that he ever had any connection in Trieste to *Il Lavoratore*. Yet, he had written articles for the irredentist paper, *Il Piccolo della Sera*, and given what amounted to a nationalist speech at the Università Popolare. In fact, his closest Triestine associates—Svevo, Francini, Prezioso, Benco, even Stanislaus—

supported the irredentist cause. But as Joyce admitted regarding Stanislaus, "I never took much interest in his politics."[44] Certainly Labriola's views, which appealed to Joyce, could not have been embraced by Triestine irredentists.

As his actions suggest, Joyce in Trieste showed decreasing interest in supporting any political faction. Not that he viewed politics as irrelevant: through newspapers he kept abreast of world events, and in Trieste he owned books by socialists and anarchists.[45] But his insistence that he found politics less and less compelling cannot be ignored. In July 1905, he had written to Stanislaus that his life was filling so quickly with duties, the biggest of which was impending parenthood, that he had "no time or patience for theories as to what the State should do."[46] He told Francini, "My political faith can be expressed in a few words. Monarchies, constitutional or not, repel me. Republics, bourgeois or democratic, also repel me. Kings are clowns. Republics are worn out slippers that fit every foot. The Pope's temporal power is gone and good riddance. What is left?"[47] Verdi's comment, "Politicians are like somebody who wishes to light one candle to Christ and another to the devil,"[48] would have received Joyce's approval.

In Rome, Joyce initially maintained his sympathy for socialism. He read *Avanti* and *L'Asino*,[49] both socialist papers, and he wrote in an October 1906 letter to Stanislaus, "I am following with interest the struggle between the various socialist parties here at the Congress."[50] But Stanislaus found Joyce's socialism "thin,"[51] and Joyce himself began to admit as much. "I have given up reading *Avanti* but enclose paragraph for Artifoni. It was too dull for me," he wrote to Stanislaus in February 1907.[52] The next month he declared to Stanislaus, "The interest I took in socialism and the rest has left me. . . . I have no wish to codify myself as anarchist or socialist or reactionary."[53] The fact was that the likelihood of any government extending financial assistance to him was slim, and Joyce hardly viewed society's problems as his burden. Joyce's advocacy of socialism, by this time, had largely vanished.

Even his own friends held conflicting views on Joyce's politics. Budgen wrote, "If Joyce was ever a Socialist in his earlier days he showed no sign of being one in Zurich."[54] Yeats claimed that Joyce never had anything to do with Irish politics and had only literary and philosophic sympathies.[55] Eugene Jolas recalled, probably more accurately, that Joyce "was little interested in pure politics and economics, although he followed events faithfully."[56]

Clearly, the events that he followed most faithfully were those in Ireland. He later wrote two articles on English-Irish relations and on Parnell for *Il Piccolo della Sera*. As late as March 1914, he sent a letter to Angelo Fortunato Formiggini, a Genoa publisher, regarding the possibility of bringing out his Italian articles on Ireland in a single volume. His reasoning was that the uproar in England over Irish efforts for independence would be of interest to Italian readers.[57] It may have been an astute observation on Joyce's part, but, probably due to the war, Formiggini evidently never responded. Money, not politics, most likely inspired Joyce's letter to Formiggini. With Europe on the brink of war, Trieste was in a near panic. Short of money as always, Joyce undoubtedly sensed that any extra income from sales of the book would help immensely. In Trieste, though, Joyce rarely had such luck.

10

The Return of the Native

Joyce's struggle to survive in Trieste did not distract him from the situation in Dublin. He often discussed family problems, literary developments, and the fortunes—and misfortunes—of Dublin friends with Stanislaus. In 1905 Joyce had stated his certainty of a return trip to Dublin,[1] and now the time had come. One problem, of course, was money—Joyce did not have any. Accordingly, he wrote to his sister Margaret (Poppie) in December 1908, suggesting a visit by Stanislaus and Giorgio the following summer. The hope was that the boy "might be a good influence" on the household,[2] particularly in persuading John Joyce to accept Joyce's relationship with Nora and the existence of their young family.

Five months later, John Joyce replied that in fact his feelings had changed somewhat toward his son,[3] and he felt a sense of pride upon seeing Giorgio's photos. His letter also demonstrated that his capacity for self-pity, as well as his ability to display rather dubious concern over his children, especially when money was needed, had not dwindled. He humbly presented himself to Joyce as an impoverished but dutiful father:

I am anxious to let you learn how matters are with us I fear the end is coming in more respects than one, as my health is fast breaking up and I feel certain I have seen my last Xmas. [He lived to see twenty-two more.] I would welcome death tonight most joyfully if I were to consult my selfish feelings, as a grateful relief from a miserable existence, but the thought of leaving my little motherless girls friendless, cast upon the wretched heartless world, without one relative to give them a meal if hungry, or shelter for the night, I am forced for their sakes to try and live and work.[4]

The letter spared no detail of the family's poverty: "My last shilling went on Sunday dinner and since then we are entirely without food, coal or light, nor do I know any means under Heaven of getting a penny as I have exhausted all my friends, and so we have another fortnights starving to do. My clothes, too, are patchwork."[5]

How moved Joyce was by his father's pleas is unknown, but he did take the step of substituting himself for Stanislaus on the trip. Stanislaus later recalled the situation: "In 1909 it had been arranged that I was to take a trip to Dublin and bring Georgie with me. At the last moment my brother wanted to go, as I had always inwardly suspected he would. He was met at the station of Westland Row in Dublin by a family group who asked him, 'Where's Stannie?' It's a question I have often asked myself."[6]

Still, Joyce faced the dilemma of how to pay for the visit. He could hardly expect Stanislaus to cover such an expense if he were not even going. As happened so often to Joyce, a solution unexpectedly presented itself. Svevo agreed to pay for a year's lessons in advance, giving Joyce exactly what he needed.[7] (Svevo once wrote to Livia, "Poor Joyce. . . . We have got a fine leech on our hands.")[8] At the end of July 1909, Giorgio and he left Trieste for Dublin, Joyce's first return journey after nearly five years in exile.

The trip home was not optional but necessary. Joyce was eager to see Dublin and his family, to show off his son, and to view the literary scene and the status of his friends in person. He was excited to be going home.

The boat arrived in Ireland on July 29, and Joyce (after spying a "fat" Gogarty at the pier)[9] brought Giorgio to the family house at 44 Fontenoy Street, where everyone was delighted by the boy[10] but found Joyce to be melancholy.[11] Padraic Colum, however, saw a markedly different effect of Joyce's years in Trieste:

In appearance, bearing, manner, Joyce was improved. If I say he was more assured I may be misunderstood, for in one sense Joyce was always assured. But there is a difference between the assurance of a man who has only intellectual capital and the assurance of a man who, besides that, has some sort of position. The Joyce I encountered in the street in 1909 had the assurance of position. He was no longer the "character," the "card," the "artist" of Dublin conversation.[12]

During his first few days in Dublin, Joyce attended to some practical matters. He arranged a meeting with George Roberts, the managing director of Maunsel, to discuss *Dubliners*. Significantly, he also obtained applications for teaching positions, indicating not only that he still looked upon himself as a transient in Trieste, but also that his "assurance of position," as Colum noted, enabled him to consider the moment opportune for a successful return of the exile.

More interesting were Joyce's personal encounters in Dublin. His father, who had never completely forgiven him for his "miserable mistake" of leaving with Nora,[13] finally reached an understanding with Joyce.[14] His meetings with old acquaintances, though, were hardly so positive. Joyce seemed to resent them, as if they had forced him out of Ireland into a life of poverty abroad. He was particularly cynical toward Gogarty, by then a wealthy doctor, and Francis Sheehy-Skeffington, an idealistic college friend. Joyce severed relations with both.

His most significant meeting was with Vincent Cosgrave, the model for Lynch in *A Portrait*. In the Dublin pubs, Cosgrave had been a frequent partner of Joyce. He was a man who loved intense discussion but, as a medical student, was less accomplished in the practical side of life.[15] Gogarty labeled Cosgrave "a 'chronic medical,' that is one who had taken lectures, walked the hospitals, but had failed to keep pace with the examinations."[16] Joyce alternately described him as a "solid" man who "always looks at things from the most sensible point of view,"[17] and as a "torpid animal."[18]

Five years earlier, Cosgrave, attracted to Nora, predicted to her that Joyce's devotion would not last.[19] For reasons that are not entirely clear, Cosgrave on August 6, 1909, told Joyce that he had had a sexual relationship with Nora around the time Joyce met her. The news jolted the unsuspecting Joyce. Crushed, he immediately sent off an emotional letter to Nora, writing, "My eyes are full of tears, tears of sorrow and mortification. My heart is full of bitterness and despair."[20] Joyce poured out the story to his friend J. F. Byrne, who found his condition extraordinary: "He wept and groaned and gesticulated in futile impotence. . . . Never in my life have I seen a human being more shattered."[21]

Quickly, Byrne assured Joyce that the story was a "blasted lie."[22] Stanislaus wrote in support of Byrne, informing his brother that Cosgrave years earlier had admitted to Stanislaus his failure with Nora. Which side was telling the truth is unknown, but Joyce felt relieved upon hearing the words of his brother and Byrne. Strangely, he did not send another letter to Nora for more than a week, although he was quite repentant; in turn, Nora sent an uncharacteristically weak letter, referring to herself as a poor, uneducated girl, possibly not good enough for Joyce. Joyce responded that she was terribly mistaken in this outlook and that his love for her was endless.[23] The two were reconciled, and Cosgrave's bombshell was behind them, if hardly forgotten.

Joyce's encounters with Gogarty and others came as no surprise to Stanislaus, who strongly doubted their sincerity toward his brother. In his later writings on Joyce, Stanislaus stated his belief that a number of Irish writers were hostile to Joyce because of his estrangement from Ireland, his outspokenness, and, ultimately, his remarkable success. Constantine Curran, though, found almost no truth in Stanislaus's "sweeping charges," pointing out that Stanislaus barely knew Joyce's literary acquaintances and was physically isolated from Ireland for the last fifty years of his life, corresponding only with his family.[24] A streak of bitterness toward Ireland does run through the comments of Stanislaus, and his objectivity here is questionable. But Joyce's own heated remarks on these writers in "The Holy Office," written before Stanislaus even came to Trieste, show that Stanislaus's personal grudges only threw fuel on an already blazing fire.

While in Dublin, Joyce maintained his connection with *Il Piccolo della Sera* by reviewing George Bernard Shaw's play *The Shewing-Up of Blanco Posnet*. His article, "La battaglia fra Bernard Shaw e la censura" (The battle between Bernard Shaw and the censor"), appeared on September 5, 1909. Joyce's imagination quickly seized on the benefits that he might find as a foreign journalist. With printed cards displaying his name and "Piccolo della Sera, Trieste," he visited the manager of the Midland Railway and convinced him that he was writing a series of articles on Ireland as a member of the Italian press and that he needed a pass to Galway.[25] In fact, Joyce intended to visit Nora's family. His guile worked—the pass was issued.

Up to mid-August, Joyce explored the possibility of remaining in Ireland as a teacher, but his efforts were useless. The only piece of good news concerned his stories: Maunsel, although not expecting *Dubliners* to be a commercial success, agreed to publish the book the following March.[26]

Joyce, though, had seen enough of Ireland, and focused on returning to Trieste. He informed Stanislaus on August 16 that their sister Eva, nine years younger than Joyce, would be with him.[27] Nora had asked if one of Joyce's sisters might come to help with the housework and child care. Joyce's sister Margaret chose Eva, devoutly religious, to go to Trieste in the hope that her presence might influence Joyce's behavior.

Paying for three tickets from Dublin to Trieste was well beyond his means, so a frustrated Joyce again sought money from Stanislaus. (Nora's mother told Joyce that his constant habit of sighing would break his heart.)[28] His demands were incessant and became nearly hysterical by the end of the month. On August 16, he wrote, "Raise all you can and send";[29] on August 20, "Raise all you can";[30] on August 21, to Nora, "Tell Stannie to send me a whole lot of money and quickly";[31] and on August 25, "When is the money coming?"[32] Finally, on August 28, Joyce lost all patience, pleading, "For Jesus Christ sake send money unless you want to send me into a madhouse. . . . Do what I tell you and I want the money by return of post. . . . *Send* the *money*."[33] Stanislaus was obliged to ask Artifoni, who had returned to the Berlitz, for a loan, a task made more uncomfortable by the fact that Stanislaus had just given his notice to leave for private teaching.[34]

Stanislaus soon assisted his brother, and Joyce's optimism returned. He assured Stanislaus, "Once we are settled back in Trieste things will fall into shape and money will begin to come in rapidly."[35] Joyce now warmly remembered Trieste as the city that had sustained him during the darkest hours of his exile. Displaying a sense of guilt over his previous impatience with the city, he wrote to Nora, "*La nostra bella Trieste!* [Our beautiful Trieste!] I have often said that angrily but tonight I feel it true. I long to see the lights twinkling along the *riva* as the train passes Miramar. After all, Nora, it is the city which has sheltered us. I came back to it jaded and moneyless after my folly in Rome and now again after this absence."[36]

Joyce missed Trieste, but he missed Nora more. A month's separation exposed the depth of Joyce's attachment to Nora, and his numerous letters showered her with touching affection. Recently she had expressed appreciation of Joyce's poems, and he wrote to her, "I like to think of you reading my verses. . . . It [*Chamber Music*] holds the desire of my youth and you, darling, were the fulfillment of that desire."[37] He described in great detail his gift to her of a chain containing a tablet with the inscription, "Love is unhappy When love is away," taken from *Chamber Music*.[38] On September 5, he implored, "Guide me, my saint, my angel. Lead me forward. *Everything* that is noble and exalted and deep and true and moving in what I write comes, I believe, from you."[39]

Being apart from Nora also presented Joyce with the problem of celibacy, and his letters, in increasingly precise detail, reflected his frustration. In an almost daily correspondence, he expressed his desire to make love to Nora. He encouraged her to "read over and over all I have written to you," admitting, "Some of it is ugly, obscene and bestial, some of it is pure and holy and spiritual: all of it is myself."[40] The letters of August and September display the strength of the emotional and physical bond that existed between Joyce and Nora, as well as help to explain why he felt compelled to return to Trieste. Interestingly, while *Ulysses* was to be banned for obscenity a decade hence, Joyce had not yet included in his fiction the types of graphic sexual references that he was using with Nora and that would culminate in the more controversial letters of December 1909, written during Joyce's next visit to Dublin. Regardless, he missed Nora dearly.

In his final letter to Nora just before leaving Ireland, his tone changed considerably. Tired after his five-week stay, Joyce issued a list of directives: "Keep that piano and get a camp bed for Eva and Georgie. Be sure and have a fine warm dinner or supper or breakfast for us when we arrive. . . . Don't begin to tell me stories about debts we owe."[41] Finally, on September 9, 1909, he departed Dublin with Eva and Giorgio.[42]

Joyce, however, had almost no chance to enjoy Nora's company before he was on his way back to Ireland, this time strictly on a profitmaking venture that had a curious genesis. Eva had found little in Trieste to her liking except for the cinemas, which did not exist in Dublin. The entrepreneur in Joyce imagined the money to be made if he could establish a successful cinema in Dublin. His idea piqued the interest of four Triestine businessmen, and he persuaded them to finance his trip to Dublin to explore the possibility of a cinema. He left Trieste once more and arrived in Dublin on October 21, 1909.

Working "morning to night,"[43] Joyce located a potential site for the theater within a week. Quickly, though, the trip became a burden for Joyce in all too familiar ways: Irish people ceaselessly annoyed him, and he was lonely without Nora. Again, from Dublin, he looked at Trieste sentimentally partly because he missed the old city but largely because Nora was there, and that made it special.

Some of his most tender and loving letters to her were written in this period. Through his writing, he spoke to Nora almost as a young man in the grasp of love for the first time. He insisted to her, "You are my only love. You have me completely in your power. I *know* and *feel* that if I am to write anything fine or noble in the future I shall do so only by listening at the doors of your heart."[44] He complained that he was a "shell of a man" and that his soul was in Trieste.

As further signs of his devotion, Joyce sent a number of gifts. For Christmas, he planned to give her a copy of *Chamber Music* that he had written on specially cut sheets of parchment.[45] He was wildly optimistic over how he would be able to treat Nora if the cinema met with success: "I will simply smother you in furs and dresses and cloaks of all kinds," he promised.[46]

Plans for the cinema, named the Cinematograph Volta, went well at first. Financial matters back in Trieste, however, were moving in the opposite direction. Stanislaus, already irritated by Joyce's trip, seeing it as another of his useless schemes, sent an urgent wire to Joyce informing him that his via Scussa landlord wanted back rent immediately or would evict everyone. Joyce promptly responded, "When I left Trieste I handed over to you the following pupils: Popper, Bolaffio,

Veneziani (Mrs.) Castelbolognese, Sordina to say nothing of Hoberth, Bartoli and Latzer. These I presume paid you or some of them in addition to your own pupils. Was nothing out of the money paid to landlord?"[47]

In fact, both brothers were under severe pressure. Stanislaus, working day and night to cover Joyce's as well as his own students, was trying to balance a hopeless budget. Joyce found his family in Dublin to be as poor as ever. His father was hospitalized with conjunctivitis, his brother Charlie was unemployed and penniless in Boston with his wife, and the landlord had given an eviction notice, effective December 1, to the Joyces.[48] "Jesus Christ, what a fearful muddle," wrote a beleaguered Joyce.[49]

He sent what money he could spare to Trieste, trusting Stanislaus to use his wits to prevent disaster. His paternal instincts aroused, he ordered Stanislaus to "prevent an eviction *at all* costs" and to "sell every stick in the house if necessary, to prevent Nora and Georgie and Lucia from being put out."[50] But the anxiety of such daily uncertainty became too great for Nora, who sent an angry letter to Joyce in mid-November, threatening to take the two children and leave him. He yielded before Nora's outburst, meekly acknowledging that he was a failure and did not deserve a woman of her stature: "It is a degradation and a shame for you to live with a low wretch like me. Act bravely and leave me. You have given me the finest things in this world but you were only casting pearls before swine," he wrote.[51] Nora, however, sent off two apologetic letters to Joyce, ending the feud.

As Joyce's stay in Ireland passed one month, the stream of letters between Nora and him flowed steadily. Joyce rarely mentioned the business aspects of his trip. Instead, he focused on his loneliness. "How wretched it is to be away from you! Have you taken your poor lover to your heart again?" he asked Nora.[52]

The separation overwhelmed both of them. During the first three weeks of December, Joyce went beyond even the intensity of his summer letters, expressing his urge to satisfy Nora completely. Nora shared his desire and wrote accordingly. Joyce's heart was entirely with Nora, and their separation tormented him. For the second time in five months, Joyce's obsession with Nora riveted his attention on Trieste.

Joyce certainly had problems other than the absence of Nora. The cinema, after a hopeful start, was encountering one snag after another, and it still had not opened as of mid-December. In his endless attempts to find sources of income, Joyce a month earlier had contracted with a Dublin company to establish an Irish tweed agency in Trieste, fulfilling his old wish.[53] The effort, though, produced minimal sales.[54] Also annoying to Joyce was the lack of correspondence from anyone in Trieste other than Nora. At various times, he complained of unanswered letters to Svevo, Count Sordina, and Stanislaus, who rarely wrote anymore.

Still, Nora was his main concern. As their separation approached two months, Joyce thought of little except her. The sexually explicit letters between them had ceased, but Joyce could not distract himself. He imagined their reunion with thorough delight: "O *how supremely* happy I shall be! God in heaven, I shall be happy there. . . . I want to go back to my love, my life, my star, my little strange-eyed Ireland!"[55] On December 22, Joyce sent her the leather-bound manuscript of

Chamber Music as a Christmas present, writing poignantly, "Even if it brought only one quick flush of pleasure to your cheek when you first see it or made your true tender loving heart give one quick bound of joy I would feel *well, well, well* repaid for my pains."[56] It was a gift she always treasured.

Mercifully for Joyce, the cinema had finally opened on December 20, 1909,[57] allowing him to focus on his return to Trieste. Of course, his travel plans meant more borrowing, in this case from Stanislaus. Two days before Christmas, he instructed Stanislaus to "wire all you can,"[58] and on the same day urged Nora to press Stanislaus for money so that his sister Eileen and he could leave Dublin by January 1.[59] Joyce was not sure how the family in Trieste would manage with Eileen, but he told Stanislaus that life at the Joyce house in Dublin was so dreadful that "it is a God's act to rescue Eileen from it." Mindful of his need for income upon his return, Joyce also noted that he had sent cards to all of his students in Trieste and expected Stanislaus to inform them of his imminent arrival.

Before going, Joyce pondered why he had left Trieste so many times. In a contemplative mood, he recalled its charm, writing to Nora, "O how I shall enjoy the journey back! Every station will be bringing me nearer to my soul's peace. O how I shall feel when I see the castle of Miramar among the trees and the long yellow quays of Trieste! Why is it I am destined to look so many times in my life with eyes of longing on Trieste?"[60]

He understood that, as usual, he would be returning to a very unstable economic situation. But, particularly after suffering another iritis attack, he was eager to go, and did so with his sister on January 2, 1910.[61] He would not see Dublin again until the summer of 1912.

11

A Brother's Keeper

The journey to Trieste could not have reassured Joyce about the immediate future. He later gave a dramatic version of his ordeal:

While I was in Dublin . . . I got a bad attack of rheumatic inflammation of the iris of the eye. I had to leave Ireland at once (with black bandages over both my eyes) and come back here where I was in bed in a half-dark room for close on two months. Had it not been for my sister who travelled with me across Europe I should certainly have ended under the wheels of some train or car.[1]

For a month, Joyce remained at the via Scussa apartment. To survive, he continued to lean on Stanislaus. Upon receiving a summons on February 12 to pay creditors, Joyce sent his brother a note, telling him, "I have no money whatsoever. . . . Kindly come here unless we are to starve."[2] A month later, Joyce sent another message to Stanislaus in which he complained that Nora and he were in imminent danger of running out of money. He reminded Stanislaus that he owed money to Joyce, adding, "I wish you would save me these continual rows as I have already too many worries."[3] The fact that Joyce rented a piano for most of 1909, though, shows that his financial worries were not nearly as deep as his debts.

Nevertheless, Joyce did seek more income. He taught at the Scuola Serale di Commercio, an evening school for professionals.[4] He also wrote two letters to El-kin Mathews in April and May regarding the lackluster sales of *Chamber Music*, now three years old. He gently chided Mathews, "I am very much surprised at the fewness of the copies sold and think the book could have been pushed more."[5] To support his claim, Joyce reported, "When I was [in Ireland] last summer very many people complained to me that it had never been in the windows at all."[6] He enclosed a leaflet, printed in Trieste at Joyce's expense, highlighting the press notices *Chamber Music* had received upon publication.

More publicity-conscious than he had been earlier in Trieste, Joyce became personally involved in sales. He noted that he had sold thirty copies of the verses "here and in other cities where I lived."[7] (He also gave away copies, including one to his friend Vidacovich in April 1910.)[8] More optimistically, he informed Mathews that through a Triestine bookseller (Schimpff) he already had obtained fifty buyers of *Dubliners*, due to be published in June 1910.[9]

Finances never distracted Joyce from literature for very long, and a well-publicized literary and political event in Trieste during this period undoubtedly caught his attention. The *serata futurista*, a meeting of futurists, was held on January 12, 1910, at the Politeama Rossetti on via dell'Acquedotto. Led by the fiery rhetoric and often bizarre behavior of founder Filippo Tommaso Marinetti, futurists rejected tradition and aggressively sought to expand the boundaries of artistic and literary expression. In his *Manifesto tecnico della letteratura futurista*, Marinetti wrote, "We utilize . . . all brutal sounds, all the expressive cries of the violent life that surrounds us. Let's courageously introduce the ugly in literature, and let's murder solemnity. . . . We must spit every day on the Altar of Art! We enter in the boundless dominions of free intuition."[10]

Marinetti's zeal for change swept beyond art and literature: he glorified modern technology and urban living, strongly favored the expansion of Italy, and viewed war as an appealing method of achieving social and cultural upheaval. One futuristic slogan was "War is the only hygiene."[11]

Futurism had adherents throughout Europe and Russia—Marinetti's writing probably influenced Vladimir Mayakovsky[12]—and had particular appeal in Trieste because of its irredentist bent. The futurists planned a series of presentations in a number of Italian cities, and Trieste, significantly, was first.[13] Well promoted, the event packed the theater and provided some noteworthy histrionics. One speaker advocated that libraries be burned, causing the boisterous crowd, evidently concerned more about ending Austrian rule than civilization itself, to shout him down.[14]

Whether or not Joyce was in the audience is unknown, but he could hardly have been unaware of the affair. The city was covered with posters, and the theater was just around the corner from his via Scussa apartment. Tullio Silvestri and Dario de Tuoni, both of whom later became good friends of Joyce, did attend and contributed to the festivities by throwing tomatoes at the speakers.[15] At some point, they easily could have discussed the night with Joyce, who was well aware of the movement and in particular of Marinetti's radical approach to writing. He possessed a copy of Marinetti's *La enquête internationale sur le vers libre et manifeste du futurisme*.[16] Discussing the "Cyclops" section of *Ulysses* with Frank Budgen in 1918, Joyce asked, "Does this episode strike you as futuristic?"[17] Although Stanislaus insisted that Marinetti's work had not affected Joyce,[18] Ezra Pound later asserted that T. S. Eliot, Joyce, and he could not have developed their writing styles without the influence of futurism.[19]

Ulysses, however, remained in a long period of gestation, and Joyce's other literary work was, for the moment, stagnant. He had to cope with the crowded Trieste household of Nora, Giorgio, Lucia, Eileen, Eva, and himself, with Stanislaus living apart but very much active in family affairs.

In spite of his failure to stabilize his finances, Joyce—almost by default—was responsible for handling the majority of family matters, a situation that continued for years. Mary Colum, who along with her husband, Padraic, often saw Joyce later in Paris, observed that he "was the one member of his family who had much practical sense. It was he who arranged every family detail, wrote every letter, engaged apartments, arranged for vacations, treatment of illnesses, and everything else, for he had a particularly helpless family."[20] According to Padraic Colum, Joyce often complained about Nora's poor housekeeping and her inability to care for the young children in Trieste without help.[21] Joyce himself, while well intentioned, tended to spoil the children. Clearly, Eileen's assistance with both the housework and the children was invaluable.[22] When she later reflected on her marriage in 1915 and subsequent separation from Joyce and his family, she stated, "I think I missed the children more than anything. . . . I had really reared Giorgio and Lucia. I used to do everything for them and we were always together."[23]

To be fair to Nora, she was not hapless or uncaring in her relationship with Joyce and the children. Indeed, so far from Ireland, Nora made her family in Trieste her life. But she clearly was no more able than Joyce to balance a budget, and she seemed largely unconcerned over any long-term planning for the family. Also, while Nora loved the children, she (and, again, Joyce) was not blessed with a strong instinct for parenting. That she needed help, particularly Eileen's, was undeniable.

Unlike Eileen, Eva could not adjust to the chaotic family life in Trieste. While both sisters were religious, Eva displayed a strong piety that the Dublin Joyces hoped would strengthen the family. Instead, Eva found her own sensitivity wounded time after time. She could not accept the unmarried status or general behavior of Joyce and Nora. Joyce maintained his aggressive skepticism toward organized religion, although he continued at times to attend the Greek Orthodox services with his sisters. Even these occasions, however, probably humiliated Eva. During Holy Week Joyce would stand alone in a corner of the church, apart from his sisters, as if to emphasize the differences in their reasons for being there.[24]

Exactly why they chose to attend Orthodox services more than others is somewhat unclear. The religious tolerance of Trieste was exhibited by its variety of houses of worship, including Greek, Serb, Anglican, Catholic, and Jewish, among others. A number of these were easily within walking distance of the Joyces' apartment, and Joyce did attend services at the churches of St. Antonio di Padova and San Giusto. But he obviously had a particular interest in the Greeks. Many of his earlier nights of drinking were spent in cheap Trieste pubs with Greek sailors, from whom Joyce picked up bits of Greek.[25] In a 1921 letter, however, he admitted jokingly, "I don't even know Greek though I am spoken of as erudite. . . . I spoke or used to speak modern Greek not too badly (I speak four of five languages fluently enough) and have spent a great deal of time with Greeks of all kinds from noblemen down to onionsellers, chiefly the latter."[26] When Padraic Colum inquired about a Greek flag hanging in Joyce's Paris apartment, Joyce replied, "The Greeks have always brought me good luck."[27] In the end, possibly the music of the Greek services was of most interest to him.

Still, the motivation of the sisters, labelled *cattolicissime* (hyper-Catholics) by Joyce,[28] to accompany him rather than attend a Catholic mass is uncertain. The church of St. Antonio di Padova, at the head of the Canal grande, was actually closer than the Greek church to their apartment.

Also upsetting to Eva was Nora's tolerance of Joyce's beliefs and her own casual approach to sex and housework. When Nora once jokingly placed a chamber pot on top of a piece of furniture, Eva was appalled by the undignified act.[29] The Joyce home in Dublin was a living hell, but to the conservative Eva, life with such an unconventional family in Trieste was no improvement. After less than two years in Trieste, she would return to Dublin in the summer of 1911.

As 1910 wore on, Joyce could see little promise for relief in Trieste, so he looked back to Ireland. It was a waste of time. The Volta project was steadily losing money, giving the owners no choice but to close it. The cinema was sold in June at a loss of 40 percent, and Joyce received almost nothing for his efforts.[30]

To distract Joyce from the Volta debacle, Svevo, in London, sent a letter that revealed both Joyce's sense of indignation and a certain innocence of character. Svevo commented,

You were so excited over the cynematograph-affair that during the whole travel I remembered your face so startled by such wickedness. And I must add to the remarks I already have done that your surprise at being cheated proves that you are a pure literary man. To be cheated proves not yet enough. But to be cheated and to present a great surprise over that and not to consider it as a matter of course is really literary. I hope you are now correcting your proofs and not frightened to be cheated by your publisher. Otherwise the book could not be a good one.[31]

Joyce, unfortunately, was making no literary progress. He had not received the *Dubliners* proofs from George Roberts, who was having doubts about the wisdom of handling work as potentially controversial as Joyce's. He asked for—and was given—some changes in the text, but Joyce's refusal to alter a passage related to Edward VII in "Ivy Day in the Committee Room" created a major conflict. When neither side offered to concede, *Dubliners* remained in limbo.[32] The June publishing date passed; six years in exile had not put Joyce any closer to being a successful writer.

In August 1910, Joyce once more moved his family, this time to an apartment at via Barriera Vecchia 32, outside the downtown Corso district but still within a ten-minute walk. The location was fortuitous for Joyce: his new home was next to the residence of Triestine composer Antonio Smareglia,[33] whose operas *Nozze Istriane* and *La Falena* were locally popular and familiar to Joyce.[34] In her memoir of her father and Joyce, Aurelia Gruber Benco recalled that not only did Benco admire Smareglia "without reserve" (Benco, in fact, wrote the libretti to some of Smareglia's works),[35] but Joyce "praised Smareglia and said that he was the only Triestine artist about whom the public and critics would talk in the future."[36] Joyce probably attended performances of Smareglia's work at Teatro Verdi. Today, a statue commemorating Smareglia stands in Piazza Giambattista Vico.

Interestingly, Joyce and Smareglia, who suffered severe vision problems, shared the same optometrist, Dr. Oscar Oblath. Oblath's sister was the wife of Giani Stuparich and a good friend of Scipio Slataper. From his conversations with Prezioso, Benco, and Svevo, Joyce must have had some knowledge of these young Triestine writers, even though much of their time was spent in Florence. Joyce evidently had no inclination to connect with them, however, despite the obvious opportunity.[37]

Meanwhile, his indifference to family finances took another bizarre turn. With Nora, Eileen, and Eva already in the apartment, Joyce hired a young woman, Mary Kirn, as a maid for the household. He was able to pry her from another job with an offer of a higher salary, twelve dollars a month,[38] which he paid punctually. Although Stanislaus, looking "sullen and silent," appeared at the apartment only twice during the year that Kirn worked there, she knew that the brothers met frequently outside because Joyce often discussed their financial disagreements with Nora and his sisters.[39] Lightening the burden a little was the publication of a Joyce article entitled "La cometa dell' 'home rule' " (The "home rule" comet) in Il Piccolo della Sera. It focused on the bankrupt policies of the English government toward Ireland and appeared in the December 22, 1910, issue.

Still, Mary Kirn remembered the Joyce family as a happy one. Nora was a cheerful person who enjoyed cooking, performed her piano lessons regularly, practiced Italian with Joyce, and went for walks along Trieste's streets with Joyce's sisters.[40] Joyce spent most mornings reading and writing on the big kitchen table, where the light was best. The main meal of the day was lunch, which Kirn prepared; Joyce's favorite was lean bacon, cabbage, and potatoes. In the afternoons, he sometimes gave lessons.

Joyce often met friends in the local restaurants, particularly the Pasticceria Caffè Pirona at via Barriera Vecchia 12, owned by Alberto Pirona and opened in 1900. Joyce met Pirona through Francini, who lived in the same building as Pirona at via dell'Olmo 1, near Joyce's flat and the cafe. The three spent hours in conversation at Pirona's apartment or cafe, savoring its large selection of wine.[41] At around 8:00 Joyce would return home and have a light dinner, after which the family often gathered to sing. Joyce, as always, enjoyed performing Italian operatic pieces, and he taught Giorgio Italian songs.[42] While the children at times were difficult, the household, excepting the absent Stanislaus, often was a buoyant, lighthearted group.

In January 1911, though, Joyce again threatened to leave Trieste. A crisis erupted between Stanislaus and him following a disagreement over some pupils. Joyce wrote to Stanislaus that he was abandoning Trieste and leaving Eva and Eileen with Stanislaus, all of whom, Joyce pointedly noted, had come to Trieste "in obedience to my summons, from your ignorant and famine-stricken and treacherous country."[43] He concluded the letter with the blunt hope that "you and your sisters will be able, with the meagre means at your disposal, to carry on the tradition I leave behind me in honour of my name and my country."[44] Joyce did not follow through with his plan to leave Trieste, but feelings of bitterness lingered.

Joyce undoubtedly directed similar sentiments toward Roberts. He had indicated to Joyce that Dubliners would be published on January 20, but Joyce, after years of disappointment, was uneasy. In a January 3, 1911, letter to Roberts, he wondered why additional proofs of "Ivy Day in the Committee Room" had been sent to him (but never received) when he had already corrected earlier proofs.[45] Instead of offering an explanation or any good news at all, Roberts abruptly replied that the publication date had been postponed again, prompting Joyce to write cynically to Stanislaus, "I know the name and tradition of my country too well to be surprised at receiving three scrawled lines in return for five years of constant service to my art."[46] In February, Roberts instructed Joyce to delete all references to the king, inspiring Joyce to investigate the possibility of suing Roberts.

His frustration over the fate of *Dubliners* and his other work was keen and inevitably led to a conflict with Nora, who was rarely enthusiastic about his writing. Eileen remembered the incident:

One day I heard them arguing in very loud voices and I went in. Just as I opened the door, Jim was saying "Very well, I'll give up the writing." And he stuffed into the stove the original of *Stephen Hero*. Nora was only laughing and she said to me, "He's mad! He's mad!" I dashed forward and pulled the copy out of the stove, but not before some of the pages got burned, and I burned my hand, too.[47]

Mary Kirn gave a rather different version, stating that the manuscript was rescued jointly by Nora, Eva, and herself.[48] Joyce simply described it as a deed performed by a "family fire brigade."[49] Repentant, he later admitted that he never could have rewritten the pages.[50]

The following months gave Joyce little reason for hope regarding *Dubliners*. Spring turned into summer, and Joyce still heard nothing from Roberts. Exasperated, Joyce warned Roberts in a July 10, 1911, letter that he would publicize his ordeal with Maunsel to the media, as well as initiate legal action, if Roberts continued to ignore him. Roberts did just that, leading the unabashed Joyce to the conclusion that the best possible arbiter of the case would be King George V, to whom Joyce sent a letter that included the text of "Ivy Day in the Committee Room" and a request for his opinion on the matter. Through his secretary, the king informed Joyce that it was inappropriate for him to comment.[51] Undaunted, Joyce proceeded to distribute a lengthy letter, detailing the protracted negotiations and disputed passages, to a number of newspapers. Only two, *Sinn Fein* and *Northern Whig*, published it.[52] The letter drew a sympathetic response from Grant Richards, who offered to review any new material of Joyce's. Roberts, though, remained quiet. Joyce's shouting from Trieste was barely heard in Ireland.

12

Irish Tempers

The beginning of 1912 found Joyce still short of money, foreshadowing what would be another dismal year financially. Unable to pay the rent, Joyce faced eviction on February 24. Nora and Joyce subsequently visited thirty apartments in an attempt to move before finally reaching an agreement with their landlord.[1]

To boost his income, Joyce became something of a public figure again during 1912 by giving speeches and writing for *Il Piccolo della Sera*. In March Joyce presented two lectures entitled "Verismo ed idealismo nella letteratura inglese (Daniele Defoe—William Blake)" (Truth and idealism in English literature [Daniel Defoe—William Blake]). The talks were given at the Università Popolare, the school where he had spoken in 1907 on Irish politics and which was increasingly becoming a center of irredentist activity.

Two months later, he wrote an article, "L'ombra di Parnell" (The shadow of Parnell), that appeared on May 16 in *Il Piccolo della Sera*. Of Parnell's vilification in Ireland, which Joyce saw as a bitter betrayal of the Irish leader, he wrote, "The Irish press emptied on him and the woman he loved the vials of their envy. The citizens of Castlecomer threw quicklime in his eyes. He went from county to county, from city to city, 'like a hunted deer,' a spectral figure with the signs of death on his forehead."[2] Joyce's tendency to blame not only outsiders but the Irish themselves for their problems was hardly the type of message irredentists were eager to hear. No one was going to confuse Joyce with Marinetti. It is clear that Joyce's friendships with Prezioso, the newspaper's editor, and Benco, its leading writer, were at least partly responsible for Joyce's continued presence in its pages.

Still, all of this activity was not going to fill the family coffers. Joyce could not ignore the fact that after nearly eight years in Trieste, he was still broke. A regular income was imperative, and again he looked away from Trieste, this time to Padua, in an attempt to find one.

Joyce had been considering the possibility of teaching in an Italian public school. In order to do so, he was required to pass exams given by the Italian government at the University of Padua. In late April, Joyce went to Padua, where he took several exams and wrote two essays. But it was all for naught. Despite scoring 421 out of a possible 450 points, Joyce was told that his University College degree was insufficient as a teaching credential.[3] His appeal of the decision went nowhere.

In the meantime, Joyce kept up his search for income. On May 30, he wrote to Mathews inquiring about any profits from sales of *Chamber Music*. Yet, five years after the book's publication, sales still had not reached three hundred copies, even though nearly fifty copies had been purchased by Joyce's friends in Trieste.[4] There were no royalties to be had.

Keeping the Joyces afloat had become something of a communal affair. To help out, Livia Svevo asked Joyce if Eileen, who had left Trieste to work as a governess with a family in Udine, a nearby town, could assist on a daily basis with Letizia.[5] Eileen declined the offer.[6] Another potential benefactor was Nora's family. Nora of late had been corresponding with her relatives in Galway, and she was enthusiastic about returning there and seeing her mother again. At the very least, Joyce was hopeful that a well-off uncle, Michael Healy, would offer to pay for Joyce to meet Nora in Ireland for a short vacation. In addition, Joyce wanted Nora to stop in Dublin to discuss *Dubliners* with George Roberts. It was decided that Nora and Lucia would make the trip, and they arrived in Ireland on July 8, 1912.

From Joyce's perspective, though, an immediate snag developed when Nora failed to promptly relay details of her arrival in Dublin. In a July 12 letter, Joyce complained bitterly to Nora, "Having left me five days without a word of news you scribble your signature with a number of others on a postcard. Not one word of the places in Dublin where I met you and which have so many memories for us both! Since you left I have been in a state of dull anger. I consider the whole affair wrong and unjust."[7]

He had no desire to stay behind in Trieste while waiting for Nora to write and for her uncle to share his wealth. Someone's wealth would need to be shared with Joyce, though, as he remained broke. Again, he looked to Svevo in an episode typical of Joyce. Following Nora's departure from Trieste, Joyce had joked with Svevo that, with his wife and daughter in Ireland, he was happily enjoying his freedom with Giorgio (the "two men") in Trieste. Two days later, Joyce went to Svevo in a completely different mood, urgently requesting money because he could not live anymore without Nora and wanted to join her immediately. Svevo complied, and Joyce then visited the captain of a commercial ship, thinking such a voyage might save some money. When the captain informed him of the cost of travel, Joyce replied, "Perhaps we did not understand each other well. When we get to England, the ship will remain yours. I did not mean to buy it."[8] Joyce managed to make more affordable travel arrangements to return to Ireland with Giorgio. It would be Joyce's final trip to his native land.

Nora, in fact, had been carrying out Joyce's wishes in Dublin. The day after her arrival, she visited Roberts with John and Charlie Joyce but made no progress.[9] The useless meeting may have revived her old feelings toward her country. She wrote dejectedly to Joyce on July 11, "I am quite tired of Ireland already . . . I got very sick of Dublin its a horrible place its quite true what you said I would soon get tired of it."[10] She was happy to see her family in Galway, but she had no intention of staying any longer than necessary.

A few days later, Joyce and Giorgio arrived in Dublin, which Joyce described to Stanislaus as "very discouraging." His sole positive impression regarded Charlie, a "decent poor fellow."[11] Joyce's meeting with Roberts only added to his pessimism, as the publisher gave Joyce the option of deleting certain passages or simply printing it under his name and at his expense. Undecided, Joyce wrote to Stanislaus, "Write and advise me at once which way you prefer,"[12] before travelling to Galway to meet Nora.

His time with Nora was a blessing. The two passed relaxing days in Galway, with Joyce doing some rowing and cycling. They also visited the Aran Islands, a trip that inspired Joyce to write two travel articles for *Il Piccolo della Sera*. "La città delle tribù: ricordi italiani in un porto irlandese" (The city of tribes: Italian echoes in an Irish port) appeared on August 11, 1912, and "Il miraggio del pescatore di Aran. La valvola dell'Inghilterra in caso di guerra" (The mirage of the fisherman of Aran. England's safety valve in case of war) was published in the September 5, 1912, issue.

News from Trieste, however, never allowed Joyce's thoughts to stray far. The nagging subject of eviction had appeared once again, immediately provoking Joyce's ire. He wrote to Stanislaus on July 27, "Whoever tries to eject me from that flat will pass a damn bad quarter of an hour," and he ordered Stanislaus to tell the landlord that they were not moving, claiming, "I am afraid he is spoiling for something he won't like when he gets it."[13]

On August 20, four days before the eviction date, Joyce had not softened his opinions toward the landlord and his agent, calling them a "pair of low brutes" and singling out the agent as a "lying thief." Finally, sensing disaster, Joyce told his brother to evacuate Joyce's table and desk to a neighbor's apartment and to give all of his papers to Francini's wife. He concluded, "For the rest let the two swindling squinting hell's bitches propose whatever they please."[14] But Stanislaus did not correspond often enough to satisfy Joyce, who complained to Nora, "I am like a man walking in his sleep. I don't know what is going on in Trieste. Stannie has not sent me what I asked him for. . . . Stannie has sent [to the Joyce sisters] nothing and Charlie nothing and me nothing. I don't know where my desk and table and MSS and books will end. . . . I don't know how we can get back to Trieste or what we shall find there."[15]

Ultimately, Stanislaus sent 110 crowns[16] and moved the possessions of Joyce and Nora to an apartment that he rented at via Donato Bramante 4. By this time, though, Joyce must have wondered if Dublin or Trieste was more frustrating.

Meanwhile, the tension between Joyce and Roberts, a man who "knew how to lose friends and alienate people," according to Padraic Colum,[17] remained. Joyce left Galway alone on August 17 and on August 20–21 negotiated with Roberts, who was noncommital, saying he could do nothing to endanger the firm. Two days later, he rejected the book altogether.

The news crushed Joyce. He wrote to Nora,

I read [Roberts' letter] and walked down the street feeling the whole future of my life slipping out of my grasp. . . . All last night I had gone over the whole book in my mind, imagined that I saw it, that those whom I know were reading it, imagined the reviews of it, friendly and unfriendly. This morning everything seemed to collapse. . . . For a long time today I thought of spending the last money I have on a revolver and using it on the scoundrels who have tortured my mind with false hopes for so many years.[18]

Worse, as always, were the finances. Joyce constantly exhorted Stanislaus to send money, emphasizing that their sisters would be without food if not for his presence, and their brother Charlie, back from Boston, was unemployed.

The dynamics of the Joyce family worked in a curious way. Joyce tried diligently to help them in Dublin, partly by coaxing money out of Stanislaus. From Trieste, Stanislaus also wanted to assist the family, but resented feeling Joyce's hand in his pocket continuously. Charlie, who wrote regularly to Stanislaus and less often to James, appreciated the help of both brothers. In his letters to Stanislaus, Charlie acknowledged that everyone in the family was struggling, but he tried to be hopeful despite the family's poverty.[19]

Adding to the crisis was the fact that Joyce's father, seeing himself as blameless in the mess, did nothing. He told his drinking companions that his family had deserted him,[20] and in a May 1914 letter he went so far as to complain of the "cruel treatment" he had received from his daughters.[21]

Joyce and his father, though, maintained a strong mutual respect. John Joyce often exclaimed that the family had "struck oil" with James,[22] who, quite unlike his brothers and sisters, admired his father immensely. They shared a wit frequently aimed at Ireland. Joyce once proudly recalled "the virulence, variety and incandescence of curses which he [the father] bestowed on his native country and all in it— a litany to which his eldest son says *Amen* from the bottom, that is to say, the nethermost or lowest part of his heart."[23] French critic Louis Gillet, a later friend of Joyce's, noted the considerable effect of the father on the son: "He [James] owed him two things: a way of flouting life and unyielding pride, an incapacity for bending his knee and capitulating. . . . It was from him that the great writer had inherited the haughty air, the prodigious faith in himself, the refusal of all compromise and concession which are the features of his work."[24]

More than once Joyce asked his father to visit the family in Trieste, and in 1914 John Joyce seriously considered a month's stay but never acted.[25] Eugene Jolas described the death of Joyce's father in 1931 as a "profound shock" to Joyce,[26] who had not seen his father for nearly twenty years. "He had an intense love for me," Joyce wrote,[27] reflecting, "I was very fond of him always, being a sinner myself, and even liked his faults. Hundreds of pages and scores of characters in my books came from him."[28] Casting an indignant glance at his siblings, he asserted, "Everyone liked him except some of his unnatural self-righteous kindred."[29] Yet, Joyce at times showed little appreciation of Stanislaus, who took the slight seriously.

Joyce's trust and faith in Nora during this crisis proved to be his main source of strength. His letters to her are touching in their sincerity and affection. One day prior to his rebuff by Roberts, Joyce pensively considered all of the places he wished to visit with Nora, writing, "You have become a part of myself—one flesh."[30] The next day, deeply despondent, he confided to Nora, "You at least will remain. Don't grieve for me."[31] Nora and the children soon left Galway to join Joyce in Dublin.

The combination of family crises and publishing disappointments consumed much of Joyce's energy and time, which may explain why he evidently had little contact with his old Dublin acquaintances, whom he mentioned rarely in his letters to Stanislaus and Nora. Undoubtedly, he also was not eager to be seen by Dublin in such trying circumstances. This concern was reflected in his rather tepid invitation to Constantine Curran, about to go abroad, to visit "my poor Trieste."[32]

Surprisingly, Joyce and Roberts in late August resumed their tortuous discussions over publication of *Dubliners*. Roberts, who twice left the room "in a temper," demanded changes in "Ivy Day in the Committee Room," "A Painful Case," and "Counterparts" and the complete omission of "An Encounter." Joyce reluctantly accepted Roberts's terms on the condition that the book be published before October 6, 1912.[33] Roberts's insistence on still more significant copy changes exhausted Joyce's patience, ending the negotiations with the understanding that Joyce would print the book privately. Roberts then informed Joyce that it would cost him thirty pounds to obtain the printed sheets of *Dubliners*,[34] and, wanting to dissociate himself entirely from the work, pressed Joyce to agree in front of witnesses that he intended to have the book published in Trieste, not Dublin.[35]

However, the printer, John Falconer, fearing his own culpability in any future lawsuits, refused to provide Maunsel with the sheets, and Roberts made little effort to retrieve them. Joyce appealed directly to Falconer who, despite having had the sheets for more than two years and standing to lose fifty-seven pounds in printing costs,[36] was unswayed and vowed to burn the text. Joyce fortunately was able to obtain a set of proofs of *Dubliners* before the other copy was destroyed by Falconer on September 11, 1912, the day that Joyce left Ireland for the last time.[37]

On his return trip to Trieste, he gave Ireland a final blast. In a train station in Holland, Joyce wrote a scathing broadside, "Gas from a Burner," evidently aimed chiefly at Falconer and, to a lesser extent, Roberts.[38] Using the printer as a stooge narrator to vent his wrath against both him and Ireland, Joyce wrote,

> But I owe a duty to Ireland:
> I hold her honour in my hand,
> This lovely land that always sent
> Her writers and artists to banishment
> And in a spirit of Irish fun
> Betrayed her own leaders, one by one.[39]

The broadside, hardly unjustified in its bitter tone, must have seemed to Joyce a highly appropriate parting shot at his native country.

Joyce returned to yet another Trieste address, which was alongside a major landmark in the city. Rising above his via Bramante apartment is the beloved hill of San Giusto, site of the church and castle whose history holds such significance for Triestines.

Built on the ruins of a Roman temple, the church is dedicated to the patron saint of the city, St. Giusto, a Christian martyr. The floor of the structure features Byzantine mosaics dating from the twelfth century. Next to the church stands the castle, constructed for defensive purposes by the Austrians in the fifteenth century. At the foot of the castle, the base of a Roman basilica can be seen.[40] San Giusto became an even stronger symbol of Trieste's Italian past when irredentist feeling in the city, following its nadir of 1907-08, grew prior to the onset of World War I, the years in which Joyce lived nearby. Joyce was well aware of the reverence Triestines paid to San Giusto. In a letter to Nora's uncle, written from Zurich in 1915, Joyce acknowledged his own respect: "Today is the feast of S. Justin Martyr, patron of Trieste, and I shall perhaps eat a cheap small pudding somewhere in his honour for the many years I lived in his city."[41]

Aside from San Giusto, another aspect of the new neighborhood intrigued Joyce. Piazza Giambattista Vico, commemorating the seventeenth-century Neapolitan philosopher, was close by Joyce's apartment and surely encouraged Joyce's interest in him. Vico's main work, *La scienza nuova*, greatly influenced the structure Joyce later chose for *Finnegans Wake*. Today, the apartment where Joyce spent nearly three productive years is remembered by Triestines: via Donato Bramante 4 bears a plaque honoring Joyce, and the Scala Joyce, a public stairwell, is located a short distance down the sloping street.

However, a figurative hill, one of debt, captured more of his immediate attention. Accustomed to his borrow-and-spend method of survival in Trieste, Joyce again depended heavily on Stanislaus. When rental problems surfaced almost at once, he urged Stanislaus to see him about "the new swindle" regarding payment for the rooms.[42] At this point in Joyce's life, a significant income still probably would not have guaranteed a balanced family budget. Joyce, in fact, did not even have the burden of income taxes, as the Trieste tax collector was a friend who conveniently overlooked his obligation to pay.[43]

Unfortunately for Joyce, he had no reason to expect profits soon from his writing. In a December 16, 1912, letter to Yeats, he asked, "Do you know of any publisher in London likely to take my unhappy book?"[44] It was not the most cheerful of holiday seasons for Joyce, who wrote again to Yeats on Christmas to ask for more assistance with *Dubliners*. Understating the dilemma, Joyce explained, "My book seems to be pursued by a strange ill-luck."[45] Yeats was not the only one unable to help. Five years after his first attempt, Joyce again tried to interest Elkin Mathews in his stories,[46] only to receive another rejection.[47] At every turn, *Dubliners* remained a failure.

Bad news continued to arrive from Dublin as well. In December, Joyce learned of the death of his uncle, William Murray, the husband of Aunt Josephine. While Joyce had fond memories of his uncle, the event reminded him of the misery he had known in Dublin. He wrote to Aunt Josephine, "He was the only member of my mother's family who seemed to take any pride out of my existence." Worse, Joyce recognized that the despair of Dublin life went on unabated for his family. "To tell the truth, I dislike to see the Dublin postmark as all the envelopes contain sad news of death, poverty or failure of some kind," he told his aunt.[48]

Slowly, events finally began to favor Joyce. His teaching, his previous work for the Università Popolare and for *Il Piccolo della Sera*, and the publication of *Chamber Music* gave Joyce growing recognition among Triestines. He was not a "man of the people" in any sense, as his students generally were wealthy and his interests beyond the reach of others. Yet among intellectuals he was respected, and the Università Popolare capitalized on his status by offering him the chance to give a series of lectures. Between November 11, 1912, and February 10, 1913, Joyce presented twelve lectures on *Hamlet* in Minerva Hall. The talks were unique in that Joyce spoke English to his largely Italian audience, many of whom undoubtedly were his own students.

The outcome must have pleased both Joyce and the school: the hall was full during the first presentation, which *Il Piccolo* praised for its "genuine brilliance," also noting the kind applause Joyce received.[49] All of the succeeding talks were well attended,[50] despite the obvious language barrier. Joyce clearly had inspired Trieste as a linguist, if not as a nationalist.

On the heels of Joyce's success, Stanislaus and friends of Joyce, including Svevo and Vidacovich, encouraged him to apply for a teaching position at the Scuola Revoltella, where Svevo had taught earlier. The spot had not been vacated yet, and in a moment of altruism Joyce insisted to Stanislaus, "I don't think any move in that direction should be made while C [Philip Cautley] has the position." Should the opening occur, on the other hand, Joyce admitted, "If they want anybody to teach the sons of bitches broken English I suppose I am good enough for that."[51] The school ultimately agreed, and Joyce secured the position.

Joyce rarely exhibited a serious attitude toward teaching, and in November 1913 he wrote an uncharacteristic letter to the school's director. He stated his belief that the academic course load of the Revoltella students was insufficient for the proper study of English. Whether Joyce simply was seeking additional teaching hours (and money) or had other motives is unclear.[52]

Gradually, Joyce's finances improved. Francini, who continued to see Joyce frequently, usually at the via Bramante apartment, observed that Joyce had purchased custom-made Danish furniture for his new home.[53] He was "living more comfortably than ever before," according to Stanislaus,[54] a statement that, in Joyce's case, hardly implied luxury. Stanislaus also had moved, renting an apartment at via San Giorgio 7, not far from his brother.[55]

Joyce had only morning classes at the Scuola Revoltella, leaving afternoons free for private students. One student he often saw was Dario de Tuoni, an apprentice at *Il Piccolo della Sera* who met Joyce through Francini in 1913.[56] Born in Innsbruck in 1892 and educated at the University of Graz in Austria, de Tuoni shared his teacher's love of literature and went on to become an accomplished scholar and writer who was well known in Trieste's literary circles, counting Svevo and Saba among his friends.[57] The two conversed while walking along via Bramante and via San Michele (toward Città Vecchia), sometimes stopping in pubs for a bottle of Joyce's favorite wine, Opollo. Joyce displayed his respect for de Tuoni by presenting him with a copy of *Chamber Music*, and de Tuoni reciprocated by giving Joyce a recently published volume of his own verse.

De Tuoni remembered Joyce's apartment as modest. Joyce gave lessons to students sitting at a simple square table in the middle of the living room. Along one of the walls was a couch that probably served as a bed, above which were two oil portraits of Joyce and Nora done by Triestine painter Tullio Silvestri. The room also contained a piano, which Joyce sometimes played. He admired the Slav sculptor Ivan Mestrovich, and several photographs showing his work, accompanied by verses of Dante chosen by Joyce, hung over the piano. There were no books in the room; if one were needed, Joyce would go to the bedroom, careful to close the door behind him, and return with the book. During the lessons, the family stayed in the kitchen, with that door also shut. De Tuoni found Nora to be very attractive and cheerful, doing her best under the difficult circumstances.

In 1914, de Tuoni was called to military service by the Austrian authorities, but his sentiments lay with Italy. During his Christmas leave in Trieste that year, he prepared to desert the Austrian army for the Italian side. On December 26, the last meeting between de Tuoni and Joyce occurred, and de Tuoni informed him of his plan. Joyce commented, with more accuracy than many at that time, "The war will be won by the country that has got the last sack of flour."[58]

Years later, in a curious sequence of events, de Tuoni learned firsthand of Joyce's tight finances in Trieste. He had loaned some books to Joyce, who neglected to return them. Following the war, Stanislaus informed de Tuoni that the books probably were still in Stanislaus's present apartment on via Sanità, where Joyce lived briefly after the war.[59] The books were found there, and in one de Tuoni discovered a card dated July 1, 1913, and addressed to Nora. It contained a pointed note from a creditor, a Mr. M. B. Katz: "I kindly invite you, in your interest, to settle your debt with me within three days, or I shall be forced to apply to my solicitor, which will cause you unnecessary troubles and increase your expenses."[60] It was a familiar message to Joyce.

Joyce in Trieste. *Courtesy of Alfonso Mottola*

Stanislaus Joyce in Trieste. *Courtesy of the Estate of Stanislaus Joyce*

Nora, Giorgio, and an unidentified woman. *Courtesy of the Croessmann Collection of James Joyce, Special Collections/Morris Library, Southern Illinois University at Carbondale*

Piazza del Ponte Rosso, where Joyce briefly lived after arriving in Trieste. *Courtesy of the Museo di Storia ed Arte*

The waterfront of Trieste and the *Graf Wurmbrand*, on which Joyce travelled from Trieste to Pola. *Courtesy of the Modiano Collection*

The bookstore of F. H. Schimpff in Trieste's Piazza della Borsa. *Courtesy of the Museo di Storia ed Arte*

The office of *Il Piccolo della Sera*, the newspaper for which Joyce wrote nine articles in Italian. *Courtesy of the Modiano Collection*

Italo Svevo with his wife, Livia, and his daughter, Letizia, all friends of Joyce. *Courtesy of Letizia Svevo Fonda Savio*

Silvio Benco, a Trieste journalist and friend of Joyce. *Courtesy of the Museo di Storia ed Arte*

The church of San Giusto. *Courtesy of the Modiano Collection*

Painting of Joyce by Tullio Silvestri. *Courtesy of Alfonso Mottola*

TRIESTE

A

JAMES JOYCE

A bust of Joyce by Trieste sculptor Marcello Mascherini, which stands across from a bust of Italo Svevo in Trieste's public garden. *Courtesy of Alfonso Mottola*

13

Mystery Lady

While he was becoming more active socially in Trieste, Joyce, through nearly ten years abroad, had maintained his fixation on Dublin in his writing. In June 1914, Svevo asked Joyce in a letter, "When will you write an Italian work about our town? Why not?"[1] Indeed, it was a question that begged an answer, and Joyce finally provided one, although under peculiar circumstances. Some of his students were young women, at least one of whom caught his fancy and inspired the short prose poem, *Giacomo Joyce*. The work is unusual in that Joyce chose Trieste, not Dublin, as the setting. More striking is that, unlike his other work, he never submitted it for publication.

The poem, which apparently marks Joyce's unwelcome passage into his thirties ("Youth has an end: the end is here")[2] describes his dreamy, lustful fixation on a young, mysterious, Jewish student in Trieste, unnamed in the text. Due to Richard Ellmann's vigorous research, Joyce's student Amalia Popper generally has been accepted as the subject of Joyce's attention in the poem. (Ellmann also noted that she may have influenced Joyce's portrayal of Molly Bloom in *Ulysses*.) However, the secrecy that long surrounded the manuscript and the controversy that arose following its publication have made a positive identification nearly impossible.

Amalia Popper was born in Trieste in 1891. Her father, Leopoldo, a successful trade merchant, was a highly cultured man who was fluent in several languages, including English. Accordingly, his two daughters, Amalia and Elisa, took English lessons from Joyce, probably in 1907 or 1908.[3]

Joyce became a familiar face to the Popper family. Although Leopoldo referred to him as a *testa matta* (literally "crazy head," or madcap), he delighted in conversing with Joyce in English. Along with Stanislaus and later Eileen, Joyce often attended the large Sunday social gatherings at the Popper house located at via Alice 16. Through his wealthy students and his friendship with Svevo, Joyce knew well the lifestyle and manners of the Triestine upper class. More sheltered was Nora, who never accompanied Joyce to the Popper house. Perhaps their "illicit" relation-

ship was an impediment in such company. But the others added to the festive atmosphere with their musical talents: all could sing well, and Joyce and Eileen
would perform duets of Puccini, Bellini, and Verdi for the guests.[4] At other times,
Joyce would play the piano and sing Irish songs.[5]

Joyce had extensive contact with numerous members of the Popper family. He
served them not only as a teacher but, more humbly, as a messenger. After departing the via Alice residence, he occasionally would walk to via Bellosguardo to
deliver a message from Amalia to an aunt (also a student of Joyce), who was per-
sona non grata at the Popper home due to her marriage to a man fifteen years
younger.[6] Then Joyce would return to via Alice with a response and leave again for
via Tigor, where he would stop at the home of Eva Venezian, a cousin of Amalia's
mother. There, he gave English lessons to four girls.[7]

Early in 1910, Amalia moved to Florence to attend school, and she continued to
study there until 1915, making brief return trips to Trieste. In 1911, she met Michele Risolo, and they were married in Florence in 1914.

When Joyce left Trieste for Paris in 1920, the manuscript of *Giacomo Joyce*
remained in Trieste with Stanislaus, and it was not published until 1968, a year
after Amalia's death. Ellmann first was drawn to Amalia Popper when he saw her
name in a list of Joyce's Triestine students given in Herbert Gorman's biography.
In 1953, he met Stanislaus in Trieste and asked him about the student, and Stanislaus provided Amalia's Florence address. (Stanislaus had been a teaching colleague
of Michele Risolo in Trieste.)[8] Initial efforts to question her produced only a perfunctory and partial response from Michele Risolo (among other mistakes, it claims
that Joyce never returned to Trieste after leaving Zurich following World War I),
which did not even concede that his wife had been a pupil of Joyce.[9] Ellmann first
saw the *Giacomo Joyce* manuscript in 1956 and, suspecting that Joyce had in mind
a real model, investigated further. He discovered the similarity of Leopoldo's name
with that of Bloom, the use of the Popper name in *Finnegans Wake*, and a letter
from Amalia to Joyce in Paris requesting permission to translate *Dubliners*. (Her
name and address also appear under *P* in Joyce's address book.)[10] While the evidence was not conclusive, it was circumstantial enough to indicate that Joyce did
have an interest in the Popper family, and possibly in Amalia.

The uncertainty surrounding the identification of the young woman arises from
three factors: the lack of any explanatory notes from Joyce, the difficulty of assign-
ing a specific date to the text, and the inconsistent information provided by Risolo
on the matter. There is no evidence that Joyce ever commented on *Giacomo Joyce*
or intended to have it published, although in an April 1917 letter from Zurich he
did refer to "some prose sketches . . . locked up in my desk in Trieste."[11] Why he
showed such reticence is unclear. He never felt the bitterness for Trieste that he had
for Dublin, so he may have judged the autobiographical aspects of the work to be
overly apparent and capable of causing him discomfort that he wished to avoid in
Trieste. (Svevo's second novel, with its barely fictionalized portrayal of a Triestine
woman, might have caused Svevo similar problems had the book received more
attention.) Possibly Joyce viewed the work to be inferior, but this stance would
have been unusual for Joyce: *Giacomo Joyce* was his only substantial work that he

did not present to the public. He hardly ignored the manuscript, however; as Ellmann noted, Joyce borrowed liberally from it in writing *Ulysses*.[12]

A precise dating of *Giacomo Joyce* is speculative. There is no indication from Joyce's acquaintances in Trieste that they knew of its existence. Based on historical and personal references in the text, the composition of the poem can be very roughly dated as sometime between 1911 and 1914, and Ellmann concluded that the poem could not have been completed before June 1914.[13]

Both Amalia and Michele Risolo were alive when Ellmann did the bulk of his research on *Giacomo Joyce*, but they did not shed any light on the issue. Amalia responded to Ellmann's inquiries only through her husband, and Michele Risolo, in his letters to Ellmann and in articles and letters published in the Italian press, simply added to the confusion. His version of events seemed to change with each of his ensuing statements. In a February 1961 letter to Ellmann, Risolo wrote that Amalia, while unable to recall the exact dates she studied with Joyce, believed they were in the periods 1904–05 and 1908–09. In another letter two weeks later, he wrote that she had seen Joyce only in 1907–08 and parts of 1909, although she did return to Trieste during school vacations up to 1915.[14] Eight years later, in an article in the Milan newspaper *Corriere della Sera*, Risolo asserted that Amalia studied with Joyce only between October 1908 and November 1909, and he recalled clearly that the last lessons were given in Joyce's via Barriera Vecchia apartment.[15] The dates are implausible, since Joyce did not move to that particular address until December 1910. Subsequent letters from Risolo indicate that Amalia and he were in Trieste on at least several occasions after 1910, including the Easter holiday in 1913 during which they became engaged.[16]

Given that Joyce was a reasonably close friend of such a sociable family, it is possible that Joyce and Amalia did see one another in this period, and there are indications that each may have had a desire to do so. In their later correspondence regarding the translation of *Dubliners*, Joyce informed Amalia that she had been his "number two" student.[17] Also, her father had remarked to Joyce during the lessons that she greatly admired her teacher.[18]

In another strange twist, Risolo agreed to be interviewed at length for a *Life* article that highlighted Amalia as the lady in *Giacomo Joyce*. The article appeared on February 2, 1968, more than one year before his own *Corriere della Sera* rebuke of Ellmann. It included four photographs of Amalia and two of Joyce and provided a detailed description of Amalia and her family and direct quotes from Risolo. He described Amalia as "gracious and lovely" with "soft eyes and beautiful hands,"[19] but maintained that while Joyce may have had a private affection for her, there was no romantic affair between the two.

While Amalia Popper generally remains accepted as the likely subject of *Giacomo Joyce*, it is possible that Joyce may not have been thinking of Amalia Popper at all. Joyce scholars in Trieste have pursued that possibility with interesting results. In his recent book, *Tutto è sciolto*, journalist Roberto Curci made a compelling case that Emma Cuzzi, a student of Joyce in Trieste, had inspired the poem. Another Joyce critic, the late Stelio Crise, presented a different scenario. Crise, a librarian at the University of Trieste who knew Stanislaus Joyce during his last years of teaching at the school, believed that a young woman named Annie Schleimer could have been the mysterious student.

Schleimer was born in 1881 in Trieste.[20] Her father, Andrea, was a successful local merchant who sold a variety of imported fruits and other foods, and the family lived in a comfortable Scorcola villa in the northern hills overlooking the harbor. Schleimer was a student of Joyce around 1905-06, a period of great personal difficulty for him, particularly concerning Nora. In late 1905, he complained bitterly to Aunt Josephine of his frustration over the restrictions he now found placed upon his free time.[21]

The possible significance of their relationship did not become known until more than fifty years later when Schleimer, unmarried and still living in Trieste, told a remarkable story about Joyce to a young Slovenian woman, Zora Koren. In 1960, Koren, who for five years had been renting a room in Schleimer's house, mentioned to her an Italian translation of *Ulysses* that she had seen in the library where she worked. Schleimer responded that she had studied English with Joyce many years earlier, and she showed Koren some books and letters that Joyce had given to her. More importantly, she revealed that Joyce had once proposed marriage to her, but Schleimer, under pressure from her father not to marry a transient English teacher, could not accept his offer. She always treasured his gifts as fond memories, however, and never lost her admiration for Joyce. Schleimer died in a nursing home in Gorizia, Italy, in 1972, and her possessions were returned to her family. The Joyce material was not saved,[22] although an obituary of Stanislaus was found in her papers.[23]

Crise noted several similarities between Schleimer and the woman depicted by Joyce. Clothing was one. Schleimer was fond of furs ("A pale face surrounded by heavy odorous furs"),[24] and often wore a green silk gown to the theater. Describing a theater scene, Joyce wrote, "All night I have watched her. . . . A green fillet upon her hair and about her body a green-broidered gown."[25] Another common point was musical interest. In her living room, Schleimer had a black piano ("A bare apartment. . . . A long black piano"),[26] and she had performed in concerts as a young pianist. Koren, in fact, chose to live with Schleimer partly because of the availability of the piano, which both played.[27] Schleimer also was in the habit of removing her hat and placing it on the piano after returning from church, as well as frequently carrying an umbrella, whether for rain or sun; Joyce wrote, "Poised on its [the piano's] edge a woman's hat, red-flowered, and umbrella, furled."[28] The villa of Schleimer's parents was located near the *palazzo* (mansion) of a Joyce student, Baron Ambrogio Ralli: "As I come out of Ralli's house I come upon her suddenly"[29] was an occurrence not at all unlikely, particularly since Schleimer was a friend of the Ralli family.[30] (Conversely, Amalia Popper's via Alice residence was on the other side of Trieste.) Finally, Schleimer was well educated, a woman who spoke four languages and kept an extensive personal library, certainly an individual who could have fit Joyce's description, "A lady of letters."[31]

Casting more doubt on the probability that Amalia Popper was the major source of Joyce's inspiration are the voices of others who knew her. Joyce was explicit in his infatuation with the subject of the work. He wrote, "Her eyes have drunk my thoughts: and into the moist warm yielding welcoming darkness of her womanhood my soul, itself dissolving, has streamed and poured and flooded a liquid and abundant seed."[32] Acquaintances of Amalia, though, found her an unlikely person to provoke such sensual feelings. Dr. Lea Rossi, a classmate from the University of Florence, described Amalia as "intelligent and cultured but neither pretty nor elegant." Another classmate, Dr. Roma Lockmer, judged her to be "cordial, studious, and intelligent," but also *una donna gelida* (an icy woman).[33]

Inconsistencies in the case supporting Schleimer, however, also exist. For example, Joyce portrayed his comfortable relationship with the student's father, a condition quite unlikely in Schleimer's case. Also, why Joyce would have been walking with her "all the way up the via San Michele" at midnight[34] is unclear. The San Michele hill does lead to Joyce's via Bramante apartment, but it is not near Schleimer's Scorcola residence or her later apartments on Corso Stadion and via Palestrina.[35] Finally, Schleimer, who was one year older than Joyce, does not fit the image of a young student as neatly as Amalia Popper or Emma Cuzzi. Nevertheless, the parallels remain intriguing.

That Joyce would have proposed marriage to anyone—including Nora—during the early Trieste years seems highly improbable, and even during the troubled period with Nora, Joyce professed, "I do not wish to rival the atrocities of the average husband and I shall wait till I see my way more clearly."[36] But the possibility that he became infatuated with another woman is not remote, particularly in light of his acknowledged discord with Nora and his yearning for more freedom. Given all of the contradictory information on the matter, it is impossible to determine precisely the extent of Amalia Popper's involvement with Joyce or her influence on the writing of *Giacomo Joyce*, or to prove that Joyce had a love affair with anyone in Trieste. The most reasonable conclusion regarding the subject of the work is that the qualities of a person or persons, probably at least Amalia Popper, were used by Joyce in conjunction with his own imaginative powers to create the woman so shrouded in mystery. To assign a percentage of her character to either of these influences would be guesswork.

As Joyce's only prose work focused solely on Trieste, *Giacomo Joyce* is striking in its lack of commentary on the city. His emphasis obviously on the person and not the place, Joyce opted not to express any specific feelings toward Trieste, as he did so strongly regarding Dublin in most of his work. (Constantine Curran once asked Joyce about returning to Ireland, to which he replied, "Why should I? Have I ever left it?"[37] He admitted to Cyril Connolly, "I am afraid I am more interested in the Dublin street names than in the riddle of the Universe.")[38] The setting in *Giacomo Joyce* clearly does not take on the same importance as does Dublin in his other works. His few local allusions are somewhat vague. His reference to irredentists as "a multitude of prostrate bugs [who] await a national deliverance" hardly suggests support of—or even respect for—the movement.[39] Indeed, given Joyce's political views at the time, his observation "They love their country when they are quite sure which country it is" appears ripe with cynicism.[40]

Otherwise, he provides no judgement on Trieste. *Giacomo Joyce* hides not only the identity of its heroine but also the attitude of the writer toward his city. Still, whoever the mysterious student was, she had clearly inspired Joyce at a time when his literary efforts—all focused on Ireland—had given him little reason for encouragement. The unknown Triestine, finally, had brought Joyce's imagination from Dublin to Trieste.

At the same time, Joyce returned to verse, composing eight poems (seven in Trieste) between 1912 and 1915. Several of the poems had a Triestine influence. A gift of a flower from the idealized student in *Giacomo Joyce* to Lucia inspired Joyce to write the poignant "A Flower Given to My Daughter":

> Frail the white rose and frail are
> Her hands that gave
> Whose soul is sere and paler
> Than time's wan wave.
>
> Rosefrail and fair—yet frailest
> A wonder wild
> In gentle eyes thou veilest
> My blueveined child.

The poem appropriately mirrors an early scene in *Giacomo Joyce*: "A flower given by her to my daughter. Frail gift, frail giver, frail blue-veined child."[41] Joyce had seen Stanislaus participate in a boating race at San Sabba and used the experience as the basis for "Watching the Needleboats at San Sabba." He sent the poem to Stanislaus on September 9, 1913;[42] it was published in *Saturday Review* on September 20, 1913.[43] A popular song of the time provided the epigraph, "O bella bionda, sei come l'onda" (O beautiful blonde, you are like a wave) for "Simples."[44] The setting of "On the Beach at Fontana" was a wooden pier built for Triestine beachgoers.[45] Joyce's other poems were "Tutto è Sciolto," "Flood," and "Nightpiece." All were later included in his volume, *Pomes Penyeach*.

A bizarre incident involving Prezioso, Joyce, and Nora around 1911–12[46] significantly influenced Joyce's only drama, *Exiles*. In the Trieste years, Nora had an attractive figure and, at times, dressed in the latest style. Tullio Silvestri called Nora the most beautiful woman he had seen. Nora was quite aware of her appeal and later told Arthur Power in Paris about her fond memories of gazing at the handsome men in Trieste.[47] Power believed that "probably after the suppressed, innuendo-riddled, sex atmosphere of Dublin the frank sex-life of an Italian seaport town stimulated her." Moreover, he understood that his friendship with Nora "helped to cement" his relationship with Joyce. The writer would not befriend anyone who did not take kindly to Nora, according to Power. "If they ignored her, he ignored them," he observed.[48]

Joyce's attitude toward Nora's sexuality, however, was complex. He enjoyed her popularity; he boasted to friends of her sexual appeal, and, according to Frank Budgen, once told Nora to go out with other men to give him something to write about.[49] At the same time, he was fiercely protective of her, a fact that Prezioso either was oblivious to or simply chose to ignore.

Prezioso and Joyce had been on good terms since Joyce's early days in Trieste. Joyce was a familiar face in Prezioso's home, where he gave lessons,[50] and Prezioso was a regular dinner guest of Joyce and Nora. Married to a woman from a respected family of wealth, the handsome, somewhat pretentious Prezioso was well known in Trieste as a newspaper editor and as a ladies' man, and it was the latter aspect that ran him afoul of Joyce. Prezioso grew affectionate toward Nora, a development apparently not displeasing to Joyce or Nora, who enjoyed innocent romantic games and openly discussed them.[51]

Prezioso, though, was not content to remain a silent worshipper of Nora, and one day he said to her, "Il sole s'è levato per Lei" (The sun has risen for you).[52] But Prezioso had crossed a boundary: if he believed he could initiate a tryst with Nora, he had badly miscalculated. Nora rejected his advance and related the episode to Joyce. Constantine Curran once wrote of Joyce, "Some things that he admired and most things that he rejected were admired or rejected by him in the teeth of his fellows."[53] Prezioso, painfully, was no exception. Joyce confronted him in Piazza Goldoni and berated him in an outburst overheard by Silvestri. The journalist was humiliated to tears, Silvestri recalled.[54]

The affair unsettled Joyce, but only temporarily: he made liberal use of it in *Exiles*, and he showed no grudge toward Prezioso, presenting him with a copy of *Dubliners* in 1914.[55] For his part, the vanquished Prezioso did not lose his nerve, maintaining friendly ties to both Joyce and Nora and continuing his English lessons. Interestingly, his letters to Joyce address him as "Jim," a casual reference that most Triestine friends, including Svevo, Benco, de Tuoni, and Francini, did not use with Joyce. Prezioso was on unique terms with Joyce. Perhaps this was true partly because Joyce understood that Prezioso, like himself, was not restrained by society's moral boundaries, although Joyce chose to trespass more in his writing than in his behavior.

Exiles, written during this period, reflects Joyce's experience with Prezioso. As he entered his thirties, Joyce was intrigued by the theme of betrayal, which he examines closely in the play. *Exiles* is set in Dublin in 1912. Richard Rowan, a writer, encourages his wife, Bertha, to meet privately with her admirer (and Richard's friend), Robert Hand, on numerous occasions. Bertha then dutifully reports the details to Richard. Further complicating the plot is the fact that both Richard and Robert have had romantic ties to Beatrice Justice, who is Robert's cousin and the music teacher of Richard's son.

Joyce drew upon a number of acquaintances in shaping Robert's character, one of the most obvious being Prezioso.[56] Robert, a journalist, flirts repeatedly with Bertha, unaware that his advances are well known to Richard. Ultimately, Richard confronts Robert over his behavior, although not with the anger that Joyce heaped upon Prezioso. Robert later asks Bertha, "Why did you lead me on? . . . You saw it. That I was ruining myself in his eyes, losing his friendship."[57] Other aspects of the play also suggest Prezioso's presence. Bertha says to Robert, "I hear you have so many admirers,"[58] which evidently was true in Prezioso's case. To assist Richard, Robert attempts to secure him a university teaching position and then writes a flattering article about him for the newspaper. Prezioso probably was among the friends who helped Joyce to join the faculty at the Scuola Revoltella, and he may have written the positive reviews of Joyce's *Hamlet* speeches that appeared in *Il*

Piccolo. Finally, the Rowans' servant tells Bertha, "Sure he [Richard] thinks the sun shines out of your face,"[59] which echoes Prezioso's fateful words to Nora.

Exiles also presents some interesting connections to *Giacomo Joyce*. For years, Richard was attracted to the intelligent and refined Beatrice, whose character contrasts sharply with that of his less urbane wife. Bertha keenly senses her inferiority to Beatrice, telling Richard, "You have given that woman very much, Dick. And she may be worthy of it. And she may understand it all, too. I know she is that kind."[60] The young student portrayed in *Giacomo Joyce*, with her privileged background, is obviously very cultured: she studies English, goes to the theater, attends Joyce's lectures on Shakespeare, and reads his first novel. Intellectually, she has little in common with Nora. Also, Bertha sarcastically refers to Beatrice as "her ladyship,"[61] which is the expression that Joyce uses, much more respectfully, for his student: "There is one below would speak with your ladyship."[62]

Another curious parallel occurs when Richard speaks to Beatrice of a work that he has written:

> Richard: Would you like to see it?
> Beatrice: Very much.
> Richard: Because it is about yourself?
> Beatrice: Yes.[63]

Given the relationship between Richard and Beatrice, the text under discussion vaguely hints of *Giacomo Joyce*. Both *Exiles* and *Giacomo Joyce* show that Joyce, around 1913–14, contemplated deeply the nature of love and betrayal, although he evidently never pursued the latter in Trieste.

14

Finally, *Dubliners*

Joyce did not feel that his future as a writer was affected in any way by the status of his friendships, Prezioso's included. He rarely allowed himself to be distracted from his determination to be a writer of fiction and to be recognized as such. In late 1913, his perseverance finally was rewarded. Resolved to see *Dubliners* published, Joyce wrote to Grant Richards on November 23 seeking his agreement to bring out the stories, for which he already had one hundred orders lined up in Trieste.[1] Joyce even offered to subsidize some of the publishing expenses. Richards replied that he would like to see the stories again.

More good news arrived on December 15 in a letter from American expatriate Ezra Pound, who was working as Yeats's secretary at Stone Cottage in Sussex, England. Pound detested much of modern literature and had a vision of revolutionizing the literary world by promoting, encouraging, and supporting writers not known or acceptable to mainstream publishers. His life was a whirlwind of activity: in addition to working with Yeats, he was the foreign editor of the new journal *Poetry*, published in Chicago by Harriet Monroe; he wrote for the *New Freewoman* (shortly to become better known as the *Egoist*), a literary and primarily feminist magazine edited by devoted suffragette Dora Marsden;[2] and he was completing an anthology of new poetry entitled *Des Imagistes*. Pound discussed the book with Yeats and asked if he was aware of any additional poets worthy of consideration, and Yeats offered Joyce's name.[3]

Joyce knew nothing of Pound, but after all of his battles against the literary and publishing establishment, he must have greatly appreciated the irascible, rebellious tone of Pound's letter. In offering to assist Joyce, Pound conceded that they likely were twin souls: "From what W.B.Y. says I imagine we have a hate or two in common."[4]

Before Joyce had even responded, Pound again wrote to express his admiration of Joyce's poem "I Hear an Army," which Yeats had "just found." Pound requested permission to include the poem in his book, offering him a guinea in payment and "whatever more your share in profits of the anthology come to." Exhibiting the same disdain for commercial publishers that Joyce obviously felt, Pound assured him that "this is not the usual graft anthology, the contributors are to share proportionately, if the book earns anything."[5]

Eager to pursue this relationship with a fellow dissenter, Joyce approved and asked about further opportunities to place his writing. On January 4, 1914, Pound wrote to thank Joyce for the poem and to offer help in circulating his other work.[6] He cited the following as potential targets for Joyce: *Smart Set* (under its new editor, H. L. Mencken),[7] the *Egoist*, *Poetry*, and the *Glebe*, dedicated to bringing out volumes of new writing such as *Des Imagistes*, which it published in February, 1914. Joyce submitted to Pound the first chapter of *A Portrait of the Artist as a Young Man*, *Dubliners*, and "A Curious History," an updated and painstakingly detailed version of the letter that he had distributed to Irish newspapers in 1911 regarding his long struggle with publishers. Sincerely interested in pulling Joyce out of obscurity in Trieste, Pound wasted no time in promoting his work. He wrote a short introduction to "A Curious History," which appeared in its entirety in the January 15, 1914, issue of the *Egoist*.[8]

As Pound had an opportunity to read Joyce, his respect grew. In a January 17 letter to Joyce, Pound described *A Portrait* as "damn fine stuff," but recognized that it would not easily find a publisher in book form. Consequently, he sent it to the *Egoist*, where it could be considered for serialization.[9] He admired the short stories and sent "An Encounter," "The Boarding House," and "A Little Cloud" to *Smart Set*.[10] Finally, anticipating that Harriet Monroe of *Poetry* would have an interest in Joyce, Pound asked if he had any more poems the quality of "I Hear an Army." (Monroe later did publish Joyce's work, although she did not meet Joyce or Pound until 1923 in Paris, at Sylvia Beach's bookshop, Shakespeare and Company.)[11]

The *Egoist* proved to be the quickest to accept Joyce's work. Several factors helped him. At the time, the magazine was softening its feminist stance in favor of a more inclusive selection designed to promote worthy examples of original literature and progressive thinking. In addition, the *Egoist*, being new and rather unstable financially, had not yet consistently attracted a large quantity of good writing,[12] although it had made a very encouraging start, with works by Ford Madox Hueffer (later Ford Madox Ford), Richard Aldington, H.D. (Hilda Doolittle), and William Carlos Williams.[13] Thus, Dora Marsden, who actually had given *A Portrait* only a cursory look, approved of the chapter.[14] Coincidentally, it appeared in the issue of February 2, Joyce's thirty-second birthday.[15]

Spurred on by the enthusiasm of Pound and by the promotion of his work by the *Egoist*, Joyce intensified his pressure on Grant Richards. In letters written on January 8 and 19, Joyce urged Richards to make a decision about *Dubliners*: "I am most anxious to have the affair concluded one way or the other," he stated.[16] After some further haggling, a conclusion indeed was reached. On January 29, Richards agreed to publish *Dubliners*.

The terms were less than favorable to Joyce, who was required to pay for the first 120 copies at trade price.[17] (Presumably some of these were intended for the

Triestines already committed to buying the book.) But after nearly a decade of disappointment, Joyce was less interested in acrimony than in simply seeing the stories published, and he acquiesced. Noting that he could "push the sale [in Trieste] very well before summer,"[18] Joyce expressed hope that the book would be available in May, a "lucky month."[19] But *Dubliners* was not published until June 15, 1914, more than eight long years after Richards had first received the manuscript. The book's publication finally allowed Joyce to present his fiction to Triestines, and he distributed copies to friends, including Svevo, and to students.

Richards requested a photo of Joyce, and on June 19 Joyce wrote that he had gone to a Triestine photographer and would send the picture the next day.[20] The photographer may have been Mario Circovich, who kept a studio on Piazza della Borsa (in the same building as Schimpff's bookstore) and did photograph Joyce, although the date is unknown.[21] Circovich's photo is one of the few taken of Joyce in Trieste.

With bitterness and exaggeration, Joyce in 1917 recalled the path of frustration *Dubliners* had followed:

Ten years of my life have been consumed in correspondence and litigation about my book *Dubliners*. It was rejected by 40 publishers; three times set up, and once burnt. It cost me about 3,000 francs in postage, fees, train and boat fare, for I was in correspondence with 110 newspapers, 7 solicitors, 3 societies, 40 publishers and several men of letters about it. All refused to aid me, except Mr Ezra Pound. In the end it was published, in 1914, word for word as I wrote it in 1905.[22]

Some friends, in fact, did rally to the defense of *Dubliners*. Pound praised it in the *Egoist*, asserting that Joyce was not "bound by the tiresome convention that any part of life, to be interesting, must be shaped into the conventional form of a 'story.'" Svevo understood the difficulty such a work would have in finding an audience in Trieste but assured him, "I shall speak about the new book with everybody I can suppose capable of being interested with an English work of Irish contents."[23]

But sales were minimal. Benco recalled the book's difficult beginnings: "*Dubliners* appeared just as the World War broke out. I did not read it at that time; I did not even know of its publication, for books could not get through to Trieste."[24] (At least some copies did make it to Trieste.) Benco did not see *Dubliners* until Stanislaus gave him a copy during the war years when both were interned in Austrian camps.[25] By the end of 1914, only 499 copies, including those purchased by Joyce, had been bought.[26] The figure must have been particularly exasperating to Joyce for he would not receive any royalties until five hundred copies were sold. It was, to Joyce, "a discreet financial failure."[27] *Dubliners*—and Joyce—remained cursed.

The fate of Joyce's novel, meanwhile, was more positive. The *Egoist* continued to publish *A Portrait* in monthly installments, giving Joyce the necessary incentive to finish the book sooner than he might have. Pound maintained his supportive vigil, informing Joyce in an April 1 letter that "Lewis [Wyndham], Hueffer and everyone with whom I have spoken of the novel have all called it good stuff."[28]

In June 1914, a significant change occurred at the *Egoist* that would greatly in-fluence Joyce's career. Dora Marsden quit, leaving the magazine in need of not only an editor but also, as its financial losses mounted, a benefactor. The breach was filled by Marsden's friend and the *Egoist*'s business manager Harriet Shaw Weaver, who agreed to become a kind of editor/financier.

Rarely was she referred to by any name other than Miss Weaver, which per-fectly suited Joyce's formal approach to women. Robert McAlmon, a writer and fellow drinker in Paris, described Joyce's manner "as that of an older day." Joyce, he wrote, "is formal, staid, dignified, and has never been known to call a woman by her first name. She is always Miss or Mrs."[29] Miss Weaver would be an immense help to Joyce for the rest of his life.

Unlike her experienced, outspoken predecessor, Miss Weaver was a reserved and practical woman who had no editorial background. But she had a remarkable degree of inner strength and faith, and, in her own quiet way, commanded great respect. Born into a well-to-do family in 1876 in England, she was raised in a strictly conservative Victorian manner. Rather shy, she nonetheless possessed a firm social conscience and felt a need to assert her independence. She developed into an ardent feminist (years later, she joined the Communist Party), but one who believed strongly in freedom of expression for all, and she naturally was attracted to the *Egoist*, where her lifelong friendship with Dora Marsden began.

Miss Weaver devoted a great deal of time and money to keep the fledgling jour-nal alive. (By 1915, the circulation of the *Egoist* was only 160 copies.)[30] As much as possible, she tried to minimize losses without sacrificing literary integrity. She had never heard of Joyce until she read the January 15 copy of the *Egoist*, but she was determined to extend publication of *A Portrait*, which she saw as an important original work that should not be suppressed.[31]

As Joyce might have guessed, Miss Weaver faced immediate publishing prob-lems. The printer objected to a passage in chapter 3; instinctively, Miss Weaver declared that the text should be printed without censorship. The printer won that particular battle and the paragraph was excised from the August 1 issue, but Miss Weaver had established where her principles lay.[32]

Now that people were learning who he was, Joyce was determined that they would not soon forget him. His writing and his own promotional efforts intensified. Along with his work on *A Portrait* and *Exiles*, he had begun his novel *Ulysses*. While he was grateful for the exposure that *A Portrait* was receiving in the *Egoist*, Joyce was more interested in seeing his "book" published in that form. Responding to a request from Grant Richards regarding his other work, Joyce mentioned *A Portrait* and the possibility of publishing the novel in its entirety. In a July 3, 1914, letter, he reminded Richards that, under the *Dubliners* contract, he had the right to publish—or reject—the novel.[33] After months of delay, Joyce's patience was re-warded: Richards agreed to see the text.

In addition to his literary activity, Joyce remained as a teacher at the Scuola Re-voltella and as an English correspondent for the Veneziani painting business, a position he had held for one year. He also continued to make friends in Trieste. One was a private student named Oscar Schwarz, who attended lessons at Joyce's apartment. (Joyce often joked that he had taught English to everyone in Trieste and would have to move to another city.)[34] Schwarz and Joyce passed time in the cafes of Trieste, and there were plenty of choices: the city now had nearly six hundred drinking establishments.[35] Schwarz recalled that Restaurant Bonavia was the site of some of Joyce's finest pontificating.[36] With dark memories of being swindled in shops and robbed in Rome, Joyce once declared that avarice was the sin of Italy.[37]

Another drinking companion was Silvestri, who met Joyce through de Tuoni. He had travelled through much of Europe as a street musician with his father before arriving in Trieste in 1906.[38] A short man with an abundance of nervous energy, Silvestri had an outgoing personality that made him a popular figure in Trieste.[39] His small studio was located on via Costantino Ressmann, where he completed the portraits of Joyce and Nora. While his artistic ability was recognized in Trieste, Silvestri had a strong character that virtually demanded respect; he sometimes chastized Joyce for any reference implying that he was less than a great painter.[40] For his part, Silvestri admired both Joyce and Svevo as cultured men but did not read their work.[41]

He shared with Joyce not only a fondness for the bottle but also incessant poverty and an uncanny knack for finding donors at critical moments. More than once, Joyce himself provided money for his friend. When the painter needed money in August 1914 to bring his family to Italy, Joyce raised one hundred crowns.[42] Silvestri's fundraising techniques were very creative. To Svevo, for example, he would present a package and claim that it contained a coat and shoes for Silvestri's daughter. Opening it, Svevo would find a painting that he naturally felt obliged to purchase.[43] In the impoverished Trieste years, necessity often did prove to be the mother of invention for Silvestri and Joyce.

15

Besieged

For Joyce, 1914 provided the first strong light in what had been a very long and dark tunnel of literary oblivion. Europe, though, was rapidly falling into its own darkness, and the tensions that preceded World War I had a marked effect on Triestine life. With the approach of war, friction between the Italians, Austrians, and Slavs in Trieste increased.

Triestine irredentists had never trusted their Austrian ruler, Prince Hohenlohe. They derisively referred to him as the "red prince" because of his sympathetic gestures toward the socialist cause and its leader, Valentino Pittoni, which Benco saw as thinly veiled attempts to suppress the irredentists.[1] Earlier displays of Triestine support for Italy, such as the large amount of aid delivered to Messina following the 1908 earthquake, the huge turnout for the funerals of Felice Venezian and Oberdan's mother in the same year, and Christmas packages sent to Italian troops in Tripoli during the 1910 Libyan conflict, irritated Hohenlohe.[2] In August 1913, Hohenlohe reacted to the irredentist pressure by enforcing a long-neglected law of 1867 and ordering the dismissal of all native Italians from public employment unless they accepted Austrian citizenship.[3] The directive led to street fighting and, ultimately, to the weekly expulsion of fifty Italians.[4]

Perhaps more troubling to the irredentists was the growing presence of the Slavs in Trieste.[5] Hohenlohe provided ample public employment to the Slavs: in fact, as more and more Italians were jailed (or expelled), the majority of police making the arrests were Slavs.[6] On March 13, 1914, the ethnic conflict touched Joyce indirectly when Italian and Slav students exchanged shots at the Scuola Revoltella, where Joyce was a teacher. There is no record of Joyce commenting on the obvious tensions between the two groups. As a pacifist, he would not have condoned the violence on either side. But given his distasteful Pola experience, his numerous Italian friendships in Trieste, and his love of Italian music and literature, it is highly probable that he sympathized with the Italians. Scipio Slataper, part Slav himself but faithful to the Italian cause, illustrated the painful complexity of Trieste's ethnic turbulence: "Either we beat the Slavs or the Slavs beat us; we must conquer to avoid being conquered,"[7] he wrote.

Fearing the worst, thousands of people from Trieste began to cross the border to support Italy should war break out.[8] The influential Teodoro Mayer had made numerous trips to Rome in an effort to secure official Italian support for the irredentists, and irredentist leader Attilio Hortis travelled to Paris and London for talks with the Allies.[9] The words of an anti-Austria propaganda leaflet were eagerly received by many Italians in Trieste: "People of Trieste! At the cry of Long Live Italy rise and you will be heard by the Mother Country, which is awaiting your voice to come and set you free."[10]

Triestines did not have long to wait before choosing sides became a necessity. The tragic events in the summer of 1914 brought war to their doorstep. At Miramare, Germany's Kaiser Wilhelm paid a visit to Austrian Archduke Francis Ferdinand[11] just before the archduke's fateful trip to Bosnia-Herzogovina and its capital, Sarajevo, where he was assassinated on June 28. His body was returned to Trieste for a state funeral,[12] while Austria and Serbia braced for fighting. Negotiations proved fruitless; Austria issued its declaration of war against Serbia one month later. While an ally of Austria, Italy remained neutral for the moment.

The escalation of the war forced Joyce to look pragmatically at his family's circumstances. At the outset of the conflict, Joyce took Giorgio to the British consulate, where he was informed that he should have no fears in Trieste as a British subject. Relieved, he then visited a student, Boris Furlan, near the Italian consulate, only to witness a mob attempting to tear down the Italian flag moments before soldiers arrived. A stunned Joyce quickly returned home, undoubtedly with increasing concern over his family's welfare.[13] Nevertheless, he showed no desire to leave Trieste early in the war. In a November 1914 letter to Miss Weaver, Joyce expressed hope that he would "remain at liberty" in Trieste, implying that the Austrian authorities had not yet disturbed him.[14]

Among the Joyces, Stanislaus was in the most immediate difficulty with the government. Unlike James, whose attentions were given to literature and family affairs, Stanislaus had embraced the irredentist movement. He openly expressed his antagonism toward the Austrians even after the start of the war, and Triestine authorities did not ignore him. He was arrested on January 17, 1915, and transferred to an Austrian detention camp for the duration of the war. Interestingly, on the same day, Hohenlohe had a letter sent to the Ministry of Culture and Education in Vienna in support of Joyce's reappointment to his teaching position for the coming year. In the letter, Joyce is described as "a quiet young man who only thinks to earn his bread."[15] Hohenlohe apparently knew of Joyce largely through his work as a teacher and journalist.

The brothers maintained regular contact. During the first half of the year Joyce wrote at least three letters, dated March 15, March 23, and June 16, to Stanislaus.[16] The last is of most interest to literary history, as it briefly describes Joyce's initial work in Trieste on *Ulysses*. The letters portray Joyce's concern for his brother's plight. He offered his assistance and, unlike earlier days, was able to send money. Stanislaus responded by sending more than a dozen letters to Joyce and Nora during his first year of internment. Despite the animosity that often marked their time in Trieste, James, Nora, and Stanislaus looked upon each other as family and acted accordingly under wartime conditions.

Joyce rarely commented upon the war. His 1914 letters, for example, offer no remarks about it. Various accounts have been given of Joyce's attitude toward the fighting. Gorman loftily proclaimed that Joyce "was above the conflict as were all the wise unimpassioned minds of the time,"[17] while Letizia Svevo saw him as anti-English.[18] Claud Sykes, an English actor with whom Joyce later established a theater company, the English Players, in Zurich during the war, considered Joyce's theatrical production of English plays an indication of his support for the Allies.

The truth was that Joyce's political statements by 1914 were coming largely through the independence that he asserted in his writing, a position that had cost him dearly with publishers. In *Dubliners*, for example, he showed with brutal frankness the hardships of life for many Irish. But he was beyond aligning himself with any political cause. In Trieste, Joyce's main concern over the war centered on how it would affect his family and his writing. The small amount of momentum that had lifted his career from years of obscurity was clearly threatened by the hostilities spreading across Europe and into Trieste. He could hardly expect to write and to maintain his family in a besieged city.

Moreover, Joyce was content to leave patriotism to the nationalists: he had no enthusiasm for flag waving or personal heroism. He once told Budgen, "I am not a bloodyminded man."[19] In the poem "Dooleysprudence," written in 1916, Joyce expressed his steadfast refusal to diminish his writing for purposes of propaganda supporting any side:

> Who is the tranquil gentleman who won't salute the State
> Or serve Nabuchodonesor or proletariat
> But thinks that every son of man has quite enough to do
> To paddle down the stream of life his personal canoe?
> > It's Mr Dooley,
> > Mr Dooley,
> > The wisest wight our country ever knew
> > 'Poor Europe ambles
> > Like sheep to shambles'
> > Sighs Mr Dooley-ooley-ooley—oo.[20]

Through the Trieste years and beyond, Joyce's interest in discussions of political movements, particularly those outside Ireland, dwindled. Numerous European acquaintances observed this change in Joyce. Benco's wife, Delia, visited Joyce in 1930 in Paris, where she found him "getting younger" and decidedly upbeat, and only politics, according to Joyce, no longer concerned him.[21] In a 1936 meeting with Stanislaus in Zurich, Joyce asserted, "For God's sake don't talk politics. I'm not interested in politics."[22] When Lady Maud Cunard, a London art patron, sent him a questionnaire the following year soliciting his views on the Spanish Civil War, Joyce's reaction was swift:

No! I won't answer it because it is politics. Now politics are getting into everything. The other night I agreed to let myself be taken to one of the dinners of the P.E.N. Club. The charter of the P.E.N. states that politics shall never be discussed there. But what happened? One person made a speech referring to an angle of politics, someone else brought up a conflicting argument, a third paper was read on more politics. I wanted the P.E.N. to take an interest in the pirating of *Ulysses* in the United States, but this was brushed aside. It was politics all the way.[23]

Joyce's Parisian friend Paul Leon, who greatly admired Joyce, nevertheless observed in a 1938 letter to Miss Weaver that Joyce might be seen as untouched by the outside world: "I can easily understand how any person who is concerned with the grave social, political and economic problems of this oppressive period will be painfully affected by its [*Finnegans Wake*] colossal triviality, its accumulation of words, meaningless, I suppose, for the ordinary intelligent reader of today. For I cannot see anywhere the slightest attempt in it to face or still less to solve these pressing problems."[24]

As had been the case in Trieste, though, Joyce was not oblivious to conditions in Europe. Jacques Mercanton, a Parisian friend, recalled Joyce's concern about the Anschluss in 1938.[25] Carola Giedion-Welcker offered a sympathetic explanation of Joyce's position:

It was not his nature to believe that he should engage in any kind of meddling or become actively involved in politics. His vocation lay in the fulfillment of a poetic mission, and he wanted to carry that mission out to the last detail, conscientiously and freely. In this sense he cursed "the disturbance of a war," not because he overvalued his cultural role and saw his special poetic work endangered but because to him, in the final analysis, war meant the victory of barbarism, with the result that any kind of cultural work—and therefore his, too—could become involved in a bloody power struggle and be destroyed.[26]

Critic Dominic Manganiello agreed: "Joyce did not discount political awareness, but rather indicated his conviction that an active role in politics would compromise his position as an artist. To be an artist entailed a sense of civic responsibility greater than that of the ordinary citizen, but not necessarily expressed at ballot boxes or in caucuses."[27]

It is difficult, however, to accurately assess Joyce in this regard. At times, he did exhibit a strong awareness of social and political affairs and acted with both compassion and courage. This side of his character is evident in four letters he wrote between June 1938 and February 1939 in which he commented upon his efforts to assist Jews in leaving Europe, hoping to secure their passage to Ireland and the United States.[28] As Giedion-Welcker emphasized, Joyce preferred to act on an individual basis rather than in support of (or in defiance of) a faceless mass. "His acts of helpfulness were never aimed at an unknown collective. Only direct assistance mattered to him, one individual helping another in a situation that could be assessed personally," she wrote.[29] Such behavior does not suggest indifference. Nevertheless, for Joyce it was more the exception than the rule.

Joyce strongly differentiated between art and patriotism, and he had no intention of altering the former for the sake of the latter. He told a friend in 1918, "As an artist I attach no importance to political conformity."[30] Perhaps an observation of Mario Vargas Llosa best characterizes the sentiments of artists like Joyce: "A writer can contribute more to politics if he dedicates himself to what he really knows how to do—write."[31] In that sense, Joyce matured politically in Trieste, although his relative anonymity in European literary circles muted his message.

Slowly, Joyce's writing career continued to blossom. On February 10, 1915, he received a letter from London literary agent J. B. Pinker, who wrote at the behest of H. G. Wells to offer his services, which Joyce accepted in April.[32] Wells later wrote to Joyce to profess his "unstinted admiration" for his work.[33]

Joyce also received a note from Mencken on April 20 stating that Joyce's stories "The Boarding House" and "A Little Cloud" would appear in the May issue of *Smart Set*, and that American publisher B. W. Huebsch hoped to bring out *Dubliners* in the United States.[34] Huebsch was devoted to publishing quality work: he once compared being a publisher to being a poet in that both were sacred callings and required complete dedication.[35] Mencken called him one of the few intelligent publishers in New York.[36] In a June 2 letter, Huebsch explained that he had been given a copy of the stories by Richards, which he read "with the keenest interest and appreciation." He reluctantly abandoned the idea of publishing them because "short stories in book form do not sell well in America." But Huebsch, as well as Pound, had earlier encouraged Mencken to use the stories. Huebsch promised that, if possible, he would publish Joyce's work later.[37] It is unclear how much of this attention Joyce shared with his Triestine friends, but it is likely that he took some pride in talking to Svevo and Francini, if not others, about his progress.

Family life was no less hectic for Joyce. In 1914, Eileen had become engaged to Frantisek Schaurek, a Czech bank cashier in Trieste, and the wedding took place in Trieste on April 12, 1915. Joyce, the best man, wore an ill-fitting suit borrowed from a teacher at the Berlitz School. He was amused to learn that "Yoyce"—the usual Triestine mispronunciation of his name—meant "eggs" in Czech, and foresaw many children for his sister. (His name was no easier for Triestines to spell: it appeared as "Joice," "Joyec," and "Yoyce" in various announcements in Trieste.)[38] The couple soon moved to Prague, where they remained throughout the war.[39]

When bad news arrived from Richards in May—he would not publish *A Portrait*—Joyce had little chance to respond. The effects of the war increasingly gripped the city. Prince Hohenlohe applied heavy censorship to the mail and press.[40] Irredentist journals were singled out: *L'Indipendente* stopped publishing early in the war, while *Il Piccolo*, with a circulation of 100,000 but a staff of only three, struggled on.[41] By contrast, the socialists' *Il Lavoratore*, which took no official stance toward the war, continued to appear daily.[42] Italian newspapers were prohibited, precipitating an active business in contraband issues (and false passports) at the Caffè Milano. Trade was severely reduced because of the mine-infested Adriatic waters, and the half-empty city often took on an eerie silence.[43] As the wounded began arriving, the Triestine people looked toward the future with trepidation.

Pressure increased on Italy to act. Although a member of the Triple Alliance,

Italy had been ignored by Austria prior to its declaration of war. Italy's decision to remain neutral disappointed Triestine irredentists, who had hoped for a quick fight against the Austrians.[44] In fact, the Italian government was talking simultaneously to the Triple Entente—Great Britain, France, and Russia—and to the Austrians, both sides coveting Italian support. Foreign Minister Sidney Sonnino pressed to secure Italy's alpine frontier to the Brenner Pass, as well as Trieste and much of Istria.

Playing a curious and unlikely role in the talks with Austria was Roberto Prezioso. By April 1915, Austria sensed that its hopes of reaching an agreement with Italy were dwindling, and the Hapsburg government wanted to learn exactly what chance of success, if any, remained. An intermediary was needed for the delicate but unofficial discussions with Italy. The Italian Prezioso was given the task apparently because his wife was a relative of Baron Klumentzkj, an Austrian official, ostensibly making Prezioso somewhat palatable to each side. In Turin, he conversed privately with former Italian prime minister Giovanni Giolitti, indicating that Austria was prepared to accede to most of Italy's demands. Giolitti passed along Prezioso's words to Sonnino, who understandably was skeptical of the Triestine's credibility.[45]

In the end, Prezioso's effort was futile. The Triple Entente accepted Italy's conditions in the event of victory, and all parties signed the secret Treaty of London on April 26, 1915.[46] Italy agreed to enter the war within one month and on May 4 denounced the Triple Alliance.

Italy's decision was not surprising, as most Italians disliked Austria. The 1882 alliance between the two had been formed for reasons of realpolitik, but the countries were historical enemies, a truth that was about to emerge—again—in the full fury of combat. On May 23, 1915, Italy declared war against Austria, which responded by immediately sealing its border, halting further Italian emigration.[47] To Austria's benefit, the Italian-Austrian border was defended initially by Slovene, Croat, and Bosnian soldiers, who, as much as the Austrians, feared Italian annexation of their lands.[48]

Reaction in Trieste was swift and chaotic. The Austrian flag was raised over the city, and anti-Italian riots broke out, lasting through the night. Mobs roamed the streets, burning the offices of *Il Piccolo* and other nationalist institutions, destroying Italian cafes and shops, and vandalizing public property.[49] Trieste's municipal council was dissolved, and Austrian authorities began deportation proceedings against Italians,[50] arresting some individuals strictly on rumor. Men up to the age of fifty were being conscripted. When the first sounds of shelling from the front in Monfalcone, only twenty kilometers away, reached Trieste,[51] many Triestines—including Joyce—prepared to depart.

Joyce's decision to leave Trieste was not difficult. The Scuola Revoltella had closed in the spring after nearly all of the teachers were called up to military duty. Joyce, who had a few private students early in the year, now had none, and to survive borrowed 300 crowns from Ralli and 250 crowns from Svevo's father-in-law.[52] He walked distractedly through Trieste's streets, Benco recalled, with "lips tight together in a hard, horizontal line. He would bow and look at one fixedly, and avoided stopping or exchanging a few words."[53]

A description of Trieste at about the time of Joyce's departure is telling:

The long paved streets are like the bed of dried-up streams: a few slow passers-by in the morning and evening, in the heat of noonday nobody at all; not a cart or a carriage either. Even the two or three shops that have stayed open in the main streets let down their shutters for a good part of the day. The silence is broken only by the rhythmic footsteps of the patrols, echoing across the empty squares. And the few soldiers remaining are the final dregs left over from the call-up . . . in faded, untidy uniforms, with muskets from the Franco-Prussian war.[54]

The confusion created by the onset of fighting was evident in the June 16 letter sent by Joyce to Stanislaus, which indicated Joyce's uncertainty as to how long he could remain in Trieste;[55] in fact, he would be departing within a week.

The American consul in Trieste, Ralph Busser, helped Joyce to obtain a passport,[56] still leaving him with the delicate task of obtaining Austrian approval to leave. When the military authorities ordered a partial evacuation of the city, Joyce requested permission to depart.[57] Fortunately, the influential Count Sordina and Baron Ralli agreed to assure local officials that Joyce posed no threat to Austria: he was allowed to go.[58] Acknowledging his debt, Joyce later presented Sordina with a copy of *A Portrait*.[59] He also remembered Ralli, giving him *A Portrait* and *Exiles*, both with personal dedications, gifts that Ralli deeply appreciated.[60]

To gain money for the trip, Joyce secured a loan on his furniture, which he left with his books and some manuscripts at the via Bramante apartment. Joyce and his family departed Trieste on June 21, 1915, headed for Switzerland. They stopped in Zurich simply because it was "the first big city after the frontier," he informed Miss Weaver.[61] Joyce's fame—and income—rose during the war years, and Zurich would become Joyce's final resting place in 1941.

16

The War Years

Despite all of the wartime problems in Trieste, Joyce abandoned the city with some regret. Francini recalled, "We separated with tears in our eyes and a heartfelt handshake."[1] Joyce referred to Trieste as his "second country,"[2] and he did not intend to be a refugee indefinitely: "I shall probably remain in Switzerland till it is possible for me to return to Trieste," he informed Pinker on June 30.[3] But, as Joyce came to realize, the situation in Trieste was deteriorating rapidly. Just two weeks later, he wrote to Pound, "I am afraid I cannot go back to Trieste for some time to come. . . . The last raid of Italian airships, as I read, was directed against the Trieste shipyard, about five minutes from my house."[4] Ultimately, he did go back to Trieste, but not until October 1919, after spending more than four eventful years in Zurich.

Joyce socialized with others from Trieste, including Ottocaro Weiss, a student at the University of Zurich and the brother of Edoardo Weiss, Italy's first psychoanalyst. He also found some private pupils, one of whom was Letizia Svevo.[5] But a severe shortage of money made Joyce's initial weeks in Zurich stressful. As usual, others came to the rescue. Michael Healy, Nora's uncle, sent fifteen pounds upon the arrival of Joyce's family in Switzerland. After receiving letters from Pound, Yeats, and British writer Edmund Gosse, the Royal Literary Fund bestowed a grant on Joyce later in 1915,[6] and more money came from the Society of Authors, a Civil List pension, and Miss Weaver. In February 1917, a group of solicitors sent Joyce a letter stating that an anonymous admirer of his would be providing a gift of two hundred pounds spread out over the following year, a period that was later extended.[7] His final benefactor was Edith Rockefeller McCormick, a wealthy American in Zurich, who gave him a large monthly stipend from March 1918 to September 1919.

While sales of his work remained slow, Joyce was gaining something of an international audience. The *Egoist* completed the serialization of *A Portrait* in September 1915, after which Miss Weaver attempted to form the Egoist Press with the intent of publishing *A Portrait* in its entirety. The plan failed when no English printer would handle the text.[8]

More helpful was B. W. Huebsch, who published the novel and *Dubliners* in the United States in 1916, as well as *Chamber Music* in 1918. In a 1917 letter to F. Scott Fitzgerald, Edmund Wilson referred to *A Portrait* as "probably one of the best novels of the century."[9] Using the American printed version, Miss Weaver finally brought out *A Portrait* in book form in 1917. Joyce's earlier poems from Trieste also received attention. In May 1917, Harriet Monroe published "Simples," "A Flower Given to My Daughter," "Tutto è Sciolto," "Flood," and "Nightpiece" in *Poetry*. "On the Beach at Fontana" appeared in the November issue.

Interest in new work by Joyce increased, and in March 1918 a New York literary magazine, the *Little Review*, edited by feminists Margaret Anderson and Jane Heap, began a serial printing of the unfinished text of *Ulysses*. Joyce's play, *Exiles*, which he had completed in Trieste,[10] was published simultaneously by Grant Richards and Huebsch in May 1918 and was performed in Munich in August 1919. Also in 1919, Miss Weaver included five installments of *Ulysses* in the *Egoist*. Joyce's writing was not bringing him the royalties he had hoped for, but in Zurich he could no longer convincingly play the role of a starving artist.

Joyce remained puzzled over the identity of his mysterious benefactor, so he contacted the solicitors in May and June of 1919. Their responses failed to name the person, but indicated that "the qualities that most interest her are your searching piercing spirit, your scorching truth, the power and startling penetration of your 'intense instants of imagination.' "[11] The knowledge that the donor was a woman did not enlighten Joyce, so Miss Weaver, sensing the unease on both sides, reluctantly acknowledged her generosity. She concluded her July 6, 1919, letter to Joyce almost apologetically: "Perhaps I had better add that it was I who sent the message through Messrs Monro Saw and Co and that I am sorry I sent it in the way and in the form I did. It is rather paralysing to communicate through solicitors. I fear you will have to withdraw all words about delicacy and self effacement: I can only beg you to forgive my lack of them."[12]

Joyce felt "great pleasure" upon learning the depth of Miss Weaver's support for him, but was somewhat embarrassed about not realizing her interest earlier. "You have probably discovered by now that I am a very stupid person—a fact which I should have preferred to conceal," he wrote.[13] Miss Weaver maintained her support of Joyce up to his death, even paying for his funeral.[14] In total, she had provided him more than $100,000.[15] After Samuel Beckett heard of Miss Weaver's death in 1961, he wrote to Sylvia Beach, "I . . . shall think of her when I think of goodness."[16]

Joyce's most serious problem in Zurich, though, was not money but his weakening eyesight. On August 12, 1917, he reported to Harriet Monroe, "I have not been able to do much this year. I have been very ill with my eyes and fear I shall never get well in this bad climate."[17] A week later, a severe attack of glaucoma required an iridectomy, the first of eleven eye operations he would undergo in a period of fifteen years. As his creative vision grew, his real vision—painfully—diminished in Zurich.

After the war, members of the Joyce family returned to Trieste. An expectant

Eileen and Frantisek left Prague with their small daughter Bozena at the end of 1918. Stanislaus, free following four years of internment, joined them in Trieste, where they shared a large apartment at via Sanità 2, near the waterfront and along-side Joyce's former haunts in Città Vecchia. Old problems between the Joyces renewed themselves quickly when Stanislaus again was burdened with handling his brother's Trieste affairs, in particular one related to the via Bramante apartment that Joyce had continued to rent during his absence. On May 25, 1919, Stanislaus wrote bitterly to Joyce in Zurich, "I have just emerged from four years of hunger and squalor, and am trying to get on my feet again. Do you think you can give me a rest?"[18]

Joyce responded by sending 150 lire to Stanislaus and berating the "rascal" of a landlord in Trieste, writing that he had paid the landlord faithfully throughout the war. But it is clear from Stanislaus's letter that Count Diodato Tripcovich, a Trieste shipping magnate whose son and daughter had been students of Joyce,[19] and Stanislaus had covered a good portion of Joyce's rent. To patch relations with Stanislaus, Joyce invited him to visit Zurich for a month.[20] Joyce, however, had no desire to remain much longer in Switzerland, particularly after Edith Rockefeller McCormick's financial support ceased at the end of the summer. But, unlike Eileen and Stanislaus, he did not look upon Trieste as home. His inclination, he told Claud Sykes, was to settle elsewhere than Trieste,[21] probably because of the rumors reaching Zurich of water shortages, typhus, high prices, and streets filled with gar-bage.[22]

His options, though, in post-World War I Europe were limited, so he reluctantly looked again to Trieste. Tiring rapidly of Zurich, Joyce informed Stanislaus on September 8 that he hoped to be leaving for Trieste on October 1 and would need a flat of "six rooms with bath and electric light," an unrealistic goal given the housing shortage in Trieste. The obvious choice was to share the flat at via Sanità 2, at least temporarily. But Stanislaus threatened to leave the apartment in such a case.[23] Schaurek also had misgivings about the family's arrival, but Eileen actively pro-moted the plan and finally prevailed.[24] On October 17, the Joyces were reunited. Acknowledging Joyce's bleak finances, Nora confided to Eileen, "We didn't have a penny left," and thanked her for her support.[25] Adjustments were made: Stanislaus switched from his study to a smaller room, and Giorgio and Lucia slept on sofas.[26]

Conditions were undeniably crowded. The new apartment sheltered Eileen, Schaurek, their two children, Joyce, Nora, Giorgio, Lucia, Stanislaus, and two maids.[27] But Bozena Delimata, one of the Schaurek children, remembered many happy moments in spite of the discomfort. Visitors were frequent, and the atmos-phere was pleasant. All of the family members enjoyed singing together, with "It's a Long Way to Tipperary" being a favorite. Joyce often played with the children and composed some music, including a song for Lucia: "Era una piccola bambina che rideva durante il giorno e non dormiva durante la notte." (She was a little girl who laughed during the day and did not sleep at night.)[28]

Inevitably, Joyce found himself again without money in Trieste. In Benco's words, he wore "one of those monastic habits with military belts which were being used as overcoats. It was too short for him and gave him rather strange proportions."[29] He admitted to Miss Weaver shortly after his arrival, "The situation in fact is extremely discouraging and but for your help to me it would be disastrous."[30]

Soon it was indeed too close to disaster for Joyce. On November 7, he appealed to Pinker to cable Huebsch for remittance of royalties, present or future. He explained,

I find myself in very difficult circumstances here, and as part of my house [on via Bramante] was ruined by air attacks and the furniture removed and many of my things stolen and moreover as it is almost impossible to find a flat owing to military congestion in the city and as the prices are extremely high, I have no resource but to ask you to do all that you can in the matter. . . . I am in most urgent need of funds at the present moment.[31]

Huebsch quickly sent the money.[32]

Joyce's adjustment to Trieste was difficult. Given a cool reception by Stanislaus, who attended with deliberation to his busy teaching schedule and his own circle of friends, Joyce "neither read nor wrote nor spoke" for the first six weeks in Trieste, he informed Frank Budgen.[33] "As for *Ulysses*—it is like me—on the rocks," he conceded.[34] Copies of *A Portrait* were slow to reach Trieste, although Joyce admitted to Miss Weaver, "I fancy that many could be sold here but perhaps the exchange, so unfavourable to Italian buyers, will be an obstacle." He added, "It is very consoling to me that you consider me a writer because every time I sit down with a pen in my hand I have to persuade myself (and others) of the fact."[35]

Joyce felt a need for companionship, but he saw friends rarely. He told Budgen, "The town is full of rumours of my success (financially chiefly) in foreign parts so that I avoid all contact with people."[36] Francini now found him to be a "serious, almost conventional" man.[37] He also stopped attending the opera because he could not afford a new suit.[38] Joyce sorely missed Budgen. Hopeful that he might consider a move to Trieste, Joyce asked, "Need I tell you what a great privation it is to me to have not here within earshot your over-patient and friendly self?"[39] Nora concurred: "We have not got over the loss of your company and often speak of you," she wrote in January 1920.[40]

There is no indication that Joyce associated with most of his contemporaries in Trieste. Poet Virgilio Giotti saw Joyce in a cafe and was struck by his self-assurance,[41] but he personally did not know Joyce.[42] Other writers, including Saba, Voghera, and Giani Stuparich, remained in Florence during Joyce's Trieste years. He apparently also never met Rainer Maria Rilke, who from 1910 to 1914 stayed occasionally as the guest of Princess Maria von Thurn und Taxis-Hohenlohe at the Duino castle, located along Trieste's northern coast.[43] But Joyce could have had the company of Svevo and other intellectuals at Caffè Garibaldi.[44] For the moment, though, he preferred to limit his discussions of *Ulysses* to those with Budgen by post.

Several explanations might account for Joyce's isolation. His students generally had come from upper-class families of businessmen, so he had little personal familiarity with the literary community, small as it was, in Trieste. Moreover, he had no emotional investment in the political and social issues of the city, as did Triestine writers. Or he simply may have felt too morose during this period to be bothered with new acquaintances. Joyce had always been highly selective in choosing readers for his manuscripts. After Constantine Curran once gave a draft of *Stephen Hero* to a mutual friend without securing Joyce's approval, Joyce wrote to Stanislaus, "It is most thoughtless of Curran to give it to anyone without my permission. . . . I must pass a week of torture until I know whether it is safe or not."[45] Few people in Trieste were privy to Joyce's work before publication, which is not surprising given the fact that Joyce craved attention most from the influential literary circles of London and Dublin. Local fame at that point, while not unwelcome, was not what he sought.

Still, Joyce needed a confidant in Trieste with whom to discuss his work. In the earlier Trieste years, Stanislaus had ably filled the role of critic. Circumstances had clearly changed, though, in that regard. Joyce wrote, "My brother [knows] something but he thinks it [*Ulysses*] a joke."[46]

Compounding the problem was Joyce's difficulty making friends. Maria Jolas observed,

You could almost count on Joyce's being silent in the presence of a newcomer rather than having anything to say to him, because he would have to sort of sniff around and find out through his pores who he had there, whether he could have confidence in him, etc. He was not at all an outgoing man, and many people have recorded their disappointment in his conversation because, particularly when he was with strangers, he was inclined to be merely perfunctory. I mean it was rather difficult to get him launched onto any subject concerning the outside world that you might think perfectly civilized people would sit down and talk to each other about. Somehow, he didn't.[47]

Curran agreed, stating, "At no time . . . do I remember him in company taking part in any general discussion. For anything approaching serious talk he preferred the company of one to many."[48]

Consequently, Joyce turned with hope toward an old Triestine friend, Silvio Benco, who had become the editor of the Italian nationalist journal *La Nazione*, which he had helped to establish in November 1918.[49] Joyce often visited him in his office to discuss *Ulysses*. Benco recalled,

He brought me the numbers of *The Little Review* in which about a third of the work had appeared. . . . The following episodes were then simply typed, and five of them were still unfinished. He showed me the loose sheets on which he prepared the material of each episode, notes as to composition, quotations, references, ideas, essays in various styles. When the rough material was ready, he devoted himself to writing out the complete episode, and this he usually did in less than a month.[50]

On numerous occasions, Joyce asked Benco to pass some time with him in the cafes of Città Vecchia. Unfortunately for Joyce, Benco was no Budgen; he simply had no time to help Joyce.[51] Despondent, Joyce complained to Budgen, "Not a soul to talk to about Bloom. Lent the chapter ["Nausikaa"] to one or two people but they know as much about it as the parliamentary side of my arse."[52] Svevo probably would have been pleased to read the manuscript, but Joyce did not approach him. Irritated by Stanislaus's indifference and by Benco's rejection, Joyce simply may have exhausted his patience in trying to find a reader.

Joyce's unhappiness resulted from more than his stale friendships. He was a restless spirit in what had become a dispirited city. Postwar Trieste was barely recognizable to Joyce and many other Triestines.

The end of World War I had seen Italy finally take power in Trieste, but at a terrible human cost. During the war, Italians, including those in Trieste, had differed in their views regarding the sacrifice that would be required to extend Italy's borders and reclaim Trieste, among other areas. In *A Farewell to Arms*, Hemingway described the polarization of Italians as they had tried to envision the postwar situation from the daily ebb and flow of the fighting. One Italian officer stated confidently that Italy would gain Corsica and all of the Adriatic coastline, and another dreamed of Italy returning to the splendors of Rome.[53] An Italian ambulance driver, however, saw much less glory ahead for his country. Conversing with fellow drivers, he asked, "What if we take San Gabriele? What if we take the Carso and Monfalcone and Trieste? Where are we then? Did you see all the far mountains today? Do you think we could take all them too? Only if the Austrians stop fighting. One side must stop fighting. . . . But no, instead there is a war."[54]

And the war around Trieste had been fierce. Air raids on the city were common, and numerous efforts by the Italians to reach Trieste by land had failed, with particularly brutal clashes near the Carso. Italian soldiers did not enter the city until November 3, 1918, barely a week before the armistice ending the fighting in Europe.

The political battle over Trieste, however, remained intense. The newly formed Kingdom of Serbs, Croats, and Slovenes (later Yugoslavia) challenged the Italians for control of both Trieste and the Istrian peninsula. By then the peninsula had become largely Slavic (58 percent)[55] due greatly to Trieste's earlier economic lure, as well as to the prewar efforts of the Austrians to neutralize the irredentist threat by encouraging population of the area with non-Italians. But in treaties signed after negotiations in 1919 and 1920, Italy secured the entire area.

Trieste, though, was no longer the prize it seemed. The once-thriving port had become a shadow of its former self. Its lifeblood, the Hapsburg empire, was gone, and with it had disappeared much of the prosperity that had given Trieste such importance for centuries. The sharp decline in commerce between Trieste and the vast Austrian territory, changes in tariff laws, and increased competition from northern European ports combined to minimize Trieste's significance.[56]

Italy did seek to help the beleaguered city, particularly in its harbor activity. The war, however, had taken an appalling toll on the country, leaving 600,000 dead, 1,000,000 wounded, and a public debt of 94 billion lire.[57] It was impossible for Italy to provide large-scale aid immediately. While initial euphoria ruled Trieste at the sight of its Italian liberators, discouragement and frustration set in as the city realized it had been reduced to economic mediocrity.

In 1919 and 1920, economic and political tension gripped the city. Poverty grew and labor strikes abounded: teachers, clerks, industrial workers, seamen, shop assistants, chemical workers, metal workers, and bank clerks all clamored for change.[58] In May 1920, Joyce complained of a clerks' strike that had closed stores in Trieste for ten days,[59] and a month later of a rail strike.[60]

The labor unrest and nationalist zeal provided fertile ground for fascist propaganda, and Trieste became one of the first areas in Italy to see considerable fascist activity.[61] At the same time, Triestine socialists increasingly favored the class struggle of the Bolshevists, a development that widened the political gulf in Trieste.[62] Turmoil spread, often involving firearms, as fascists and other nationalists gained political control of Trieste.[63]

Ultimately, a violent clash jolted the city on July 13, 1920, less than a week before Joyce left Trieste permanently. Two Italians had been killed by Slavs in the Istrian port of Split on July 12, and the fascists held a demonstration in Piazza Grande, just two blocks from Joyce's via Sanità apartment, the following day. After an Italian was stabbed to death by an unknown assailant during the rally, the crowd marched on the Balkan Hotel, headquarters of the Slav nationalists. Shots were exchanged and, within one hour, the building was in flames.[64] Fascists confronted firemen at the scene and allowed the hotel to burn, resulting in the death of innocent people.[65]

Joyce, living so nearby, may have heard or even seen the violence. Essentially disinterested in the local political situation and not at all one to support the use of such force, Joyce probably looked upon the event as another reason to leave. Equally nettling to him was Stanislaus's outspoken opposition to fascism, which undoubtedly was voiced following the Balkan incident. It was hardly an environment that Joyce, engrossed in *Ulysses*, wanted to endure.

The extent of Trieste's transformation left a marked impression on Joyce. In 1922 in Paris, he was approached by an Irish politician about returning to his country. "I told him not for the present," he wrote to Stanislaus. "One redeemed city (and inhabitants thereof) will last me for a few years more."[66] Trieste, as Joyce knew it, was gone.

17

Fame Beckons

The postwar strife in Trieste probably contributed to the fond memories Joyce later held regarding the orderly and efficient Austrian administration. Judging from the number of friends who recall Joyce reminiscing about the old days in Trieste, it is clear that he spoke often on the subject. Maria Jolas stated, "Joyce always said about life in Trieste, that it was a most charming existence. It was the end, of course, of the Austro-Hungarian empire, but it was apparently a very warm, friendly moment in history. He, in fact, remembered it as a model of what life had been at that time, when people were not trying to oppress one another."[1]

Mary Colum heard similar sentiments. Joyce, she wrote, left Trieste "with sadness, for (he) loved the old Austrian Empire, and he and his family had their happiest days in Trieste. 'They called the Austrian Empire a ramshackle empire,' he said to us later in Paris. 'I wish to God there were more such empires.' "[2] He praised the generosity of the Austrian authorities who allowed him to leave Trieste in 1915, according to Budgen,[3] who observed that Joyce "certainly had more than a sneaking affection for the Austro-Hungarian monarchy."[4] Joyce showed somewhat uncharacteristic sentimentality when he later remarked, "I experienced more kindness in Trieste than ever before or since in my life."[5]

Joyce was not alone in these feelings. Even today, nostalgia for the Hapsburgs exists in Trieste, and to some extent the influence of Austria remains. Alongside works of Joyce and Svevo, numerous bookstores offer window displays of pre-World War I historical books on Trieste. A summer operetta festival features classics by Strauss and other Danube masters, and the local cuisine combines Italian dishes with Eastern European tastes.[6] In public schools, many Triestine students continue to learn German as a foreign language, although Joyce would be surprised by the number who can speak English. Older Triestines can still remember Austrian rule: as of 1991, Trieste had nearly ten thousand citizens over seventy years of age.[7] Much of the city's downtown area remains unchanged from Joyce's days in Trieste, featuring architecture resembling more an Austrian than an Italian city.

Several reasons may explain Joyce's wistful memories. In the Trieste years he was a young man, defiant, a proud father, and, with some notable lapses, in love with an attractive Irish woman. Even in the midst of the endless complications he endured, life to Joyce in Trieste must have had a certain vitality that could not have existed for him in Dublin. While Trieste was not one of the great capitals of Europe, it was no backwater. All of Joyce's addresses and places of employment were located within a twenty-minute walk of the busy harbor and Corso business district. Joyce shared the city's passion for opera, perfected his Italian, made a number of friends, and, most importantly, wrote prodigiously. Thus, he had sufficient cause for reflecting warmly upon his Triestine experience, even while overlooking its more vexing moments.

Joyce's spirits eventually rose despite the unsettled conditions in Trieste, and he again focused on his work. Joyce corresponded regularly with Milan critic Carlo Linati, who had translated plays of Yeats and Synge, regarding an Italian translation of *Exiles*, and in November 1919 he resumed work on *Ulysses* with the goal of finishing it the following year.

He temporarily took up teaching once more at the Scuola Revoltella, which was being transformed into the new Università di Trieste. (Joyce called it the "revolver university.")[8] His schedule was light—one hour per day—but teaching was as dreary to Joyce as ever.[9] One of his students, Lojce Berce, described him as often being distracted or inattentive, smiling abstractly or staring blankly at students during class, hardly an inspirational figure. On one occasion, when a student asked about the length of time necessary to reach fluency in a foreign language, Joyce replied, "I have been studying Italian for fifteen years and am at last beginning to know it."[10] It was not unusual for Joyce to give students the lowest passing grade.[11] The school irked Joyce further by not paying him for four months.[12]

Joyce drifted back into closer relationships with Triestine friends. With Nora and the children, he began to join the Francinis for dinner each week, after which Joyce would display his old enthusiasm by regaling the group with church songs. Benco, who lived in the same building, was a guest one evening and noted that Joyce "seemed lost in his own singing."[13] He practiced Latin with Francini and saw Benco and Svevo on occasion.

He also renewed his friendship with Oscar Schwarz; when Schwarz asked how he had passed the war years, a disinterested Joyce answered, "Oh yes, I was told there was a war going on in Europe." Silvestri was another good companion. One night at the Restaurant Dreher in the Piazza della Borsa, Joyce suggested that Silvestri do his portrait. Silvestri completed the painting but, probably not to his surprise, did not receive payment until a year later.[14]

In other ways, though, Joyce's dissatisfaction in Trieste remained. On March 11, 1920, he wrote to American lawyer and publisher John Quinn, "I have not a very pleasant existence at present for this city is overcrowded and we are packed into one flat with seven other people."[15] To Budgen he lamented, "We now cook for ourselves in this household. Till yesterday I was paying about 35 lire a day to my brother-in-law. Now I pay him half rent, gas, coal and we pig for ourselves. Jolly!"[16] He reported that a birthday party for him had ended in an argument with "meinem Schwager," a reference to Eileen's husband.[17] His pleas to Budgen regarding a trip to Trieste showed the extent to which he had already imagined the change: "I will have a room ready for you. Re studio I think you could have [Tullio] Silvestri's. I can introduce you to many of your craft here. I can get you lessons here, not tiresome, at 6 or 7 lire an hour. You will learn Italian. You will see the Mediterranean. You will surely find something to paint in this colourfull place. Food is not so dear. You will see ME."[18]

While he considered Joyce to be a "consistent and helpful friend,"[19] Budgen did not see Trieste as a step forward in his career and instead hoped to go to London.[20] Joyce declared "Conditions here rotten," and compelled him to "Write! Write!! Write!!!"[21] but remained alone in Trieste with his thoughts of *Ulysses*, wondering when "this bloody state of affairs" would end.[22]

Joyce's rather unorthodox lifestyle during this period led to some bizarre speculation on the part of his neighbors, which he recounted in a 1921 letter to Miss Weaver: "Triestines, seeing me emerge from my relative's house . . . for about twenty minutes every day and walk to the same point . . . and back (I was writing *Nausikaa* and *The Oxen of the Sun* in a dreadful atmosphere) circulated the rumour, now firmly believed, that I am a cocaine victim."[23] He acknowledged, though, that "the task I set myself technically in writing a book from eighteen different points of view and in as many styles, all apparently unknown or undiscovered by my fellow tradesmen, that and the nature of the legend chosen would be enough to upset anyone's mental balance."[24] In any case, Joyce was not one to chat with neighbors, so their gawking probably only amused him.

Amid the chaos in both his apartment and the city, Joyce's work progressed and continued to attract attention. He completed the "Nausikaa" section of his novel and sent it to Pound and Budgen in early February, quickly moving on to "Oxen of the Sun," which he found to be the most difficult part of the book.[25] He guessed that this episode cost him one thousand hours of work, and it was with great relief and satisfaction that he wrote to Budgen on May 18, "The oxen of the bloody bleeding sun are finished."[26] In the previous month, Linati's translation of *Exiles* appeared in the Milan journal *Convegno* in the first of three installments, and Joyce's poem "A Memory of the Players in a Mirror at Midnight" was included in the April 15 issue of *Poesia* (founded by Marinetti in 1905),[27] again with Linati's assistance.[28]

News from the United States regarding copies of the *Little Review*, which contained the serialized text of *Ulysses*, was far less encouraging. In 1919, the January and May issues were confiscated and burned by postal authorities on the grounds of obscenity. Margaret Anderson recalled, "It was like a burning at the stake."[29] John Quinn protested the matter to the solicitor of the Post Office Department to no avail.[30] *Ulysses* would not be cleared for publication in the United States until 1933.

In Trieste, summer was approaching, and Joyce had little interest in suffering through another hot season. He wrote to Budgen in March that he was contemplating going to England and Ireland around June or July.[31] In May, though, all plans changed. Pound, in Venice, intended to meet Joyce there or in Trieste, but an illness of Pound's wife, Dorothy, required the couple to relocate to a milder climate, so they moved on to Lago di Garda, near Sirmione, Italy.[32] Pound suggested they meet at his place, and Joyce agreed.

On June 5, he arrived at the Trieste train station only to learn that a train accident had made travel to Sirmione impossible. Consequently, Joyce composed a long letter to Pound that detailed his circumstances in Trieste and his reasons for wanting to leave:

I am in need of a long holiday (by this I don't mean abandonment of *Ulysses* but quiet in which to finish it) away from here. Without saying anything about this city (*de mortuis nil nisi bonum* [of the dead say nothing but good]) my own position for the past seven months has been very unpleasant. I live in a flat with eleven other people and have had great difficulty in securing time and peace enough to write those two chapters. The second reason is: clothes. I have none and can't buy any. The other members of the family are still provided with decent clothes bought in Switzerland. I wear my son's boots (which are two sizes too large) and his castoff suit which is too narrow in the shoulders, other articles belong or belonged to my brother and to my brother-in-law. I shall not be able to buy anything here. A suit of clothes, they tell me, costs 600–800 francs. A shirt costs 35 francs. I can just live with what I have but no more. Since I came here I suppose I have not exchanged 100 words with anybody. I spend the greater part of my time sprawled across two beds surrounded by mountains of notes. I leave the house at 12:22 and walk the same distance along the same streets buy the *Daily Mail* which my brother and wife read and return. Idem in the evening. I was once inveigled into a theatre. I was once invited to a public dinner, as professor of the Scuola Superiore here, and next day received from there a request to subscribe 20,000 or 10,000 or even 5000 lire of Italian war loan. I must buy clothes so I think I ought to go to Dublin to buy them.

He concluded, "I must finish my book in quiet even if I sell off the furniture."[33]

Pound realized that a meeting—and maybe a move—was imperative. He counseled Joyce, "I don't think you need regard yourself as tied to Trieste by your job, If you are fed up with the place & want to pull out of it."[34] Pound's words were not lost on Joyce, who later told Miss Weaver, "Mr. Pound wrote to me so urgently from Sirmione . . . that in spite of my dread of thunderstorms [Pound had reported a severe storm in the area] and detestation of travelling I went there bringing my son with me to act as a lightning conductor."[35] Joyce and Giorgio arrived on June 8. The meeting was productive: both writers agreed that Joyce should leave Trieste and remain for at least a brief period with Pound in Paris, where he had important literary contacts.

Pound recorded his observations of Joyce in a June 19 letter to John Quinn, expressing some surprise that Joyce was not the rebel that he might have expected. He found him

pleasing; after the first shell of cantankerous Irishman, I got the impression that the real man is the author of *Chamber Music*, the sensitive. The rest is the genius; the registration of realities on the temperament, the delicate temperament of the early poems. A concentration and absorption passing Yeats'. . . . Also great exhaustion, but more constitution than I had expected, and apparently good recovery from eye operation. . . . He is, of course, as stubborn as a mule or an Irishman, but I failed to find him at all unreasonable.[36]

Joyce returned to Trieste and began making the elaborate preparations necessary for another trip across Europe. In a July 1 letter to Linati, he described himself as "in great haste and half dead through the formalities of Consulates and others."[37] He informed the Scuola Revoltella of his decision. (Stanislaus filled the position the following year.) After packing what they could—Joyce left behind more than six hundred books[38] and "a heap of MS"[39] in the apartment—and saying farewell to friends, Joyce and his family went to the train station accompanied by the Schaureks. Using his remaining savings,[40] Joyce left for Paris in early July 1920, destined for literary fame.

Stanislaus, annoyed again with his brother, declined to see them off.[41] Through letters they subsequently made peace. Following his brother's departure, Stanislaus forwarded a letter of apology for not being in a very sociable mood during Joyce's short postwar stay in Trieste.[42] Joyce acknowledged, "I regretted to observe the barometric depression to which you allude."[43]

But they were to remain in different spheres. Joyce had a life of celebrity awaiting him in Paris, while Stanislaus continued his quiet teaching career in Trieste. There had been a mutual brotherly influence, both positive and negative, in earlier years in Trieste, but by 1920 they had little patience for each other. The relationship had always contrasted with those between Joyce and his Triestine friends, who addressed him respectfully and obviously enjoyed his company. Now, James and Stanislaus separated with no regrets, although they maintained a sincere interest in each other, largely through letters, over the next two decades.

18

Paris-Trieste

With a remarkable array of writers that included Pound, Hemingway, and T. S. Eliot (who found Joyce arrogant but impressive in his artistic self-confidence),[1] Paris in the 1920s had a far more suitable literary environment than Trieste for Joyce. The economic situation also was an improvement. The cost of living was lower,[2] and Joyce had the good fortune to secure for three months a rent-free apartment. Still, he relied heavily upon Pound for financial survival[3] and asked Stanislaus to collect "850 or 1000 lire" owed to Joyce by the Scuola Revoltella.[4] Following his stay in Paris, Joyce planned to go back to Trieste to finish *Ulysses*,[5] but, probably with the memory of a depressed postwar Trieste still fresh in his mind, his inclination to return faded. When the rent subsidy expired, he admitted that he had no idea where he might go.[6] In an October 28 letter to Stanislaus, he mentioned the possibility of a return to Trieste but gave no hint as to when.[7] The trip never materialized: Joyce had seen Trieste for the last time.

Most of his exile had been spent in Trieste, however, and Joyce did not wish to lose his ties to the old city. Initially he kept in touch with Stanislaus, Francini, and Benco and finally sent one hundred lire to pay Silvestri for his earlier sketch of Joyce.[8] The Joyce family continued to speak Italian among themselves at home, often using the Triestine dialect. Nora employed what journalist Nino Frank called "the lisping speech of those who dwelt in the shadow of San Giusto."[9] Following her visit with Joyce in Paris, Delia Benco reported that Joyce still spoke of many old Triestine students and recalled with fondness the streets and cafes of Città Vecchia.[10]

He did not forget his struggles in Trieste, though. Reflecting on his eight months in the city after the war, he told Budgen, "Trieste was a very bad mark," but conceded, "I did two big chapters [of *Ulysses*] in it all the same."[11] Aware of the ongoing political and social tumult between the fascists and socialists in Trieste, Joyce cynically cautioned Stanislaus, "I see Trieste is in riot. Keep out of the way of both their lousy projectiles."[12] Raising his ire was the minimal response to his correspondence. He wrote to Pound on December 12, "I have no news from Trieste. . . . They are a very friendly lot, I must say."[13]

Joyce nonetheless did stay on good terms with Italo Svevo. Despite Joyce's early praise of his work, Svevo had not gained any recognition: he was still seen locally as a successful businessman who dabbled in writing. From Paris, Joyce first contacted Svevo by letter on January 5, 1921, with a request of no small significance. He asked Svevo to pick up his *Ulysses* notes from the Trieste apartment and bring them to Paris.[14] In March, Svevo delivered the valuable package.

In a Herculean effort, often writing for seventeen hours a day, Joyce finally completed the manuscript, estimating that it took nearly twenty thousand hours to finish.[15] But the issue of who would publish such a book was unresolved. Again, a woman rescued Joyce. Sylvia Beach agreed to help, and *Ulysses* was first published in its entirety by Shakespeare and Company in Paris on February 2, 1922, Joyce's fortieth birthday.[16] As his notoriety grew, he commented to Francini, "Is it possible that I am worth something? Who would have said so after my last experience in Trieste?"[17]

In fact, his star in Trieste had not yet risen. When Joyce's Parisian friends compiled an advance list of buyers for the limited edition of the controversial novel, Baron Ralli was the only Triestine to respond. Joyce wrote caustically to Francini, "When you find a Triestine . . . who will pay 300 lire for a book of Zois light a candle to Saint Anthony the Worker of Miracles."[18] As a member of the press, Francini himself had asked Joyce for a complimentary copy of the work. It was a problem Joyce knew well. In a conversation between Robert Hand and Richard Rowan in *Exiles*, Joyce wrote:

> Robert: He [the vice chancellor] has read your
>   book.
> Richard: Did he buy it or borrow it?[19]

Stanislaus could not even interest Benco, the city's leading literary critic, in reading the book. To prod Benco, Joyce asked Miss Weaver to send the Triestine a copy of a favorable English review "marked with red pencil."[20] Ultimately Benco, who had written the first Italian review of *A Portrait* in 1918,[21] responded. In the April 1, 1922, issue of *La Nazione*, Benco, first again with an Italian review, praised *Ulysses*.[22] He later remarked about Joyce, "he himself, perhaps, imagined that I had not seen the genius in him. In that case, he was wrong."[23]

Svevo did not get a copy of *Ulysses* until 1924.[24] He eagerly informed Joyce, "I shall read it chapter by chapter. . . . I have your brother's promise that after I have worked over each chapter thoroughly he will give me his assistance. I think that next to you I could not have a better guide."[25] Stanislaus as a teacher may have warranted Svevo's praise, but as a critic he did not try to hide his initial disgust with *Ulysses*. He told his brother, "Everything dirty seems to have the same irresistable attraction for you that cow-dung has for flies."[26] But Joyce was undeterred. Ellmann observed that "his confidence persisted as he grew older, and his putative kingdom continued to include the posterity for whom he thought his books would be required texts."[27]

In quite a different context, Joyce was the recipient of some rather unflattering publicity in Trieste. Apparently in need of money, Francini presented a speech on Joyce, entitled "Joyce intimo spogliato in piazza" ("Joyce Stripped Naked in the Piazza"), in February 1922. Stanislaus attended and found it to be a "vulgar and silly" caricature of his brother. He reported to Joyce that the hall was only half-full, and the general response was not positive.[28]

The speech represented the first in a series of curious turns in the relationship between Francini and Joyce after 1920. In Herbert Gorman's biography, edited heavily by Joyce, Joyce included a footnote[29] that implies his disapproval of Francini's portrayal.[30] Yet, on July 23, 1924, more than two years after the speech, Joyce sent a note of greetings to Francini and his family.[31] Fifteen years later, he asked Jacques Mercanton to visit Francini during a trip to Florence, where the Tuscan was teaching. After receiving a warm welcome, Mercanton heard of Francini's disillusionment with Joyce's writing, particularly regarding its criticism of the Catholic Church. Francini's faith had remained strong (he wrote two books on theology), and he did not try to hide his disappointment in Joyce: he told Mercanton, "I used to hope . . . that as a result of experience, of having a family, of misfortune, he would become reconciled with the Church. That is not what has happened." Reluctantly, he gave Mercanton a copy of "Stripped Naked," which was delivered to Joyce.[32]

De Tuoni, who had exchanged letters with Francini since the end of World War I, also found him to be unimpressed with Joyce's writings and rather bitter about both the work and the criticism from Stanislaus.[33] Still, as late as March 1940, Joyce indicated his intention to continue corresponding with Francini.[34]

Stanislaus, on the other hand, grew only more resentful of Francini. In a lengthy letter to Joyce on August 7, 1924, he recalled with great clarity the evening's details and scorned Francini, concluding, "I am now thoroughly sick of this bloody fool."[35] Stanislaus also continued to unleash his temper on Joyce. Tired of being Joyce's creditor while playing the role of a dutiful, younger brother, Stanislaus vented his anger in a letter. "I am no longer a boy," he pointedly reminded Joyce.[36] A month later, Joyce responded that he was sorry for Stanislaus's financial plight and would send money but stressed that he too had little to spare.[37] It was an aspect of their lives that had barely changed since Trieste.

Regardless, their correspondence, while somewhat irregular, continued. In a long August 1924 letter, Stanislaus thanked Joyce for sending "the Transatlantic Review, the French translation of your novel, Gorman's study of you and many papers."[38]

Stanislaus's initial reaction to *Finnegans Wake* was total disdain, as he stated, "I for one would not read more than a paragraph of it, if I did not know you." He acknowledged that the work imposed a barrier between them: "My only excuse for saying what I think is that it is what I think, and it is so little pleasure to me to say that this is perhaps the chief reason why I cannot bring myself to write to you." Still, unlike others, he took the novel seriously enough to read it. More positively, Stanislaus displayed a change of heart toward *Ulysses*, the "greater part" of which he now liked. "Dublin lies stretched out before the reader, the minute living incidents start out of the pages. Anybody who reads can hear the people talk and feel himself among them," he commented. His major complaint was that "there is no serenity or happiness anywhere in the whole book." He closed by indicating his intention to accept Joyce's offer to visit Paris when possible.[39]

The trip did not materialize in 1924, but Stanislaus's engagement the following year to a student, Nelly Lichtensteiger, afforded Joyce a chance to extend another invitation, which he did with enthusiasm:

I was very glad to hear the news of your engagement. . . . At least I have a house now and it ought to be easier for you to pay us a visit. Can you come this autumn, for example? I will send you the fare and you could pass a pleasant time here. I have to undergo another eye operation this month, but I will time it according to your answer. Let me have a line by return, if you can.[40]

In early 1926, Stanislaus finally confirmed that he would journey to Paris in April, ending a separation of nearly six years. "We are glad to hear you are coming and will all be very glad to see you again," Joyce responded.[41]

His connection with Svevo also remained strong. Svevo sent Joyce his new book, *La coscienza di Zeno* (The Confessions of Zeno), as a Christmas gift in 1923. Joyce expressed his pleasure in reading the novel and proclaimed it to be "by far" Svevo's best work. Using the opportunity to aid his old friend, Joyce advised him to send copies to Valery Larbaud, Benjamin Crémieux, T. S. Eliot, Ford Madox Ford, and Gilbert Seldes, all of whom Joyce volunteered to contact.[42]

Upon seeing the work, Larbaud concurred with Joyce and agreed to write a review, but months of inaction passed. Reacting to a final plea from Svevo ("After taking this step with M. Larbaud, let's both let it go"),[43] who had heard nothing also from the Italian critics to whom he had submitted copies,[44] Joyce reminded Larbaud in June of his earlier assurance. In January 1925, Larbaud finally responded with a note to Svevo, addressing him as "Esteemed Sir and Master" and outlining his effort to promote *La coscienza*. Svevo felt forty years of literary frustration lifted, and he immediately replied to Larbaud with a promise to forward copies of *Una vita* and *Senilità*.[45] (Larbaud actually had been in Trieste in 1899, just after the original publication of *Senilità*, but had heard nothing of the work.)[46] Crémieux, who had a keen interest in Italian literature, was similarly impressed.[47]

Although in his sixties, Svevo displayed the excitement of a child as attention came his way.[48] He stopped in Paris in May on his way to London with Livia and met his French supporters. At a dinner arranged by Joyce, Svevo charmed everyone with his friendly manner. The following night he was invited to the aristocratic literary salon of Princess Bassiano Caetani in her Villa Romana at Versailles, where he again conversed with Larbaud and Crémieux.[49] In Paris—the artistic capital of the 1920s—Svevo had found acceptance as a writer. Indeed, his photo hung in what was recognized as one of the literary shrines of the period, Sylvia Beach's bookshop, Shakespeare and Company.[50]

Word of the discovery of Svevo spread. The name Svevo entered serious literary discussions in both Italy and France. In December 1925 the Milan literary magazine *L'Esame* published a ten-page article on Svevo by Eugenio Montale. In

February 1926, the Parisian journal *Le Navire d'argent* published a Svevo issue that included a four-page article by Crémieux, and Larbaud later wrote a complimentary piece on Svevo.[51]

Not all Italian readers and critics, though, joined in the chorus of praise for Svevo: some Triestines commented that Svevo's work was popular abroad only because it improved in translation,[52] and Italian critics in general were not impressed by the French "discovery" of, in their view, so minor a talent.[53] Sales of his books, while improved, were undeniably sluggish.[54] "You are an author who doesn't go," a bookstore employee told Svevo.[55] After Svevo's death in 1928, a reviewer in the *New York Times* resurrected the old criticism of his work: "The absence of such elements as imagination, passion, and elegance of style makes him boresome and hostile to the tastes of the Italian reader."[56]

Joyce and Svevo subsequently maintained sporadic but amiable contact. Due to his serious eye ailments, Joyce declined an invitation in late 1925 to see Svevo in London but indicated that Lucia hoped to visit Trieste the next year.[57] In February 1926, Svevo sent Joyce his impressions of a performance of *Exiles* that he had viewed in London,[58] and in September he forwarded an article by Montale on *Dubliners*.[59] Svevo gave a speech on *Ulysses* in Milan in 1927. Shortly thereafter, seeing Joyce in Paris, he was surprised to find him barely interested in *Ulysses* and completely devoted to his new novel.[60]

Both writers took great pleasure in Svevo's acclaim. They met only infrequently, but Joyce greatly enjoyed Svevo's company. Nino Frank recalled a dinner conversation in Paris that had a distinctly Triestine flavor:

From the start we spoke Italian, and in Joyce's and Svevo's mouths the language quickly turned into the Trieste dialect, which I understood. But Crémieux, accustomed to the pedantic Tuscan idiom and slowed besides by his way of speaking, was a little lost. Although a descendant of the papal Jews of Avignon, he was the foreigner, doubly so, since the conversation came around to Apulia, where I was born, and Svevo and Joyce teased me, following the custom that those from the upper Adriatic have of baiting those from the lower: we three formed an exclusive country of our own. I am afraid our loud voices and laughter in the narrow room of this gathering-place for gastronomes caused something of a scandal. Actually, we no longer felt that we were in Paris but instead were by the "infinitely briny" sea sung by d'Annunzio, and the Irishman was not the least fervent of the three of us. Poor Crémieux tried to follow us, and, in an attempt to join in our harmony, he ordered sea urchins, which he swallowed enthusiastically before our somewhat disgusted eyes, for this echinoderm is disdained along the Adriatic.[61]

Svevo basked in his literary glory. Due largely to the efforts of Joyce, Larbaud, and Crémieux, the P.E.N. Club in Paris honored him with a dinner on March 15, 1928.[62] To encourage an English translation of Svevo's work, Joyce sent letters to publishers Jonathan Cape and B. W. Huebsch. Svevo in turn offered him the portrait of Livia done by Svevo's old friend, Umberto Veruda.[63] Joyce, in his final communication with Svevo, replied, "I will gladly accept your gift and may the portrait of Anna Livia bring me both memories and luck,"[64] and he displayed it in his apartment.[65]

Back in Trieste, though, tragedy struck the Joyce family. Svevo earlier had asked Joyce if he would be at Stanislaus's wedding, planned for October 1926. But the suicide of Eileen's husband dramatically altered family affairs. To Miss Weaver, Joyce bluntly described the events: "My brother-in-law in Trieste blew his brains out while my sister was on her way from Ireland to Trieste. He was dead when she was here and neither she nor my wife . . . knew about it, only my children who are too young to understand. I had a dreadful time playing up to them and was almost in the 'jimjams' for about a month after."[66] Stanislaus, obliged to assist Eileen and her two children (as Joyce did), postponed the wedding.[67]

Subsequently, an overly optimistic Joyce sent a gift of six thousand lire to Stanislaus in November 1926 with the hope that "your marriage will soon come off and that it will be a very happy one."[68] Stanislaus did not marry, though, until August 1928. Eileen's situation remained difficult. A discouraged Joyce wrote to Stanislaus, "Do not tell me for the moment any more details, but propose to me some temporary plan and say what you suggest I do, say, till March."[69] Stanislaus apparently advised sending money, for Joyce responded in January 1927, "Yes, allright. I will arrange for L10 a quarter to be sent to Eileen in Dublin from the time she arrives. . . . I hope things are better now."[70] A year later, Eileen and her children left Trieste to settle in Ireland.[71]

Svevo died on September 13, 1928, following an auto accident the previous day. Joyce sent his condolences to Livia in a heartfelt September 24 letter, offering to help "at any time."[72] The Florence journal *Solaria* memorialized Svevo in its March-April issue, which included a brief but respectful note from Joyce, who stated, "I retain the memory of a lovable person, and an admiration of long standing that matures, rather than weakens, with the years."[73]

In 1930, a somewhat surprising disagreement arose between Joyce and Livia Svevo, with Stanislaus uncomfortably stuck in the middle. Remembering Joyce's earlier pledge to help if possible, Livia asked him to write a preface to *Senilità*, which was about to appear in English. But Joyce, in a polite letter, declined the request; he had a policy of never writing prefaces for any work, even his own. In lieu of himself, he provided Livia with the name of Ford Madox Ford, who was living in Paris and had consented to do the preface. Joyce also suggested replacing the title's English translation, *Senility*, with *As a Man Grows Older*, which, in the end, was adopted.[74] The publisher did not accept Ford as a substitute, and Livia appealed in two letters to Larbaud for his help in persuading Joyce to cooperate. Larbaud raised the point with Joyce to no avail.[75]

While circumspect in his correspondence with Livia, Joyce, feeling unappreciated, was far less sensitive in his comments to Stanislaus on the Svevo matter. Again, his animosity toward Trieste surfaced. In April 1931, he wrote sarcastically—but truthfully—"I hope the ceremony of the 26 [the April 26, 1931, ceremony in Trieste honoring Svevo] will be a crowning affair for whenever I mentioned S's name to any of my semi-literate pupils they laughed in my face."[76] On May 12, 1931, he wrote, "If Mrs. S. told you I promised to write a preface for any book of I. S. she lies."[77]

Despite a compromise that resulted in Stanislaus writing the preface, Joyce did not let up on the Svevos. He stated in a March 1932 letter to Stanislaus that Svevo was cheap (even though in Trieste Svevo often had loaned money to him), their relationship had existed only on a formal basis, and Livia had been "longsighted" when Nora was near.[78] Already stung by the perception that he was snubbing Svevo, Joyce was insulted further by the account in *Il Piccolo* on the April 26 ceremony for Svevo. The newspaper made no mention of the telegram regarding Svevo that Joyce had sent to Livia for the occasion. The message read, "With you today on which Trieste honors memory Italo Svevo its illustrious son my old friend. James Joyce."[79] Joyce pointedly suggested that any preface to Svevo's book should note this oversight.[80]

Joyce's dispute with the Svevos surely affected Gorman's biography, the first written on Joyce. Svevo's name is barely seen in the 350-page book, written after the conflict with Livia and containing Joyce's own corrections. At the time of Gorman's work, Stanislaus was assisting Gorman and devoting "practically all" of his spare time to preparing Joyce's letters for Gorman's use in the book.[81] Joyce wrote sympathetically to his brother, "I am sorry you have to toil amid that damn dreary correspondence and hope you are soon 'through' with it."[82] Stanislaus was well acquainted with the Svevos and later wrote an article on the Joyce-Svevo relationship. It is highly unlikely that he would have overlooked Svevo in recounting Joyce's years in Trieste, so the omission can be seen only as the intention of Joyce.

The reasons for Joyce's animosity toward the Svevos are unclear, but several possibilities exist. Livia was, most likely, on a formal basis with Nora. There is no record of any correspondence between them even though they knew each other for more than forty years. Joyce easily may have bristled at Livia's attitude toward Nora. Still, prior to their disagreement, Joyce had always referred respectfully to Livia. He went so far as to borrow her name and her flowing hair in creating the character of Anna Livia Plurabelle in *Finnegans Wake*. In their memoirs, both Livia and Letizia praised Joyce.

His stance toward Svevo is equally difficult to explain. Clearly, Svevo was immensely fond of Joyce, who was pleased by Svevo's belated success. It is possible that Joyce, an international figure, felt that he had created Svevo: without Joyce's help, Svevo would have been just another neglected writer. The posthumous acclaim heaped on Svevo, with little acknowledgement of Joyce's pivotal role, could have triggered Joyce's anger. His change of heart, in any case, was dramatic.

Joyce, however, had known Livia for half of his life, and he did not allow the grudge to become permanent. He sent her Christmas greetings in 1931, 1935, 1936,[83] and 1938 (the last announcing the completion of *Finnegans Wake*),[84] and wished her "peace and happiness" for the Easter holidays in April 1939.[85] Joyce's final letter to Livia, sent in May 1939, states his respect for Svevo, and shows the toll of a life spent trying to survive as a writer. After noting that *Finnegans Wake* would be published shortly, Joyce pondered, "It is I who am perhaps an ass . . . to have devoted eighteen years of my life to completing that monster of a book. But what is one to do? One is born that way. Yet, by God, I have had enough. And that's that!"[86] The novel's infamous reference to Trieste—"And trieste, ah trieste ate I my liver!"—recalls Joyce's years as a struggling young artist in the Austrian city.[87]

As was the tragic case with many European families, World War II devastated the Svevos. All three of Letizia's sons died in the fighting, two of them in the Soviet Union. Letizia and Livia, classified as Jews, left Trieste for greater safety in the village of Arcade. In February 1945, Allied bombing destroyed the Villa Veneziani.[88] They returned to Trieste after the war; Livia died there in 1957, and Letizia in 1993. A bust of Joyce, designed by Triestine sculptor Marcello Mascherini for the 1982 centennial celebration of Joyce's birth, now stands alongside one of Svevo in Trieste's public garden.

In his final years, Joyce renewed ties with other Triestine friends. He invited Benco to Paris in 1937.[89] Three years later, Joyce spotted a newspaper article on Larbaud written by his old companion, Dario de Tuoni. In February 1940, Joyce sent a cordial greeting to the Triestine writer, with whom he had not been in contact since World War I. Writing with obvious fondness of the former days in Trieste, Joyce indicated that he had recently heard from Francini and also inquired about Silvestri, noting that he kept four or five of his paintings in his apartment.[90] After a lengthy delay, de Tuoni received the letter and responded swiftly, but it is not known whether his reply ever reached Joyce in wartime France.[91]

With Stanislaus, Joyce maintained a sincere relationship in the last decade of his life, largely through the mail. Serious difficulties arose for both brothers in the mid-1930s. Joyce was most troubled by the severe emotional problems of Lucia and his daughter-in-law, Helen, while Stanislaus, an antifascist, received an expulsion order from the Italian authorities in April 1936 "without notice, without warning, without explanation." He wrote to Joyce on April 12,

I cannot understand it. At my lessons at the university and elsewhere I am very careful not to say anything that might be interpreted as a political allusion. I go nowhere, to no cafe, bar, or restaurant. I live a more retired life than you did here before the war. I see only my private pupils, who all come here. . . . I have a rather nicely furnished flat—the result of thirty years of incessant work—and, though still in debt owing to the ruin of Schaurek's end, have lived fairly comfortably, sometimes even taking a holiday. Now I feel my feet cut from under me. I am doing what I can to have the order recinded. I shall be very anxious to hear from you.[92]

Nearly two weeks later he reported to Joyce on his attempts to stay in Trieste, but admitted that a reunion with Joyce might be the only alternative: "If I fail I shall have no choice but to come to Paris."[93] Joyce evidently did not discourage such a possibility.

On May 11, Stanislaus informed him that the order had been suspended for an indefinite time, a concession quite unsatisfactory to Stanislaus. Having already lost both his position at the university and his evening classes, he again wrote to Joyce about the possibility of moving to Paris.[94]

The brothers met for the last time in Zurich in the summer of 1936.[95] Joyce repeatedly asked Carola Giedion-Welcker, who lived in Switzerland, to assist Stanislaus in relocating. Although Stanislaus earlier had pledged to do his "utmost" to remain in Trieste, he admitted in November, "I must get out of Trieste. . . . It is clear to me that I shall not be able to hold out here during the coming summer and autumn." He explained why: "A great many pupils who would be willing to study privately with me are afraid to compromise themselves. This is not, as you will probably think, a hotheaded supposition of mine. Things English (and in this category they include things Joyce) are still taboo. Things Joyce doubly so."[96]

Stanislaus's problems as a "Joyce" in Trieste may have resulted partially from a mistake contained in some fascist propaganda. Mussolini resented the growing influence of the United States and in 1929 allowed a campaign against Americanism, characterized as a "grease stain which is spreading through the whole of European life." American writers in particular were singled out for criticism, and Joyce's name was cited as an example.[97]

In addition, some of Stanislaus's students in Trieste undoubtedly were supporters of fascism, and they may have been reacting to his earlier criticism of the Italian government. It is not clear, though, exactly what caused the animosity Stanislaus encountered. Joyce simply professed his ignorance. "I . . . don't understand the allusions in his letter to 'anti-Joyce.' But if it is so, it is so," he wrote to Giedion-Welcker.[98]

Joyce was not optimistic regarding Stanislaus, telling Giedion-Welcker, "The horizon looks to me so dark that I would be very glad to hear that my brother has definitely settled in Switzerland."[99] Ultimately, the Italian government did permit Stanislaus to remain in Trieste, where he stayed until the war.

Notably, Joyce's last piece of correspondence, written on January 4, 1941, nine days prior to his death, was a postcard in Italian to Stanislaus offering the names of four individuals (including Francini) who might be able to help Stanislaus if his predicament worsened during the war years in Trieste.[100] After Joyce died, Stanislaus wrote several remembrances of his brother. His own death came on Bloomsday, June 16, 1955, in Trieste, four years after Nora had passed away in Zurich.

Conclusion

Joyce's feelings toward Trieste varied widely during and after his years there, but his stay in the Adriatic city benefitted him in a number of ways. Most importantly, of course, he wrote prodigiously, developing his literary genius to the point of transforming modern literature. In Trieste, he completed *Dubliners*; wrote twelve chapters of *Stephen Hero*, which he later finished as *A Portrait of the Artist as a Young Man*, as well as *Exiles*, nine articles for *Il Piccolo della Sera*, seven poems, *Giacomo Joyce*, and scores of letters; and made great progress on *Ulysses*.

The multilingual dimension of the city, particularly the numerous foreign phrases and slang expressions that peppered the Italian dialect of Triestines, fascinated him. Philippe Soupault wrote of the "passionate attention" with which Joyce listened to the Triestine dialect,[1] and he eventually spoke it with ease.[2] Joyce borrowed Triestine words and names liberally when writing *Ulysses* and *Finnegans Wake*. His children, both born in Trieste, received Italian names, and Italian remained the family language for the Joyces after they left Trieste.

Friends also served Joyce well in Trieste. While none were as close as Frank Budgen in Zurich (Stanislaus, in fact, was Joyce's most trusted confidant during much of the Trieste period), friends such as Francini and Silvestri, as well as the working-class patrons he met in the Città Vecchia pubs, provided lively companionship for Joyce. Others, including Svevo, Benco, Count Sordina, and Baron Ralli, were more formal with Joyce but no less sincere.

The city was well suited to accommodate Joyce's lifestyle. His main pleasures were reading and writing, enjoying his family, attending the theater, and dining and drinking with friends, and Trieste provided more than adequately for those few. His numerous apartments, ranging from lower middle to middle class, were comfortable enough and, more importantly to an urban type like Joyce, were within easy walking distance of downtown Trieste.

In later years, he expressed a fondness for Italian life that was not readily apparent while he lived among Trieste's largely Italian population. Mercanton recalled that Joyce "loved Italian ways, their style of living, their language, the opera."[3] In 1947 Francini wrote of Joyce's "obvious, luminous, and conscious love" of Italy.[4] Joyce's interest in Dante, D'Annunzio, Vico, and Aquinas, among other Italians, supports Francini's point.

But of his years in Trieste, what did Joyce think? The older Joyce reflected sentimentally on both Austria, the city's ruler, and Italy, its cultural ideal. Certainly the number of ethnic groups represented in Trieste—and the city's tolerance of them—permitted Joyce to assimilate and to feel accepted as a "Triestine" more easily than might have been the case in other, less cosmopolitan, cities. Trieste's diversity, which Joyce could hardly have imagined in Dublin, also found expression in his work: Molly, for example, recalls from her Gibraltar days "the Spanish girls laughing in their shawls and their tall combs and the auctions in the morning the Greeks and the jews and the Arabs and the devil knows who else from all the ends of Europe."[5] Joyce's description, with the possible exception of the Spanish girls, would have seemed none too strange to Triestines of Joyce's time—they lived daily among such people.

He could not forget, however, the obstacles that for years blocked his work from publication and, in part, reduced him so often to scrounging for income in Trieste. Following a difficult eye operation in 1924, Joyce, in a letter to Miss Weaver, placed responsibility for his weakened condition squarely on the stress of that period: "The long drudgery and disappointment in Trieste (I scarcely ate anything, taught until late every night and bought one suit of clothes in nine years . . .) and then the labour of *Ulysses* must have undermined my strength. I was poisoned in more ways than one."[6] Padraic Colum evidently heard similar words: "I know by the way he speaks about those days [in Trieste] that the temptation to turn to another career must have been a bitter one," he recalled.[7] Lack of money, family problems, housing emergencies, employment difficulties, publishing frustrations, drinking—all contributed to his daily struggles in Trieste. His accomplishments there were significant, but he could not fully appreciate his Triestine years until they were well behind him.

Even though Joyce became somewhat involved in Trieste affairs through his writing and teaching, he never allowed the city to influence him as Dublin did. In Trieste, for example, Joyce attended performances at Teatro Verdi, lectured at the Università Popolare, wrote for *Il Piccolo della Sera*, taught at the Scuola Revoltella, passed many hours at the Villa Veneziani—each place strongly associated with irredentism—and remained largely untouched by the movement. He lived in Trieste for years before any of his writing focused on the city, and even then, only in a minor way.

Yet, Joyce must have had a strong sense that Trieste, for him, was unique. It is noteworthy that although he did leave Trieste frequently between 1904 and 1920, in every instance, up to his move to Paris, he returned. It was *his* decision to be there. Why? What Joyce needed most was a place—away from Ireland—in which he could write. Pound commented to Joyce after he completed *A Portrait* in Trieste that he probably could not have done so in the "lap of luxury" or in the chaos of a large city.[8] Curran agreed: "As always, he went where he could live and write with least disturbance," he wrote.[9] Joyce understood that Trieste was valuable as the place from which he could clearly view Dublin, the focus of his life's work. Svevo, in his Milan speech on Joyce, observed, "A piece of Ireland was ripening under our sun."[10]

Joyce exaggerated somewhat when he told Claud Sykes in Zurich that as long as he could write, he could live anywhere.[11] His actions show that Trieste was most preferable for him. It did not antagonize him as Pola and Rome—and Dublin—had. Its ambience generally was compatible with Joyce's character, as evidenced by his accomplishments and by the length of time he stayed there. It is difficult to imagine him writing as well or remaining for so long in any of these other three cities.

In summary, Joyce chose exile largely to assert his independence from Ireland and to establish himself as a writer. He was able to meet those goals in Trieste: it was there that his artistic genius reached its mature expression. Soupault wrote, "The Trieste period . . . is without doubt the most important of all his life. He completed *A Portrait*, but it was also at this time that he became aware of the grandeur and importance of his life's work; it was at this period that he detached himself definitively from our world in order to conceive the Joycean universe."[12] Looking back, Joyce would have appreciated Saba's words about his native city:

> My city that is alive in every part,
> has a little corner that is made for me, for my life.[13]

Notes

I have used certain abbreviations in the notes. *Letters of James Joyce*, volumes 1, 2, and 3, are cited as *I*, *II*, and *III*, respectively, and *Selected Letters* as *SL*. Stanislaus Joyce's book *My Brother's Keeper* is *MBK*, and *The Complete Dublin Diary of Stanislaus Joyce* is *CDD*. The *James Joyce Quarterly* is *JJQ*.

Some individual writers and recipients of letters are cited by initials: JJ for James Joyce, NB for Nora Barnacle, SJ for Stanislaus Joyce, GR for Grant Richards, EP for Ezra Pound, HSW for Harriet Shaw Weaver, and FB for Frank Budgen.

The Richard Ellmann Collection is located in the Department of Special Collections at the McFarland Library, University of Tulsa. Joyce's Cornell letters are located in the Rare Book and Manuscript Collections at the Carl A. Kroch Library, Cornell University.

The annual Trieste address directories, referred to in the notes as *Guida generale di Trieste*, are located in the Biblioteca Civica in Trieste.

1. ROMAN ROOTS

1. The historical information on pp. 1–2 came from the following sources: Laura Ruaro Loseri, *Guida di Trieste* (Trieste: Edizioni Lint, 1985); Attilio Tamaro, *Storia di Trieste*, 2 vols. (Trieste: Edizioni Lint, 1976).

2. Mario Stock, *Trieste's Trade with America: The Beginnings* (Trieste: Edizioni Fachin, 1985), 71.

3. Loseri, *Guida di Trieste*, 66.

4. Bogdan C. Novak, *Trieste, 1941–1954* (Chicago: University of Chicago Press, 1970), 14.

5. Silvio Benco, *Trieste e il suo diritto all'Italia* (Trieste: Cappelli, 1952), 83.

6. John Gatt-Rutter, *Italo Svevo: A Double Life* (New York: Oxford University Press, 1988), 14.

7. Ibid., 36.

8. The information in the following paragraphs about Mayer and *Il Piccolo* is from Silvio Benco, Il Piccolo *di Trieste* (Rome: Edizioni Fratelli Treves, 1931), 7, 10, 14, 13.

9. Gatt-Rutter, *Italo Svevo*, 55.

10. Christopher Seton-Watson, *Italy from Liberalism to Fascism* (London: Methuen & Co., 1967), 354.

11. Vladimir Dedijer, *The Road to Sarajevo* (New York: Simon and Schuster, 1966), 171.

12. Benco, *Il Piccolo*, 28.

13. Ibid., 38.

14. Ibid., 58.

15. Benco, *Trieste*, 91.

16. George R. Marek, *The Eagles Die* (New York: Harper and Row, 1974), 375.

17. Novak, *Trieste*, 20.

18. Leo Valiani, *The End of Austria-Hungary* (New York: Alfred A. Knopf, 1972), 304.

19. Ibid., 305.

20. Shepard B. Clough and Salvatore Saladino, *A History of Modern Italy* (New York: Columbia University Press, 1968), 288.

21. Ibid.

22. Ivo Vidan, "Joyce and the South Slavs," in *Atti del Third International James Joyce Symposium*, ed. Niny Rocco-Bergera (Trieste: Università degli Studi, Facoltà di Magistero, 1974), 120.

23. Denis Mack Smith, *Italy* (Ann Arbor: University of Michigan Press, 1969), 289; Seton-Watson, *Italy*, 355.

24. Seton-Watson, *Italy*, 356.

25. Ernest Hemingway, *A Farewell to Arms* (New York: Charles Scribner's Sons, 1957), 7.

26. Novak, *Trieste*, 8.

27. Vidan, "Joyce and the South Slavs," 120.

28. Vladimir Dedijer et al., *History of Yugoslavia* (New York: McGraw-Hill Book Co., 1974), 439.

29. Benco, *Trieste*, 92.

30. Tamaro, *Storia*, vol. 2, 459.

31. Giani Stuparich, *Sequenze per Trieste* (Trieste: Edizioni Dello Zibaldone, 1968), 117.

32. Benco, *Trieste*, 93.

33. Scipio Slataper, *Scritti politici* (Rome: Alberto Stock, 1925), 18.

34. Gatt-Rutter, *Italo Svevo*, 184.

2. THE DUBLINER

1. Giorgio Valussi, *Le Regioni d'Italia: Friuli—Venezia Giulia*, vol. 5 (Turin: Tipografia Sociale Torinese, 1961), 436.

2. Cyril Pearl, *Dublin in Bloomtime* (New York: Viking Press, 1969), 42.

3. Ibid., 44.

4. Frank Tuohy, *Yeats* (New York: Macmillan Publishing Co., 1976), 133.

5. JJ to NB, September 16, 1904, *II*, 53.

6. JJ to SJ, November 13, 1906, *II*, 189.

7. Chester G. Anderson, *James Joyce* (London: Thames & Hudson, 1967), 10.

8. Stanislaus Joyce, *My Brother's Keeper* (New York: Viking Press, 1958), 35.

9. Bozena Berta Delimata, "Reminiscences of a Joyce Niece," *JJQ* (Fall 1981): 53.

10. Stanislaus Joyce, *MBK*, 50, 51.

11. Ibid., 133, 134.

12. Ibid., 234.

13. J. F. Byrne, *Silent Years* (New York: Farrar, Straus, and Young, 1953), 86.

14. Oliver St. John Gogarty, "The Joyce I Knew," *Saturday Review of Literature,* January 25, 1941, 4.

15. Alice Curtayne, "Pappy Never Spoke of Jim's Books," interview with Eileen Joyce Schaurek in *James Joyce: Interviews and Recollections,* ed. E. H. Mikhail (New York: St. Martin's Press, 1990), 61.

16. "Sister," interview with May Joyce Monaghan in Mikhail, *James Joyce,* 183.

17. Padraic O'Laoi, *Nora Barnacle Joyce: A Portrait* (Galway: Kennys Bookshops and Art Galleries, 1982), 8.

18. Ibid., 3.

19. JJ to SJ, January 22, 1911, *II,* 289.

20. Marvin Magalaner and Richard M. Kain, *Joyce: The Man, the Work, the Reputation* (Oxford: Plantin, 1990), 52.

21. Arthur Power, "James Joyce—The Internationalist," in *A Bash in the Tunnel,* ed. John Ryan (Brighton: Clifton Books, 1970), 181.

22. JJ to NB, August 29, 1904, *II,* 48.

23. Eugene Jolas, "My Friend James Joyce," in *James Joyce: Two Decades of Criticism,* ed. Seon Givens (New York: Vanguard Press, 1963), 12.

24. Brenda Maddox, *Nora: The Real Life of Molly Bloom* (Boston: Houghton Mifflin Company, 1988), 344.

25. Frank Budgen, "James Joyce," in Givens, *James Joyce,* 21.

26. Richard Ellmann, "Joyce and Yeats," *Kenyon Review* (Autumn 1950): 624.

27. Ibid., 625, 626, 627.

28. Budgen, "James Joyce," 25.

29. Stanislaus Joyce, *MBK,* 179.

30. JJ to William Butler Yeats, July 17, 1915, *I,* 83.

31. Jolas, "My Friend," 14.

32. Ellmann, "Joyce and Yeats," 636.

33. James Joyce, *The Critical Writings of James Joyce,* ed. Ellsworth Mason and Richard Ellmann (Ithaca: Cornell University Press, 1989), 102.

34. James Joyce, *Ulysses* (New York: Random House, 1961), 216.

35. Lady Augusta Gregory, *Seventy Years: 1852–1922* (New York: Macmillan Publishing Co., 1974), 507.

36. Leon Edel, *Stuff of Sleep and Dreams* (New York: Harper and Row, 1982), 90.

37. JJ to SJ, [May 2 or 3, 1905], *II,* 89.

38. JJ to NB, September 10, 1904, *II,* 51.

39. James Joyce, *A Portrait of the Artist as a Young Man,* ed. Chester G. Anderson (New York: Penguin Books, 1982), 203.

40. Ibid.

41. Byrne, *Silent Years,* 145.

42. Ibid., 144.

43. JJ to NB, September 29, 1904, *II,* 57.

44. Mary Colum and Padraic Colum, *Our Friend James Joyce* (Garden City, N.J.: Doubleday & Company, 1958), 72.

45. Richard Ellmann, "James Joyce, Irish European," *Umana* (May/September 1971): 13.

46. Jacques Mercanton, "The Hours of James Joyce," in *Portraits of the Artist in Exile,* ed. Willard Potts (New York: Harcourt Brace Jovanovich, 1986), 220.

47. JJ to NB, September 16, 1904, *II,* 53.

48. Stanislaus Joyce, *MBK,* 153.

49. Ibid.

50. JJ to NB, September 19, 1904, *II*, 55.

51. JJ to NB, August 21, 1909, *II*, 237.

52. Constantine Curran, memorial to Joyce, *Irish Times*, January 14, 1941, in Ryan, *Bash*, 243.

3. EXILE

1. Richard Ellmann, *James Joyce* (New York: Oxford University Press, 1982), 179.

2. Padraic O'Laoi, *Nora Barnacle Joyce: A Portrait* (Galway: Kennys Bookshops and Art Galleries, 1982), 57.

3. JJ to Joyce family, December 6, 1902, *II*, 19.

4. Arthur Symons to JJ, May 4 [1904], *II*, 42.

5. JJ to SJ, October 11, 1904, *II*, 66.

6. Ibid.

7. Ellmann, *James Joyce*, 184.

8. Herbert Gorman, *James Joyce* (New York: Farrar & Rinehart, 1939), 131.

9. Stelio Crise, *Epiphanies and Phadographs: Joyce e Trieste* (Milan: All'Insegna del Pesce d'Oro, 1967), 194.

10. Ibid., 35.

11. Ibid., 40.

12. Richard Ellmann, *Four Dubliners* (New York: George Braziller, 1987), 78.

13. Gianni Pinguentini, *James Joyce in Italia* (Verona: Linotipia Veronese di Ghidini e Fiorini, 1963), 25.

14. Brenda Maddox, *Nora: The Real Life of Molly Bloom* (Boston: Houghton Mifflin Company, 1988), 51.

15. James Joyce, *Giacomo Joyce* (London: Faber & Faber, 1984), 8.

16. NB to JJ, [about August 4, 1917], *II*, 401.

17. Pinguentini, *James Joyce*, 54.

18. Ibid., 25.

19. Patricia Hutchins, *James Joyce's World* (London: Methuen & Co., 1957), 168.

20. JJ to SJ, October 31, 1904, *II*, 68.

21. Ibid.

22. Ellmann, *James Joyce*, 189.

23. JJ to SJ, October 31, 1904, *II*, 68.

24. Pinguentini, *James Joyce*, 25.

25. Silvio Benco, "James Joyce in Trieste," in *Portraits of the Artist in Exile*, ed. Willard Potts (New York: Harcourt Brace Jovanovich, 1986), 50.

26. Alessandro Francini-Bruni, "Joyce Stripped Naked in the Piazza," in Potts, *Portraits*, 11.

27. Ellmann, *James Joyce*, 186.

28. Pinguentini, *James Joyce*, 44.

29. Ivo Vidan, "Joyce and the South Slavs," in *Atti del Third International James Joyce Symposium*, ed. Niny Rocco-Bergera (Trieste: Università degli Studi, Facoltà di Magistero, 1974), 117.

30. Giacomo Scotti, "Gente di Pola," *Trieste Oggi*, October 2, 1992, 19.

31. JJ to John Stanislaus Joyce, November 10, 1904, *II*, 69.

32. JJ to SJ, November 19, 1904, *II*, 70.

33. Francini-Bruni, "Joyce Stripped," 8.

34. Ellmann, *James Joyce*, 187.

35. Constantine Curran, *James Joyce Remembered* (New York: Oxford University Press, 1968), 40.

36. JJ to SJ, December 15, 1904, *II*, 74.

37. Stanislaus Joyce, *My Brother's Keeper* (New York: Viking Press, 1958), 166.

38. Maddox, *Nora*, 56.

39. Francini-Bruni, "Joyce Stripped," 12.

40. Francini-Bruni, "Recollections of Joyce," in Potts, *Portraits*, 39.

41. Ellmann, *James Joyce*, 188.

42. JJ to SJ, December 28, 1904, *II*, 75.

43. JJ to SJ, December 3, 1904, *II*, 73.

44. JJ to SJ, January 19, 1905, *II*, 78.

45. Alice Curtayne, "Pappy Never Spoke of Jim's Books," interview with Eileen Joyce Schaurek in *James Joyce: Interviews and Recollections*, ed E. H. Mikhail (New York: St. Martin's Press, 1990), 65.

46. Arthur Power, "James Joyce—The Internationalist," in *A Bash in the Tunnel*, ed. John Ryan (Brighton: Clifton Books, 1970), 186.

47. Frank Budgen, *James Joyce and the Making of* Ulysses (Bloomington: University of Indiana Press, 1960), 36.

48. JJ to SJ, February 7, 1905, *II*, 80.

49. Hutchins, *James Joyce's World*, 68.

50. JJ to Mrs. William Murray, December 31, 1904, *I*, 57.

51. JJ to SJ, December 3, 1904, *II*, 73.

52. JJ to SJ, December 28, 1904, *II*, 75.

53. Ellmann, *James Joyce*, 189.

54. JJ to Grant Richards, May 5, 1906, *II*, 134.

55. JJ to Constantine Curran, [? 1904], *I*, 55.

56. Curran, *James Joyce Remembered*, 54.

57. JJ to SJ, January 13, 1905, *II*, 76.

58. JJ to SJ, October 31, 1904, *II*, 68.

59. JJ to SJ, January 13, 1905, *II*, 76.

60. JJ to SJ, November 6, 1906, *II*, 186.

61. Ellmann, *James Joyce*, 194.

62. JJ to SJ, February 7, 1905, *II*, 79, 80.

63. JJ to SJ, July 12, 1905, *II*, 96.

64. Francini-Bruni, "Recollections," 40.

65. Vidan, "Joyce and the South Slavs," 119.

66. Ellmann Collection, box 143, "Stanislaus Joyce diary," January 4, 1907.

67. JJ to SJ, February 7, 1905, *II*, 80.

68. JJ to SJ, February 28, 1905, *II*, 84.

69. JJ to SJ, December 3, 1904, *II*, 73.

70. JJ to SJ, December 28, 1904, *II*, 75.

4. A TRIESTINE

1. Carola Giedion-Welcker, "Meetings with Joyce," in *Portraits of the Artist in Exile*, ed. Willard Potts (New York: Harcourt Brace Jovanovich, 1986), 261.

2. JJ to SJ, [? May 2 or 3, 1905], *II*, 88.

3. JJ to SJ, July 12, 1905, *II*, 93.

4. JJ to SJ, [? May 2 or 3, 1905], *II*, 89.

5. Michele Pozzetto, *1912 pianta topografica della città di Trieste* (1912; reprint, Tri-

este: Linea Studio, 1988).

6. Corinna del Greco Lobner, *James Joyce's Italian Experience: Trovatore in Trieste* (Ann Arbor: University Microfilms International, 1981), 41.

7. Constantine Curran, *James Joyce Remembered* (New York: Oxford University Press, 1968), 39.

8. JJ to SJ, April 4, 1905, *II*, 86.

9. Alessandro Francini-Bruni, "Joyce Stripped Naked in the Piazza," in Potts, *Portraits*, 35.

10. Bianca Maria Favetta, *Il "Verdi": Mito di un teatro* (Trieste: n.p., 1971), 9.

11. Ibid., 14.

12. Philippe Soupault, "James Joyce," in Potts, *Portraits*, 113.

13. Curran, *James Joyce Remembered*, 42.

14. Jacques Mercanton, "The Hours of James Joyce," in Potts, *Portraits*, 248.

15. Richard M. Kain, "An Interview with Carola Giedion-Welcker and Maria Jolas," *JJQ* (Winter 1974): 102.

16. Ellmann Collection, box 144, "Stanislaus Joyce diary," September 25, 1907.

17. James Joyce, *Giacomo Joyce* (London: Faber & Faber, 1984), 12.

18. Jan Morris, *Destinations* (New York: Oxford University Press, 1980), 211.

19. P. N. Furbank, *Italo Svevo: The Man and the Writer* (Berkeley: University of California Press, 1966), 17.

20. Joseph Cary, *A Ghost in Trieste* (Chicago: University of Chicago Press, 1993), 93.

21. JJ to SJ, [? May 2 or 3, 1905], *II*, 90.

22. Giani Stuparich, *Trieste nei miei ricordi* (Milan: Edizioni Garzanti, 1948), 19.

23. Scipio Slataper, *Scritti politici* (Rome: Alberto Stock, 1925), 23.

24. Thomas F. Staley, "Italo Svevo and the Ambience of Trieste," in *Atti del Third International James Joyce Symposium*, ed. Niny Rocco-Bergera (Trieste: Università degli Studi, Facoltà di Magistero, 1974), 207.

25. Slataper, *Scritti politici*, 5.

26. JJ to SJ, April 4, 1905, *II*, 87.

27. JJ to SJ, September 25, 1906, *II*, 167.

28. JJ to SJ, July 12, 1905, *II*, 94.

29. Ibid.

30. del Greco Lobner, *James Joyce's Italian Experience*, 56.

31. Nora Poliaghi, "Il loggione di Joyce," *Gazzetta di Parma*, January 23, 1969, 3.

32. Pozzetto, *pianta topografica*.

33. Mary Colum and Padraic Colum, *Our Friend James Joyce* (Garden City, N.J.: Doubleday & Company, 1958), 45.

34. Richard Ellmann, *James Joyce* (New York: Oxford University Press, 1982), 196.

35. Colum and Colum, *Our Friend*, 44.

36. Alyce Barry, ed., *Djuna Barnes/Interviews* (Washington, D. C.: Sun and Moon Press, 1985), 294.

37. James Joyce, *The Critical Writings of James Joyce*, ed. Ellsworth Mason and Richard Ellmann (Ithaca: Cornell University Press, 1989), 174.

38. Dominic Manganiello, *Joyce's Politics* (London: Routledge & Kegan Paul, 1980), 46.

39. Silvio Benco, "James Joyce in Trieste," in Potts, *Portraits*, 54.

40. Stanislaus Joyce, *My Brother's Keeper* (New York: Viking Press, 1958), 170.

41. JJ to SJ, [? May 2 or 3, 1905], *II*, 89.

42. Stanislaus Joyce, *MBK*, 169–70.

43. JJ to SJ, [about August 12, 1906], *II*, 148.

44. JJ to SJ, [? May 2 or 3, 1905], *II*, 89.

45. Ibid.

46. J. F. Byrne, *Silent Years* (New York: Farrar, Straus, and Young, 1953), 149.

47. JJ to SJ, May 27, 1905, *II*, 90.

48. JJ to SJ, July 12, 1905, *II*, 93.

49. Letter from Annamaria Mottola to author, November 15, 1991.

50. JJ to SJ, April 4, 1905, *II*, 87.

51. Ibid.

52. JJ to SJ, July 12, 1905, *II*, 94.

53. Gianni Pinguentini, *James Joyce in Italia* (Verona: Linotipia Veronese di Ghidini e Fiorini, 1963), 56.

54. Ivo Vidan, "Joyce and the South Slavs," in Rocco-Bergera, *Atti*, 121.

55. Vitaliano Brancati, "Recollections of Professor Joyce," *JJQ* (Fall 1981): 80.

56. JJ to SJ, [October 16, 1905], *II*, 123.

57. Francini-Bruni, "Joyce Stripped," 20.

58. JJ to SJ, July 12, 1905, *II*, 94.

59. Stanislaus Joyce, *MBK*, 65.

60. JJ to SJ, May 27, 1905, *II*, 90.

61. JJ to SJ, postmark June 11, 1905, *II*, 91.

62. Stanislaus Joyce, *MBK*, 159.

63. Bruno Coceani and Cesare Pagnini, *Trieste della "belle époque"* (Trieste: Libreria "Universitas" Editrice, 1971), 118.

64. JJ to SJ, postmark June 11, 1905, *II*, 91.

65. Ibid.

66. JJ to SJ, May 27, 1905, *II*, 90.

67. JJ to SJ, July 8, 1905, *II*, 92.

68. JJ to SJ, July 12, 1905, *II*, 93.

69. JJ to SJ, September 25, 1906, *II*, 167.

70. Eílis Dillon, "The Innocent Muse: An Interview with Maria Jolas," *JJQ* (Fall 1982): 47.

71. The information in the following paragraphs is from JJ to SJ, July 12, 1905, *II*, 93–98.

72. JJ to SJ, July 19, 1905, *II*, 99.

73. JJ to SJ, July 29, 1905, *II*, 101.

74. Stanislaus Joyce, *MBK*, 136.

75. JJ to SJ, [July 27, 1905], *II*, 100.

76. SJ to JJ, July 31, 1905, *II*, 102.

77. Ellmann, *James Joyce*, 204.

5. ANOTHER JOYCE IN TRIESTE

1. Richard Ellmann, *James Joyce* (New York: Oxford University Press, 1982), 204.

2. Stanislaus Joyce, *My Brother's Keeper* (New York: Viking Press, 1958), 152.

3. JJ to SJ, postmark June 7, 1905, *II*, 91.

4. Ellmann, *James Joyce*, 198.

5. JJ to SJ, [about October 18, 1905], *II*, 124.

6. JJ to SJ, [about September 24, 1905], *II*, 111.

7. Ibid.

8. JJ to SJ, July 19, 1905, *II*, 99.

9. JJ to SJ, [about September 24, 1905], *II*, 109.

10. JJ to SJ, July 19, 1905, *II*, 98.

11. JJ to SJ, [about September 24, 1905], *II*, 109.

12. JJ to SJ, [about September 30, 1905], *II*, 113.

13. JJ to SJ, [September] 18, 1905, *II*, 107.

14. JJ to SJ, [about September 24, 1905], *II*, 110.

15. JJ to John Stanislaus Joyce, November 10, 1904, *II*, 69.

16. JJ to SJ, [about September 30, 1905], *II*, 113.

17. JJ to NB, August 29, 1904, *II*, 48.

18. Stanislaus Joyce, *MBK*, 65.

19. Ibid., 49.

20. Stanislaus Joyce, *The Complete Dublin Diary of Stanislaus Joyce* (Ithaca: Cornell University Press, 1971), 5.

21. JJ to NB, August 29, 1904, *II*, 48.

22. Stanislaus Joyce, *CDD*, 6, 7, 24, 28.

23. Stanislaus Joyce, *MBK*, 32.

24. John Stanislaus Joyce to JJ, July 19, 1907, *II*, 223.

25. Constantine Curran, *James Joyce Remembered* (New York: Oxford University Press, 1968), 68.

26. Stanislaus Joyce, *CDD*, 32.

27. Bozena Berta Delimata, "Reminiscences of a Joyce Niece," *JJQ* (Fall 1981): 48.

28. JJ to SJ, February 7, 1905, *II*, 80.

29. JJ to SJ, July 12, 1905, *II*, 95.

30. JJ to NB, [about September 1, 1904], *II*, 51.

31. Stanislaus Joyce, *MBK*, 103.

32. JJ to SJ, July 15, 1905, *II*, 98.

33. Stanislaus Joyce, *CDD*, 26.

34. JJ to SJ, July 19, 1905, *II*, 100.

35. *II*, 109, n. 1.

36. JJ to GR, August 17, 1905, *II*, 104.

37. GR to JJ, September 26, 1905, *II*, 112, n. 1.

38. JJ to SJ, February 7, 1905, *II*, 80.

39. JJ to GR, October 15, 1905, *II*, 122.

40. JJ to Mrs. William Murray, December 4, 1905, *II*, 128.

41. JJ to SJ, [About October 12, 1905], *II*, 121.

42. Brenda Maddox, *Nora: The Real Life of Molly Bloom* (Boston: Houghton Mifflin Company, 1988), 67.

43. Ellmann, *James Joyce*, 213.

44. Stanislaus Joyce, *MBK*, 245.

45. Stanislaus Joyce, *CDD*, 101.

46. JJ to SJ, August 7, 1906, *II*, 146.

47. John Gatt-Rutter, *Italo Svevo: A Double Life* (New York: Oxford University Press, 1988), 227.

48. Alessandro Francini-Bruni, "Joyce Stripped Naked in the Piazza," in *Portraits of the Artist in Exile,* ed. Willard Potts (New York: Harcourt Brace Jovanovich, 1986), 30.

49. Ibid., 32.

50. JJ to NB, October 27, 1909, *II*, 256.

51. Herbert Gorman, *James Joyce* (New York: Farrar and Rinehart, 1939), 159.

52. Frank Budgen, "James Joyce," in *James Joyce: Two Decades of Criticism*, ed. Seon Givens (New York: Vanguard Press, 1963), 20.

53. Ellmann Collection, box 5, "Alessandro Francini-Bruni."

54. Francini-Bruni, "Joyce Stripped," 33.

55. Richard M. Kain, "An Interview with Carola Giedion-Welcker and Maria Jolas," *JJQ*

(Winter 1974): 95.

56. Italo Svevo, *Saggi e pagine sparse* (n.p.: Mondadori, 1954), 237.

57. JJ to NB, December 3, 1909, *II*, 270.

58. JJ to Mrs. William Murray, December 4, 1905, *II*, 129.

59. Patricia Hutchins, *James Joyce's World* (London: Methuen & Co., 1957), 69.

60. Maddox, *Nora*, 68.

61. Eílìs Dillon, "The Innocent Muse: An Interview with Maria Jolas," *JJQ* (Fall 1982): 48.

62. JJ to NB, December 23, 1909, *II*, 279.

63. Ellmann Collection, box 5, "Alessandro Francini-Bruni."

64. Ivo Vidan, "Joyce and the South Slavs," in *Atti del Third International James Joyce Symposium*, ed. Niny Rocco-Bergera (Trieste: Università degli Studi, Facoltà di Magistero, 1974), 121.

65. Stelio Crise, "Joyce e Trieste," *Accademie e biblioteche d'Italia* 29 (1961): 6.

66. Stanislaus Joyce, *MBK*, 200.

67. Francini-Bruni, "Joyce Stripped," 27.

68. Ibid., 28.

69. JJ to GR, March 13, 1906, *II*, 132.

70. GR to JJ, February 17, 1906, *II*, 130, n. 1.

71. GR to JJ, April 23, 1906, *II*, 132, n. 2.

72. JJ to GR, April 26, 1906, *I*, 60.

73. JJ to GR, May 5, 1906, *II*, 133.

74. JJ to GR, May 13, 1906, *II*, 137.

75. JJ to GR, May 20, 1906, *I*, 62.

76. JJ to GR, May 13, 1906, *II*, 137.

77. JJ to GR, July 9, 1906, *II*, 143.

78. Mrs. William Murray to SJ, June 6, 1906, *II*, 138.

79. Ellmann Collection, box 143, "Stanislaus Joyce diary," January 1, 1907.

80. JJ to GR, February 28, 1906, *II*, 131.

81. Gorman, *James Joyce*, 159.

82. Ellmann, *James Joyce*, 222.

6. ITALIAN INTERLUDE

1. JJ to GR, June 10, 1906, *II*, 140.

2. JJ to SJ, August 7, 1906, *II*, 145.

3. JJ to SJ, August 2, 1906, *II*, 144.

4. JJ to SJ, August 7, 1906, *II*, 145.

5. JJ to SJ, postmark July 31, 1906, *II*, 144.

6. JJ to SJ, August 7, 1906, *II*, 146.

7. JJ to SJ, postmark August 19, 1906, *II*, 152.

8. JJ to SJ, August 31, 1906, *II*, 153.

9. JJ to SJ, postmark August 19, 1906, *II*, 151.

10. Arthur Power, "James Joyce—The Internationalist," in *A Bash in the Tunnel*, ed. John Ryan (Brighton: Clifton Books, 1970), 184.

11. JJ to SJ, [October 9, 1906], *II*, 172.

12. JJ to SJ, postmark August 16, 1906, *II*, 149.

13. JJ to SJ, postmark August 19, 1906, *II*, 151.

14. JJ to SJ, August 31, 1906, *II*, 153, 155.

15. JJ to SJ, September 6, 1906, *II*, 156.

16. JJ to SJ, August 7, 1906, *II*, 147.

17. JJ to SJ, November 6, 1906, *II*, 189.

18. JJ to SJ, postmark December 3, 1906, *II*, 198.

19. JJ to SJ, [? March 1, 1907], *II*, 218.

20. JJ to SJ, December 7, 1906, *II*, 201.

21. JJ to SJ, postmark September 16, 1906, *II*, 161.

22. JJ to SJ, September 18[-20], 1906, *II*, 162.

23. JJ to SJ, October 18, 1906, *II*, 180.

24. Ellmann Collection, box 143, "Stanislaus Joyce diary," January 19, 1907.

25. JJ to SJ, December 7, 1906, *II*, 203.

26. JJ to SJ, December 24, 1906, *II*, 204.

27. JJ to SJ, postmark January 10, 1907, *II*, 206.

28. Karl Beckson, "Letters from Arthur Symons to James Joyce," *JJQ* 4 (1966/67): 97.

29. JJ to SJ, January 15, 1907, *II*, 206.

30. JJ to SJ, [? March 1, 1907], *II*, 219.

31. Peter Costello, *James Joyce: The Years of Growth 1882–1915* (New York: Pantheon Books, 1992), 228.

32. Richard Ellmann, *James Joyce* (New York: Oxford University Press, 1982), 230.

33. JJ to SJ, February 6, 1907, *II*, 209.

34. JJ to SJ, February 11, 1907, *II*, 211–12.

35. JJ to SJ, November 20, 1906, *II*, 197.

36. JJ to SJ, September 25, 1906, *II*, 166.

37. Robert Spoo, "Joyce's Attitudes Toward History: Rome, 1906-07," *Journal of Modern Literature* (Spring 1988): 488.

38. JJ to SJ, February 14, 1907, *II*, 214.

39. JJ to SJ, [postmark February 16, 1907], *II*, 214.

40. Ellmann Collection, box 143, "Stanislaus Joyce diary," February 15, 1907.

41. JJ to SJ, February 16, 1907, *II*, 215.

42. JJ to SJ, [about September 24, 1905], *II*, 110.

43. JJ to SJ, [? March 1, 1907], *II*, 217.

7. JOYCE AS JOURNALIST

1. Richard Ellmann, *James Joyce* (New York: Oxford University Press, 1982), 254, 241.

2. Frank Budgen, *Myselves When Young* (New York: Oxford University Press, 1970), 185.

3. JJ to SJ, November 6, 1906, *II*, 187.

4. JJ to HSW, August 26, 1919, *II*, 450.

5. Niny Rocco-Bergera and Carlina Rebecchi-Piperata, *Itinerary of Joyce and Svevo through Artistic Trieste* (Trieste: Azienda Autonoma Soggiorno e Turismo, 1970), 10.

6. Giani Stuparich, *Sequenze per Trieste* (Trieste: Edizioni Dello Zibaldone, 1968), 28.

7. Bruno Coceani and Cesare Pagnini, *Trieste della "belle époque"* (Trieste: Libreria "Universitas" Editrice, 1971), 219.

8. *Guida generale di Trieste 1907*, 726.

9. Ellmann Collection, box 143, "Stanislaus Joyce diary," March 9, 1907.

10. Ibid.

11. Silvio Benco, Il Piccolo *di Trieste* (Rome: Edizioni Fratelli Treves, 1931), 148.

12. Ellmann Collection, box 5, "Alessandro Francini-Bruni."

13. Ellmann Collection, box 143, "Stanislaus Joyce diary," March 9, 1907.

14. Silvio Benco, *Trieste e il suo diritto all'Italia* (Trieste: Cappelli, 1952), 96.

15. Ellmann Collection, box 5, "Alessandro Francini-Bruni."

16. Cesare Pagnini, *I giornali di Trieste* (Milan: Centro Studi, 1959), 342.

17. Coceani and Pagnini, *Trieste*, 23.

18. Silvio Benco, "James Joyce in Trieste," in *Portraits of the Artist in Exile*, ed. Willard Potts (New York: Harcourt Brace Jovanovich, 1986), 52.

19. Ibid., 55.

20. Aurelia Gruber Benco, "Between Joyce and Benco," *JJQ* (Spring 1972): 329.

21. Ellmann, *James Joyce*, 255.

22. Ibid., 258.

23. Scipio Slataper, *Scritti politici* (Rome: Alberto Stock, 1925), 18.

24. Stelio Crise, *And Trieste, Ah Trieste* (Milan: All'Insegna del Pesce d'Oro, 1971), 30.

25. Ellmann Collection, box 143, "Stanislaus Joyce diary," April 25, 1907.

26. Ibid., April 27, 1907.

27. Ibid., May 15, 1907.

28. Stanislaus Joyce, *My Brother's Keeper* (New York: Viking Press, 1958), 175.

29. James Joyce, *Chamber Music*, ed. William York Tindall (New York: Columbia University Press, 1954), 99.

30. Stanislaus Joyce, "Ricordi di James Joyce," *Letteratura* (July/September 1941): 43.

31. Ellmann, *James Joyce*, 260.

32. Ibid., 262.

33. SJ to G. Molyneux Palmer, July 20, 1907, *II*, 224.

34. JJ to G. Molyneux Palmer, July 19, 1909, *I*, 67.

35. JJ to G. Molyneux Palmer, June 11, 1910, *I*, 70.

36. J. B. Lyons, "Thrust Syphilis Down to Hell," in *James Joyce: The Centennial Symposium*, ed. Morris Beja et al. (Chicago: University of Illinois Press, 1986), 175.

37. Ellmann Collection, box 143, "Stanislaus Joyce diary," May 23, 1907.

38. Ibid., April 6, 1907.

39. Ibid., August 1, 1907.

40. Ibid., May 23, 1907.

41. Ibid., July 12, 1907.

42. Ellmann, *James Joyce*, 262.

43. Ellmann Collection, box 143, "Stanislaus Joyce diary," July 27, 1907.

44. Brenda Maddox, *Nora: The Real Life of Molly Bloom* (Boston: Houghton Mifflin Company, 1988), 83.

45. Crise, *And Trieste*, 18.

46. This information is contained under "Joyce" in the Libro dei Parti 1907, Trieste.

47. Harry T. Moore, *The Priest of Love: A Life of D. H. Lawrence* (New York: Penguin Books, 1981), 260.

48. Ellmann, *James Joyce*, 262.

49. Ulick O'Connor, *Oliver St. John Gogarty* (London: Jonathan Cape, 1963), 82–83.

50. Stanislaus Joyce, "Ricordi," 36.

51. Ellmann, *James Joyce*, 264.

52. JJ to Elkin Mathews, September 24, 1907, *II*, 224.

53. "Major Dermot Freyer's Report on *Dubliners*," *JJQ* (Summer 1973): 457.

54. JJ to Elkin Mathews, February 9, 1908, *II*, 225.

55. JJ to Carlo Linati, September 21, 1920, *I*, 146.

56. Georges Borach, "Conversations with James Joyce," in Potts, *Portraits*, 69.

57. Ellmann, *James Joyce*, 265.

58. Ibid.

59. Corinna del Greco Lobner, *James Joyce's Italian Experience: Trovatore in Trieste* (Ann Arbor: University Microfilms International, 1981), 4.

60. Ellmann, *James Joyce*, 267.

61. JJ to W. B. Yeats, September 14, 1916, *I*, 95.

62. John Gatt-Rutter, *Italo Svevo: A Double Life* (New York: Oxford University Press, 1988), 44.

63. Corinna del Greco Lobner, *James Joyce's Italian Connection* (Iowa City: University of Iowa Press, 1989), 18.

64. Bianca Maria Favetta, *Il "Verdi": Mito di un teatro* (Trieste: n.p., 1971), 15.

65. Ellmann Collection, box 144, "Stanislaus Joyce diary," October 3–18, 1908.

66. Alessandro Francini-Bruni, "Joyce Stripped Naked in the Piazza," in Potts, *Portraits*, 30.

67. Ellmann Collection, box 144, "Stanislaus Joyce diary," January 12, 1908.

8. SCHMITZ-SVEVO

1. Livia Veneziani Svevo, *Memoir of Italo Svevo* (Marlboro, Vermont: Marlboro Press, 1990), 7.

2. Lina Galli, "Svevo and Irredentism," *Modern Fiction Studies* (Spring 1972): 114.

3. Veneziani Svevo, *Memoir*, 12.

4. Silvio Benco, "Italo Svevo," *Pegaso* 1 (January 1929): 48.

5. Veneziani Svevo, *Memoir*, 32.

6. Ibid., 15.

7. Ibid., 18.

8. P. N. Furbank, *Italo Svevo: The Man and the Writer* (Berkeley: University of California Press, 1966), 34.

9. Veneziani Svevo, *Memoir*, 23.

10. Richard Ellmann, "Speaking of Books: Italo Svevo and Joyce," *New York Times Book Review*, January 21, 1968, 2.

11. John Gatt-Rutter, *Italo Svevo: A Double Life* (New York: Oxford University Press, 1988), 113.

12. Veneziani Svevo, *Memoir*, 21.

13. James Joyce, *Giacomo Joyce* (London: Faber & Faber, 1984), 1.

14. Stanislaus Joyce, *The Meeting of Svevo and Joyce* (Trieste: Del Bianco, 1965), 9.

15. Thomas F. Staley, "Italo Svevo and the Ambience of Trieste," in *Atti del Third International James Joyce Symposium*, ed. Niny Rocco-Bergera (Trieste: Università degli Studi, Facoltà di Magistero, 1974), 206.

16. Gatt-Rutter, *Italo Svevo*, 169.

17. Ibid., 161.

18. Benco, "Italo Svevo," 53.

19. Letizia Svevo Fonda Savio, "A Daughter's Tribute," *Modern Fiction Studies* (Spring 1972): 3.

20. Stanislaus Joyce, *Meeting*, 7.

21. Veneziani Svevo, *Memoir*, 52.

22. Alessandro Francini-Bruni, "Recollections of Joyce," in *Portraits of the Artist in Exile*, ed. Willard Potts (New York: Harcourt Brace Jovanovich, 1986), 43.

23. Ellmann Collection, box 143, "Stanislaus Joyce diary," April 16, 1907.

24. Stanislaus Joyce, *Meeting*, 6.

25. "La prima conferenza Joyce," *Il Piccolo*, November 12, 1912, 3.

26. Silvio Benco, "James Joyce in Trieste," in Potts, *Portraits*, 50.

27. Veneziani Svevo, *Memoir*, 66.

28. Livia Veneziani Svevo, "Ricordo di James Joyce" (Trieste: Tip. Moderna, 1956), 76.

29. Stanislaus Joyce, *Meeting*, 6.

30. Ellmann Collection, box 144, "Stanislaus Joyce diary." January 19, 1908.

31. Stanislaus Joyce, *Meeting*, 7.

32. Stanislaus Joyce, "Joyce and Svevo," *Stork*, September 1932, 16.

33. Gatt-Rutter, *Italo Svevo*, 221.

34. Ibid., 243.

35. Stanislaus Joyce, *Meeting*, 9.

36. Niny Rocco-Bergera, "Italo Svevo and Trieste," *Modern Fiction Studies* (Spring 1972): 113.

37. Richard Ellmann, *James Joyce* (New York: Oxford University Press, 1982), 272.

38. Corinna del Greco Lobner, *James Joyce's Italian Experience: Trovatore in Trieste* (Ann Arbor: University Microfilms International, 1981), 83.

39. Bruno Maier, "Joyce, Trieste, e Svevo," *Rotary*, April 1982, 20.

40. Ettore Schmitz to JJ, June 26, 1914, *II*, 334.

41. Letizia Svevo Fonda Savio, "Svevo, un 'miracolo,' " *Il Piccolo*, January 13, 1991, 5.

42. Thomas F. Staley, "James Joyce and Italo Svevo," *Italica* 40 no. 4 (1963): 336.

43. Italo Svevo, *James Joyce*, trans. Stanislaus Joyce (New York: New Directions, 1950), 2.

9. OF BLOOM AND POLITICS

1. Ellmann Collection, box 144, "Stanislaus Joyce diary," December 29, 1907.

2. JJ to SJ, November 17, 1909, *II*, 263.

3. Richard Ellmann, *James Joyce* (New York: Oxford University Press, 1982), 269.

4. Ellmann Collection, box 144, "Stanislaus Joyce diary," August 12-October 31, 1908.

5. Ellmann Collection, box 144, "Stanislaus Joyce diary," October 1, 1908.

6. Ettore Schmitz to JJ, February 8, 1909, *II*, 227.

7. Ellmann, *James Joyce*, 274.

8. Stanislaus Joyce, "Joyce and Svevo," *Stork*, September 1932, 16.

9. John Gatt-Rutter, *Italo Svevo: A Double Life* (New York: Oxford University Press, 1988), 144.

10. Author interview with Dragomir Elia Giorgi, July 13, 1993.

11. Mario Stock, *Nel segno di Geremia* (Udine, Italy: Istituto per l'Enciclopedia del Friuli—Venezia Giulia, 1979), 78.

12. Author interview with Giorgio Voghera, July 6, 1993.

13. Ira B. Nadel, *Joyce and the Jews* (Iowa City: University of Iowa Press, 1989), 201.

14. Ellmann Collection, box 144, "Stanislaus Joyce diary," September 18, 1907.

15. P. N. Furbank, *Italo Svevo: The Man and the Writer* (Berkeley: University of California Press, 1966), 17.

16. Ibid., 6.

17. Frank Budgen, "James Joyce," in *James Joyce: Two Decades of Criticism*, ed. Seon Givens (New York: Vanguard Press, 1963), 23.

18. Stanislaus Joyce, *The Meeting of Svevo and Joyce* (Trieste: Del Bianco, 1965), 18.

19. Nadel, *Joyce and the Jews*, 70.

20. Oscar Schwarz to JJ, n.d., Cornell.

21. Umberto Saba, "Tre Vie," in *Scrittori triestini del Novecento*, ed. O. H. Bianchi et al. (Trieste: Edizioni Lint, 1968), 564.

22. Ellmann Collection, box 144, "Stanislaus Joyce diary," September 15, 1907.

23. Interview with Giorgi.

24. Stanislaus Joyce, "Joyce and Svevo," 20.

25. Ellmann, *James Joyce*, 374.

26. Peter Costello, *James Joyce: The Years of Growth 1882–1915* (New York: Pantheon Books, 1992), 68.

27. Gatt-Rutter, *Italo Svevo*, 361.

28. James Joyce, *Giacomo Joyce* (London: Faber & Faber, 1984), 6.

29. Interview with Voghera.

30. Thomas F. Staley, "James Joyce and Italo Svevo," *Italica* 40, no. 4 (1963): 335.

31. Lina Galli, "Svevo and Irredentism," *Modern Fiction Studies* (Spring 1972): 114.

32. Livia Veneziani Svevo, *Memoir of Italo Svevo* (Marlboro, Vermont: Marlboro Press, 1990), 71.

33. Galli, "Svevo and Irredentism," 116.

34. Furbank, *Italo Svevo*, 105.

35. Bogdan C. Novak, *Trieste, 1941–1954* (Chicago: University of Chicago Press, 1970), 19.

36. Gatt-Rutter, *Italo Svevo*, 227.

37. Leo Valiani, *The End of Austria-Hungary* (New York: Alfred A. Knopf, 1972), 304.

38. Bruno Coceani and Cesare Pagnini, *Trieste della "belle époque"* (Trieste: Libreria "Universitas" Editrice, 1971), 129.

39. JJ to SJ, November 6, 1906, *II*, 187.

40. Dominic Manganiello, *Joyce's Politics* (London: Routledge & Kegan Paul, 1980), 26.

41. JJ to SJ, October 18, 1906, *II*, 183.

42. JJ to SJ, November 6, 1906, *II*, 188.

43. Harry Levin, *James Joyce* (New York: New Directions, 1960), 8.

44. JJ to Carola Giedion-Welcker, November 18, 1936, *III*, 393.

45. Richard Ellmann, *The Consciousness of Joyce* (New York: Oxford University Press, 1977), 82.

46. JJ to SJ, July 12, 1905, *II*, 95.

47. Alessandro Francini-Bruni, "Joyce Stripped Naked in the Piazza," in *Portraits of the Artist in Exile*, ed. Willard Potts (New York: Harcourt Brace Jovanovich, 1986), 38.

48. T. R. Ybarra, *Verdi* (New York: Harcourt, Brace and Company, 1955), 179.

49. JJ to SJ, [? September 12, 1906], *II*, 160; JJ to SJ, postmark August 19, 1906, *II*, 151.

50. JJ to SJ, [October 9, 1906], *II*, 173.

51. JJ to SJ, November 6, 1906, *II*, 187.

52. JJ to SJ, February 6, 1907, *II*, 210.

53. JJ to SJ, [? March 1, 1907], *II*, 217.

54. Frank Budgen, *Myselves When Young* (New York: Oxford University Press, 1970), 198.

55. William Butler Yeats to Edmund Gosse, August 28, [1915], *II*, 362.

56. Eugene Jolas, "My Friend James Joyce," in Givens, *James Joyce*, 4.

57. JJ to Casa Editrice Formiggini, March 25, 1914, in James Joyce, *Poesie e prose*, ed. Franca Ruggieri (Milan: Arnoldo Mondadori, 1992), 517.

10. THE RETURN OF THE NATIVE

1. JJ to SJ, [October 16, 1905], *II*, 124.

2. JJ to Margaret Joyce, December 8, 1908, *II*, 226.

3. John Stanislaus Joyce to JJ, May 16, 1909, *II*, 228.

4. Ibid.

5. Ibid., 229.

6. SJ to Herbert Gorman, August 8, 1931, *III*, 226.

7. JJ to SJ, August 28, 1909, *II*, 241.

8. P. N. Furbank, *Italo Svevo: The Man and the Writer* (Berkeley: University of California Press, 1966), 83.

9. JJ to NB, postmark July 29, 1909, *II*, 230.

10. Ibid.

11. JJ to SJ, August 4, 1909, *II*, 231.

12. Mary Colum and Padraic Colum, *Our Friend James Joyce* (Garden City, N.J.: Doubleday & Company, 1958), 76.

13. John Stanislaus Joyce to JJ, April 24, 1907, *II*, 221.

14. Richard Ellmann, *James Joyce* (New York: Oxford University Press, 1982), 276.

15. Ulick O'Connor, *Oliver St. John Gogarty* (London: Jonathan Cape, 1963), 53.

16. Oliver St. John Gogarty, "The Joyce I Knew," *Saturday Review of Literature*, January 25, 1941, 3.

17. JJ to NB, September 29, 1904, *II*, 57.

18. JJ to SJ, February 7, 1905, *II*, 79.

19. Ellmann, *James Joyce*, 160.

20. JJ to NB, August 6, 1909, *II*, 232.

21. J. F. Byrne, *Silent Years* (New York: Farrar, Straus, and Young, 1953), 156.

22. JJ to NB, August 19, 1909, *II*, 235.

23. JJ to NB, August 31, 1909, *II*, 242.

24. Constantine Curran, *James Joyce Remembered* (New York: Oxford University Press, 1968), 74.

25. JJ to SJ, August 21, 1909, *II*, 238.

26. JJ to SJ, August 16, 1909, *II*, 234.

27. Ibid.

28. JJ to NB, September 2, 1909, *II*, 243.

29. JJ to SJ, August 16, 1909, *II*, 234.

30. JJ to SJ, postmark August 20, 1909, *II*, 236.

31. JJ to NB, August 21, 1909, *II*, 237.

32. JJ to SJ, August 25, 1909, *II*, 240.

33. JJ to SJ, August 28, 1909, *II*, 241.

34. Ellmann, *James Joyce*, 285.

35. JJ to SJ, September 4, 1909, *II*, 247.

36. JJ to NB, September 7, 1909, *II*, 249.

37. JJ to NB, August 21, 1909, *II*, 236.

38. JJ to NB, September 3, 1909, *II*, 246.

39. JJ to NB, September 5, 1909, *II*, 248.

40. JJ to NB, September 7, 1909, *II*, 249.

41. Ibid., 251.

42. JJ to SJ, September 9, 1909, *II*, 252.

43. JJ to NB, [? October 25, 1909], *II*, 254.

44. Ibid.

45. JJ to NB, November 1, 1909, *II*, 258.

46. JJ to NB, October 27, 1909, *II*, 257.

47. JJ to SJ, November 17, 1909, *II*, 262.

48. Ibid.

49. Ibid., 265.

50. Ibid.

51. JJ to NB, November 18, 1909, *II*, 265.

52. JJ to NB, November 22, 1909, *II*, 268.

53. JJ to SJ, November 3, 1909, *II*, 259.
54. Herbert Gorman, *James Joyce* (New York: Farrar & Rinehart, 1939), 200.
55. JJ to NB, December 16, 1909, *II*, 276.
56. JJ to NB, December 22, 1909, *II*, 278.
57. JJ to NB, December 20, 1909, *II*, 276.
58. JJ to SJ, December 23, 1909, *II*, 279.
59. JJ to NB, December 23, 1909, *II*, 278.
60. Ibid.
61. Ellmann, *James Joyce*, 308.

11. A BROTHER'S KEEPER

1. JJ to Theodore Spicer-Simson, June 8, 1910, *II*, 285.
2. JJ to SJ, February 12, 1910, *II*, 282.
3. JJ to SJ, March 9, 1910, *II*, 283.
4. *Guida generale di Trieste 1911*, 565.
5. JJ to Elkin Mathews, May 15, 1910, *I*, 68.
6. JJ to Elkin Mathews, May 21, 1910, *II*, 283.
7. Ibid.
8. Stelio Crise, "Quasi mai il suo cuore si apriva ad affetti sinceri," *Il Piccolo*, June 13, 1971, 3.
9. Ibid.; JJ to George Roberts, January 3, 1911, *II*, 288.
10. Corinna del Greco Lobner, *James Joyce's Italian Connection* (Iowa City: University of Iowa Press, 1989), 96.
11. Ibid., 89.
12. Edward J. Brown, *Mayakovsky* (New York: Paragon House, 1988), 50.
13. "La serata di poesia al Politeama Rossetti," *Il Piccolo*, January 12, 1910.
14. "La serata di poesia futurista," *Il Piccolo*, January 13, 1910, 2.
15. Ellmann Collection, box 11, "Dario de Tuoni."
16. Richard Ellmann, *The Consciousness of Joyce* (New York: Oxford University Press, 1977), 118.
17. Frank Budgen, *James Joyce and the Making of* Ulysses (Bloomington: University of Indiana Press, 1960), 153.
18. Stelio Crise, *Epiphanies and Phadographs: Joyce e Trieste* (Milan: All'Insegna del Pesce d'Oro, 1967), 19.
19. Gianni Pinguentini, *James Joyce in Italia* (Verona: Linotipia Veronese di Ghidini e Fiorini, 1963), 176.
20. Mary Colum, *Life and the Dream* (Garden City, N.J.: Doubleday & Company, 1947), 388.
21. Mary Colum and Padraic Colum, *Our Friend James Joyce* (Garden City, N.J.: Doubleday & Company, 1958), 227.
22. Alice Curtayne, "Pappy Never Spoke of Jim's Books," interview with Eileen Joyce Schaurek in *James Joyce: Interviews and Recollections*, ed. E. H. Mikhail (New York: St. Martin's Press, 1990), 63.
23. Ibid., 66.
24. Richard Ellmann, *James Joyce* (New York: Oxford University Press, 1982), 310.
25. Sylvia Beach, *Shakespeare and Company* (Lincoln: University of Nebraska Press, 1980), 38.
26. JJ to HSW, June 24, 1921, *I*, 167.
27. Colum and Colum, *Our Friend*, 112.

28. JJ to SJ, January 12, 1911, *II*, 288.

29. Arthur Power, *Conversations with James Joyce* (Chicago: University of Chicago Press, 1982), 70.

30. Ellmann, *James Joyce*, 311.

31. Ettore Schmitz to JJ, June 15, 1910, *II*, 286.

32. Ellmann, *James Joyce*, 311.

33. JJ to G. Molyneux Palmer, December 23, 1911, *II*, 294.

34. Herbert Gorman, *James Joyce* (New York: Farrar & Rinehart, 1939), 196.

35. Ellmann Collection, box 3, "Silvio Benco."

36. Aurelia Gruber Benco, "Between Joyce and Benco," *JJQ* (Spring 1972): 331.

37. Stelio Crise and Bruno Chersicla, "Antonio Smareglia," in *è tornato Joyce* (Milan: Nuova Rivista Europca, 1982).

38. Thomas F. Staley, "James Joyce in Trieste," *Georgia Review* (October 1962): 446.

39. Ibid., 449, 447.

40. Ibid., 448.

41. "Qui nacque l'Ulisse di Joyce," *Trieste Oggi*, March 14, 1992.

42. Staley, "James Joyce in Trieste," 448.

43. JJ to SJ, January 12, 1911, *II*, 288.

44. Ibid.

45. JJ to George Roberts, January 3, 1911, *II*, 288.

46. JJ to SJ, January 22, 1911, *II*, 289.

47. Curtayne, "Pappy," 65.

48. Staley, "James Joyce in Trieste," 449.

49. JJ to HSW, January 6, 1920, *I*, 136.

50. Curtayne, "Pappy," 65.

51. JJ to the editor, August 17, 1911, *II*, 292.

52. Gorman, *James Joyce*, 208.

12. IRISH TEMPERS

1. JJ to SJ, postmark August 7, 1912, *II*, 298.

2. James Joyce, *The Critical Writings of James Joyce*, ed. Ellsworth Mason and Richard Ellmann (Ithaca: Cornell University Press, 1989), 227.

3. Louis Berrone, *James Joyce in Padua* (New York: Random House, 1977), xxii.

4. JJ to Elkin Mathews, May 30, 1912, *II*, 296.

5. JJ to Eileen Joyce, May 30, 1912, *II*, 295.

6. JJ to SJ, postmark August 7, 1912, *II*, 299; NB to Eileen Joyce, August 14, 1912, *II*, 302.

7. JJ to NB, [? July 12, 1912], *II*, 297.

8. Letizia Svevo Fonda Savio to author, February 7, 1992.

9. NB to JJ, July 11, 1912, *II*, 297.

10. Ibid., 296.

11. JJ to SJ, postmark July 17, 1912, *II*, 298.

12. Ibid.

13. JJ to SJ, postmark July 27, 1912, *II*, 298.

14. JJ to SJ, [August 20, 1912], *II*, 305.

15. JJ to NB, [August 21, 1912], *II*, 308.

16. JJ to SJ, postmark ? August 26, 1912, *II*, 314.

17. Mary Colum and Padraic Colum, *Our Friend James Joyce* (Garden City, N.J.: Doubleday & Company, 1958), 89.

18. JJ to NB, postmark August 23, 1912, *II*, 311.

19. Charles Joyce to SJ, September 6, 1912, *II*, 317.

20. Stanislaus Joyce, *My Brother's Keeper* (New York: Viking Press, 1958), 240.

21. John Stanislaus Joyce to JJ, May 5, 1914, *II*, 331.

22. Patricia Hutchins, *James Joyce's World* (London: Methuen & Co., 1957), 36.

23. JJ to Mrs. William Murray, October 23, 1922, *I*, 191.

24. Louis Gillet, "Farewell to Joyce," in *Portraits of the Artist in Exile*, ed. Willard Potts (New York: Harcourt Brace Jovanovich, 1986), 167.

25. John Stanislaus Joyce to JJ, May 5, 1914, *II*, 331.

26. Eugene Jolas, "My Friend James Joyce," in *James Joyce: Two Decades of Criticism*, ed. Seon Givens (New York: Vanguard Press, 1963), 9.

27. JJ to T. S. Eliot, January 1, 1932, *I*, 311.

28. JJ to HSW, January 17, 1932, *I*, 312.

29. JJ to HSW, January 28, 1932, *I*, 313.

30. JJ to NB, [postmark August 22, 1912], *II*, 310.

31. JJ to NB, postmark August 23, 1912, *II*, 311.

32. JJ to Constantine Curran, August 19, 1912, *I*, 71.

33. JJ to SJ, postmark ?August 26, 1912, *II*, 314.

34. JJ to SJ, postmark August 30, 1912, *II*, 315.

35. Charles Joyce to SJ, September 6, 1912, *II*, 317.

36. Charles Joyce to SJ, September 11, 1912, *II*, 319.

37. JJ to SJ, postmark September 11, 1912, *II*, 320.

38. Robert Scholes, "The Broadsides of James Joyce," in *A James Joyce Miscellany*, ed. Marvin Magalaner (Carbondale: Southern Illinois University Press, 1962), 10.

39. James Joyce, *Critical Writings*, 243.

40. Niny Rocco-Bergera and Carlina Rebecchi-Piperata, *Itinerary of Joyce and Svevo through Artistic Trieste* (Trieste: Azienda Autonoma Soggiorno e Turismo, 1970), 8.

41. JJ to Michael Healy, November 2, 1915, *I*, 86.

42. JJ to SJ, [? October 1912], *II*, 321.

43. Richard Ellmann, *James Joyce* (New York: Oxford University Press, 1982), 386.

44. JJ to William Butler Yeats, December 16, 1912, *II*, 322.

45. JJ to William Butler Yeats, December 25, 1912, *II*, 322.

46. JJ to Elkin Mathews, February 26, 1913, *II*, 323.

47. JJ to Elkin Mathews, Easter Day 1913, *I*, 73.

48. JJ to Mrs. William Murray, December 9, 1912, *I*, 72.

49. "La prima conferenza Joyce," *Il Piccolo*, November 12, 1912, 3.

50. "Le conferenze del dott. James Joyce," *Il Piccolo*, February 11, 1913, 2.

51. JJ to SJ, [? January 1913], *II*, 322.

52. JJ to director of Scuola Superiore di Commercio Revoltella, November 24, 1913, in Comitato Per L'Anno Joyciano, *Il ritorno di Joyce* (Trieste: n.p., 1982).

53. Alessandro Francini-Bruni, "Recollections of Joyce," in Potts, *Portraits*, 41.

54. SJ to Herbert Gorman, August 8, 1931, *III*, 225.

55. *Guida generale di Trieste 1914*, 181.

56. Carla Galinetto, "Viaggiando coi vagabondi," *Il Piccolo*, November 24, 1992, 3.

57. The information in this and the following paragraph is from Dario de Tuoni, *Ricordo di Joyce a Trieste* (Milan: All'Insegna del Pesce d'Oro, 1966), 63, 57, 56, 10, 11, 14.

58. Dario de Tuoni, "L'ultima casa di Joyce a Trieste," *La Fiera Letteraria*, no. 18, 1961, 2.

59. de Tuoni, *Ricordo di Joyce*, 20.

60. Niny Rocco-Bergera, review of *Ricordo di Joyce a Trieste*, by Dario de Tuoni, *JJQ* (Summer 1969): 389.

13. MYSTERY LADY

1. Ettore Schmitz to JJ, June 26, 1914, *II*, 335.

2. James Joyce, *Giacomo Joyce* (London: Faber & Faber, 1984), 16.

3. Helen Barolini, "The Curious Case of Amalia Popper," *New York Review of Books*, November 20, 1969, 49; Stelio Crise and Bruno Chersicla, "Amalia Popper," in *è tornato Joyce* (Milan: Nuova Rivista Europea, 1982).

4. Roberto Curci, "Chi? Quella fiamma triestina," *Il Piccolo*, January 13, 1991.

5. Eileen Lanouette Hughes, "The Mystery Lady of 'Giacomo Joyce,' " *Life*, February 2, 1968, 40.

6. Ibid.

7. Michele Risolo, "Mia moglie e Joyce," *Corriere della Sera*, February 26, 1969, 11.

8. Roberto Curci, "Sylvia, scrittrice ritrovata," *Il Piccolo*, May 8, 1993, 3.

9. Barolini, "Curious Case," 48.

10. Stelio Crise, *And Trieste, Ah Trieste* (Milan: All'Insegna del Pesce d'Oro, 1971), xx.

11. JJ to EP, April 9, 1917, *I*, 101.

12. See Richard Ellmann, *James Joyce* (New York: Oxford University Press, 1982), 342–47.

13. See Ellmann, introduction to James Joyce, *Giacomo Joyce*.

14. Barolini, "Curious Case," 49.

15. Risolo, "Mia moglie e Joyce," 11.

16. Barolini, "Curious Case," 50.

17. Ibid.

18. Gianni Pinguentini, *James Joyce in Italia* (Verona: Linotipia Veronese di Ghidini e Fiorini, 1963), 225.

19. Hughes, "Mystery Lady," 37.

20. The information regarding Annie Schleimer came from an unpublished manuscript of Stelio Crise that was based on an interview with Zora Koren Skerk.

21. JJ to Mrs. William Murray, December 4, 1905, *II*, 129.

22. Alfonso Mottola interview with Stelio Crise, August 1991.

23. Alfonso Mottola interview with Eddy Schleimer, October 1993.

24. James Joyce, *Giacomo Joyce*, 1.

25. Ibid., 12.

26. Ibid., 16.

27. Alfonso Mottola interview with Zora Koren Skerk, July 1993.

28. James Joyce, *Giacomo Joyce*, 16.

29. Ibid., 14.

30. Mottola interview with Skerk.

31. James Joyce, *Giacomo Joyce*, 12.

32. Ibid., 14.

33. Hughes, "Mystery Lady," 40.

34. James Joyce, *Giacomo Joyce*, 6.

35. Archivio dell'Anagrafe comunale, Trieste.

36. JJ to Mrs. William Murray, December 4, 1905, *II*, 129.

37. Constantine Curran, memorial to Joyce, *Irish Times*, January 14, 1941, in *A Bash in the Tunnel*, ed. John Ryan (Brighton: Clifton Books, 1970), 244.

38. Cyril Connolly, *The Selected Essays of Cyril Connolly* (New York: Persea Books, 1984), 181.

39. James Joyce, *Giacomo Joyce*, 8.

40. Ibid., 9.

41. Ibid., 3.

42. JJ to SJ, September 9, 1913, *II*, 323.

43. JJ to G. Molyneux Palmer, October 6, 1913, *I*, 74.

44. Niny Rocco-Bergera, "James Joyce and Trieste," *JJQ* (Spring 1972): 345.

45. Ibid.

46. Ellmann, *James Joyce*, 316.

47. Arthur Power, "James Joyce—The Internationalist," in Ryan, *Bash*, 186.

48. Ibid., 187.

49. Richard Ellmann, *a long the riverrun* (New York: Alfred A. Knopf, 1989), 40.

50. Ellmann Collection, box 5, "Alessandro Francini-Bruni."

51. Ellmann, *James Joyce*, 316.

52. Ibid.

53. Constantine Curran, *James Joyce Remembered* (New York: Oxford University Press, 1968), 34.

54. Ellmann Collection, box 186, "Tullio Silvestri."

55. Roberto Prezioso to JJ, August 26, 1913, Cornell.

56. For further discussion, see Ellmann, *a long*, 33–45.

57. James Joyce, *Exiles* (New York: Penguin Books, 1983), 97.

58. Ibid., 36.

59. Ibid., 116.

60. Ibid., 68.

61. Ibid., 94.

62. James Joyce, *Giacomo Joyce*, 1.

63. James Joyce, *Exiles*, 17.

14. FINALLY, *DUBLINERS*

1. JJ to GR, November 23, 1913, *II*, 324.

2. Julian Symons, *Makers of the New: The Revolution in Literature, 1912–1939* (New York: Random House, 1987), 73.

3. Ezra Pound, *Pound/Joyce: The Letters of Ezra Pound to James Joyce*, ed. Forrest Read (New York: New Directions, 1967), 1.

4. EP to JJ, December 15, 1913, *Pound/Joyce*, 18.

5. EP to JJ, December 26, 1913, *Pound/Joyce*, 19.

6. EP to JJ, January 4, 1914, *Pound/Joyce*, 19.

7. For an interesting history of the publication, see Carl R. Dolmetsch, *The Smart Set* (New York: Dial Press, 1966).

8. JJ to GR, January 19, 1914, *II*, 328.

9. EP to JJ, January 17–19, 1914, *II*, 327.

10. Richard Ellmann, *James Joyce* (New York: Oxford University Press, 1982), 350.

11. Harriet Monroe, *A Poet's Life* (New York: Macmillan, 1938), 433.

12. Jane Lidderdale and Mary Nicholson, *Dear Miss Weaver* (New York: Viking Press, 1970), 83.

13. Ibid., 76.

14. Ibid., 83.

15. JJ to HSW, July 12, 1915, *I*, 83.

16. JJ to GR, January 19, 1914, *II*, 328.

17. JJ to GR, January 24, 1914, *II*, 329.

18. JJ to GR, March 4, 1914, *I*, 75.

19. JJ to GR, May 16, 1914, *II*, 334.

20. JJ to GR, June 19, 1914, *II*, 334.

21. Stelio Crise, *And Trieste, Ah Trieste* (Milan: All'Insegna del Pesce d'Oro, 1971), II.

22. JJ to John Quinn, July 10, 1917, *I*, 105.

23. Ettore Schmitz to JJ, June 26, 1914, *II*, 334.

24. Silvio Benco, "James Joyce in Trieste," in *Portraits of the Artist in Exile*, ed. Willard Potts (New York: Harcourt Brace Jovanovich, 1986), 55.

25. Ibid., 56.

26. JJ to GR, May 7, 1915, *II*, 340, n. 2.

27. JJ to James B. Pinker, July 7, 1915, *II*, 351.

28. EP to JJ, [April 1], 1914, *Pound/Joyce*, 25.

29. Robert McAlmon and Kay Boyle, *Being Geniuses Together* (London: Hogarth Press, 1984), 255.

30. Lidderdale and Nicholson, *Dear Miss Weaver*, 106.

31. Ibid., 83, 87.

32. Ibid., 92.

33. JJ to GR, July 3, 1914, *II*, 335.

34. Silvio Benco, "James Joyce in Trieste," 55.

35. Bruno Coceani and Cesare Pagnini, *Trieste della "belle époque"* (Trieste: Libreria "Universitas" Editrice, 1971), 290.

36. Ellmann, *James Joyce*, 382.

37. Ibid.

38. Dario de Tuoni, *Ricordo di Joyce a Trieste* (Milan: All'Insegna del Pesce d'Oro, 1966), 24.

39. Ibid., 26.

40. Ibid., 33.

41. Ibid., 36.

42. Ellmann, *James Joyce*, 383.

43. Ibid., 382.

15. BESIEGED

1. Gianni Pinguentini, *James Joyce in Italia* (Verona: Linotipia Veronese di Ghidini e Fiorini, 1963), 46.

2. Attilio Tamaro, *Storia di Trieste*, vol. 2 (Trieste: Edizioni Lint, 1976), 479.

3. Christopher Seton-Watson, *Italy from Liberalism to Fascism* (London: Methuen & Co., 1967), 406.

4. Tamaro, *Storia*, vol. 2, 477.

5. Ibid., 461.

6. Ibid., 450.

7. Seton-Watson, *Italy*, 407.

8. Silvio Benco, *Trieste e il suo diritto all'Italia* (Trieste: Cappelli, 1952), 99.

9. Silvio Benco, Il Piccolo *di Trieste* (Rome: Edizioni Fratelli Treves, 1931), 187.

10. Stelio Crise, *And Trieste, Ah Trieste* (Milan: All'Insegno del Pesce d'Oro, 1971), 23.

11. John Gatt-Rutter, *Italo Svevo: A Double Life* (New York: Oxford University Press, 1988), 270.

12. Ibid., 271.

13. Richard Ellmann, *James Joyce* (New York: Oxford University Press, 1982), 380.

14. JJ to HSW, November 11, 1914, *I*, 76.

15. Stelio Crise, "Il professore Zois? No, solo Jacomo," *Il Piccolo*, February 2, 1982, I.

16. Stelio Crise, *Epiphanies and Phadographs: Joyce e Trieste* (Milan: All'Insegna del Pesce d'Oro, 1967), 198.

17. Herbert Gorman, *James Joyce* (New York: Farrar & Rinehart, 1939), 257.

18. Letizia Svevo Fonda Savio and Antonio Fonda Savio, "James Joyce: Two Reminiscences," *JJQ* (Spring 1972): 321.

19. Frank Budgen, *James Joyce and the Making of* Ulysses (Bloomington: University of Indiana Press, 1960), 256.

20. James Joyce, *The Critical Writings of James Joyce*, ed. Ellsworth Mason and Richard Ellmann (Ithaca: Cornell University Press, 1989), 248.

21. Silvio Benco, "James Joyce in Trieste," in *Portraits of the Artist in Exile*, ed. Willard Potts (New York: Harcourt Brace Jovanovich, 1986), 50.

22. Ellmann, *James Joyce*, 697.

23. Ezra Pound, *Pound/Joyce: The Letters of Ezra Pound to James Joyce*, ed. Forrest Read (New York: New Directions, 1967), 258.

24. Jane Lidderdale and Mary Nicholson, *Dear Miss Weaver* (New York: Viking Press, 1970), 372.

25. Jacques Mercanton, "The Hours of James Joyce," in Potts, *Portraits*, 241.

26. Carola Giedion-Welcker, "Meetings with Joyce," in Potts, *Portraits*, 269.

27. Dominic Manganiello, *Joyce's Politics* (London: Routledge & Kegan Paul, 1980), 2.

28. JJ to Daniel Brody, June 16, 1938, *III*, 424; JJ to B. W. Huebsch, September 20, 1938, *III*, 430; JJ to Daniel Brody, October 5, 1938, *III*, 432; JJ to Edmund Brauchbar, February 23, 1939, *III*, 436.

29. Giedion-Welcker, "Meetings," 271.

30. Georges Borach, "Conversations with James Joyce," in Potts, *Portraits*, 71.

31. Llosa quoted in "Righting a mistake," *Boston Globe*, November 13, 1993, 24.

32. JJ to James B. Pinker, April 1, 1915, *II*, 338.

33. JJ to GR, April 5, 1915, *I*, 78.

34. H. L. Mencken to JJ, April 20, 1915, *I*, 79.

35. Ann McCullough, "Joyce's Early Publishing History," in *James Joyce: The Centennial Symposium*, ed. Morris Beja et al. (Chicago: University of Illinois Press, 1986), 184.

36. H. L. Mencken to JJ, April 20, 1915, *I*, 79.

37. B. W. Huebsch to JJ, June 2, 1915, *I*, 81.

38. Crise, *And Trieste*, 14.

39. Ellmann, *James Joyce*, 385.

40. Benco, *Il Piccolo*, 207.

41. Ibid., 202.

42. Ennio Maserati, "Il socialismo triestino," *Trieste*, November/December 1964, 9.

43. Benco, *Il Piccolo*, 219.

44. Tamaro, *Storia*, vol. 2, 484.

45. Claudio Silvestri, "La missione di Prezioso," *Trieste*, September/October 1960, 27.

46. Janet Penrose Trevelyan, *A Short History of the Italian People* (New York: Putman Publishing Co., 1956), 378.

47. Crise, *And Trieste*, 23.

48. Bogdan C. Novak, *Trieste, 1941–1954* (Chicago: University of Chicago Press, 1970), 24.

49. Gatt-Rutter, *Italo Svevo*, 277.

50. Benco, *Trieste*, 100.

51. Gatt-Rutter, *Italo Svevo*, 283.

52. JJ to A. Llewelyn Roberts, July 30, 1915, *II*, 357.

53. Benco, "James Joyce in Trieste," 55.

54. H. and B. Astori, *La passione di Trieste*, quoted in P. N. Furbank, *Italo Svevo: The Man and the Writer* (Berkeley: University of California Press, 1966), 102.

55. Crise, *Epiphanies*, 198.

56. Ellmann Collection, box 6, "Ralph C. Busser Jr."

57. JJ to A. Llewelyn Roberts, July 30, 1915, *II*, 357.

58. JJ to HSW, October 28, 1919, *II*, 455.

59. Stelio Crise and Bruno Chersicla, "Francesco Sordina," in *è tornato Joyce* (Milan: Nuova Rivista Europea, 1982).

60. Ambrogio Ralli to JJ, March 19, 1919, Cornell; Ambrogio Ralli to JJ, May 27, 1920, Cornell.

61. JJ to HSW, June 30, 1915, *I*, 82.

16. THE WAR YEARS

1. Alessandro Francini-Bruni, "Recollections of Joyce," in *Portraits of the Artist in Exile*, ed. Willard Potts (New York: Harcourt Brace Jovanovich, 1986), 43.

2. Richard Ellmann, *James Joyce* (New York: Oxford University Press, 1982), 389.

3. JJ to James B. Pinker, June 30, 1915, *II*, 349.

4. JJ to EP, [about July 15, 1915], *II*, 353.

5. Letizia Svevo Fonda Savio and Antonio Fonda Savio, "James Joyce: Two Reminiscences," *JJQ* (Spring 1972): 321.

6. James Longenbach, *Stone Cottage: Pound, Yeats and Modernism* (New York: Oxford University Press, 1988), 182.

7. Slack, Monro, Saw and Co. to JJ, February 22, 1917, *II*, 389.

8. Jane Lidderdale and Mary Nicholson, *Dear Miss Weaver* (New York: Viking Press, 1970), 117.

9. Edmund Wilson, *Letters on Literature and Politics 1912–1972*, ed. Elena Wilson (New York: Farrar, Straus, Giroux, 1977), 30.

10. JJ to B. W. Huebsch, July 7, 1915, *II*, 350.

11. Monro, Saw and Company to JJ, June 24, 1919, *II*, 445.

12. Lidderdale and Nicholson, *Dear Miss Weaver*, 160.

13. JJ to HSW, July 20, 1919, *SL*, 240.

14. Lidderdale and Nicholson, *Dear Miss Weaver*, 380.

15. Mary T. Reynolds, "Joyce and Miss Weaver," *JJQ* (Summer 1982): 384.

16. Lidderdale and Nicholson, *Dear Miss Weaver*, 455.

17. JJ to Harriet Monroe, August 12, 1917, *II*, 403.

18. SJ to JJ, May 25, 1919, *II*, 443.

19. Stelio Crise and Bruno Chersicla, "Diodato Tripcovich," in *è tornato Joyce* (Milan: Nuova Rivista Europea, 1982).

20. JJ to SJ, [July 31, 1919], *II*, 446.

21. Patricia Hutchins, *James Joyce's World* (London: Methuen & Co., 1957), 100.

22. JJ to SJ, [July 31, 1919], *II*, 446.

23. Ellmann, *James Joyce*, 470.

24. Alice Curtayne, "Pappy Never Spoke of Jim's Books," interview with Eileen Joyce Schaurek in *James Joyce: Interviews and Recollections*, ed. E. H. Mikhail (New York: St. Martin's Press, 1990), 66.

25. Bozena Berta Delimata, "Reminiscences of a Joyce Niece," *JJQ* (Fall 1981): 47.

26. Ellmann, *James Joyce*, 471.

27. Delimata, "Reminiscences," 47.

28. Ibid.

29. Silvio Benco, "James Joyce in Trieste," in Potts, *Portraits*, 57.

30. JJ to HSW, October 28, 1919, *II*, 455.

31. JJ to James B. Pinker, November 7, 1919, *I*, 130.

32. JJ to James B. Pinker, December 7, 1919, *II*, 456.

33. JJ to FB, January 3, 1920, *I*, 134.

34. JJ to FB, November 7, 1919, *I*, 130.

35. JJ to HSW, January 6, 1920, *I*, 136.

36. JJ to FB, [? end 1919], *I*, 131.

37. Francini-Bruni, "Recollections," 44.

38. JJ to FB, January 3, 1920, *I*, 135.

39. JJ to FB, [? end 1919], *I*, 131.

40. NB to FB, January 27, 1920, *II*, 457.

41. P. A. Quarantotti Gambini, "Giotti, Ferravilla, e Svevo," *Il Piccolo*, May 1, 1960, 3.

42. Alfonso Mottola interview with Tanda Giotti, December 1991.

43. Donald Prater, *A Ringing Glass: The Life of Rainer Maria Rilke* (New York: Oxford University Press, 1986), 171.

44. Giani Stuparich, *Trieste nei miei ricordi* (Milan: Edizioni Garzanti, 1948), 10.

45. JJ to SJ, postmark October 3, 1905, *II*, 113.

46. JJ to FB, January 3, 1920, *I*, 134.

47. Richard M. Kain, "An Interview with Carola Giedion-Welcker and Maria Jolas," *JJQ* (Winter 1974): 100.

48. Constantine Curran, *James Joyce Remembered* (New York: Oxford University Press, 1968), 35.

49. Stelio Crise, *And Trieste, Ah Trieste* (Milan: All'Insegna del Pesce d'Oro, 1971), 14.

50. Benco, "James Joyce in Trieste," 57.

51. Ibid., 58.

52. JJ to FB, January 3, 1920, *I*, 134.

53. Ernest Hemingway, *A Farewell to Arms* (New York: Charles Scribner's Sons, 1957), 74.

54. Ibid., 50.

55. Charles Jelavich and Barbara Jelavich, *The Establishment of the Balkan National States* (Seattle: University of Washington Press, 1977), 301.

56. Muriel Grindrod, *Italy* (New York: Frederick A. Praeger, 1968), 166.

57. Gerardo Zampaglione, *Italy* (New York: Frederick A. Praeger, 1956), 91.

58. John Gatt-Rutter, *Italo Svevo: A Double Life* (New York: Oxford University Press, 1988), 296.

59. JJ to Carlo Linati, May 2, 1920, *II*, 463.

60. JJ to EP, June 5, 1920, *II*, 467.

61. Adrian Lyttelton, *The Seizure of Power: Fascism in Italy 1919–1929* (Princeton: Princeton University Press, 1987), 53.

62. Ennio Maserati, "Il socialismo triestino durante la grande guerra," *Trieste*, November/December 1964, 10.

63. Gatt-Rutter, *Italo Svevo*, 299.

64. Carlo Schiffrer, "Fascisti e militari nell'incendio del Balkan," *Trieste*, May/June 1963, 16.

65. Gatt-Rutter, *Italo Svevo*, 297.

66. JJ to SJ, March 20, 1922, *III*, 61.

17. FAME BECKONS

1. Richard M. Kain, "An Interview with Carola Giedion-Welcker and Maria Jolas," *JJQ* (Winter 1974): 103.

2. Mary Colum, *Life and the Dream* (Garden City, N.J.: Doubleday & Company, 1947),

383.

3. Frank Budgen, *James Joyce and the Making of* Ulysses (Bloomington: University of Indiana Press, 1960), 12.

4. Frank Budgen, *Myselves When Young* (New York: Oxford University Press, 1970), 198.

5. Herbert Gorman, *James Joyce* (New York: Farrar & Rinehart, 1939), 143.

6. Paul Hofmann, *Cento città* (New York: Henry Holt and Company, 1988), 14.

7. "La città piu vecchia," *Il Piccolo*, April 1991.

8. JJ to SJ, July 25, 1920, *III*, 10.

9. JJ to FB, January 3, 1920, *I*, 134.

10. Richard Ellmann, *James Joyce* (New York: Oxford University Press, 1982), 472.

11. Ibid., 473.

12. JJ to FB, [early February 1920], *III*, 458.

13. Silvio Benco, "James Joyce in Trieste," in *Portraits of the Artist in Exile*, ed. Willard Potts (New York: Harcourt Brace Jovanovich, 1986), 58.

14. Ellmann, *James Joyce*, 472.

15. JJ to John Quinn, March 11, 1920, *II*, 460.

16. JJ to FB, January 3, 1920, *I*, 134.

17. JJ to FB, [early February 1920], *II*, 458.

18. JJ to FB, March 15, 1920, *I*, 138.

19. Frank Budgen, "James Joyce," in *James Joyce: Two Decades of Criticism*, ed. Seon Givens (New York: Vanguard Press, 1963), 20.

20. Budgen, *Myselves When Young*, 200.

21. JJ to FB, [early February 1920], *II*, 458.

22. JJ to FB, January 3, 1920, *I*, 134.

23. JJ to HSW, June 24, 1921, *I*, 165.

24. Ibid., 167.

25. JJ to HSW, February 25, 1920, *I*, 136.

26. JJ to FB, May 18, 1920, *II*, 464.

27. Corinna del Greco Lobner, *James Joyce's Italian Connection* (Iowa City: University of Iowa Press, 1989), 94.

28. JJ to Carlo Linati, March 11, 1920, *II*, 462, n. 1.

29. Margaret Anderson, *My Thirty Years' War* (New York: Horizon Press, 1969), 175.

30. B. L. Reid, *The Man from New York: John Quinn and His Friends* (New York: Oxford University Press, 1968), 441.

31. JJ to FB, March 15, 1920, *I*, 138; JJ to FB, [? March 20, 1920], *I*, 139.

32. JJ to Carlo Linati, May 11, 1920, *I*, 140.

33. JJ to EP, June 5, 1920, *II*, 467.

34. EP to JJ, June 7–8, 1920, in Ezra Pound, *Pound/Joyce: The Letters of Ezra Pound to James Joyce*, ed. Forrest Read (New York: New Directions, 1967), 177.

35. JJ to HSW, July 12, 1920, *I*, 142.

36. EP to John Quinn, June 19, 1920, in Ezra Pound, *Selected Letters 1907–1941*, ed. D. D. Paige (New York: New Directions, 1971), 153.

37. JJ to Carlo Linati, July 1, 1920, *I*, 142.

38. Richard Ellmann, *The Consciousness of Joyce* (New York: Oxford University Press, 1977), 6.

39. JJ to Sylvia Beach, n.d., 1927, *I*, 253.

40. Sylvia Beach, *Shakespeare and Company* (Lincoln: University of Nebraska Press, 1980), 38.

41. Ellmann, *James Joyce*, 481.

42. JJ to SJ, July 25, 1920, *III*, 11, n. 1.

43. JJ to SJ, July 25, 1920, *III*, 11.

18. PARIS-TRIESTE

1. Peter Ackroyd, *T. S. Eliot: A Life* (New York: Simon and Schuster, 1984), 102.
2. JJ to Alessandro Francini-Bruni, July 19, 1920, *III*, 8.
3. JJ to James B. Pinker, July 15, 1920, *I*, 143.
4. JJ to SJ, July 25, 1920, *III*, 10.
5. JJ to HSW, July 12, 1920, *I*, 143.
6. JJ to Jenny Serruys, October 20, 1920, *III*, 25.
7. JJ to SJ, October 28, 1920, *III*, 26.
8. JJ to SJ, October 28, 1920, *III*, 26.
9. Nino Frank, "The Shadow That Had Lost Its Man," in *Portraits of the Artist in Exile*, ed. Willard Potts (New York: Harcourt Brace Jovanovich, 1986), 83.
10. Silvio Benco, "James Joyce in Trieste," in Potts, *Portraits*, 50.
11. JJ to FB, July 27, 1920, *I*, 144.
12. JJ to SJ, September 14, 1920, *III*, 22.
13. JJ to EP, December 12, 1920, *III*, 34.
14. JJ to Ettore Schmitz, January 5, 1921, *I*, 154.
15. JJ to HSW, June 24, 1921, *I*, 166.
16. Sylvia Beach, *Shakespeare and Company* (Lincoln: University of Nebraska Press, 1980), 84.
17. JJ to Alessandro Francini-Bruni, June 7, 1921, *III*, 44.
18. JJ to Alessandro Francini-Bruni, December 30, 1921, *III*, 56.
19. James Joyce, *Exiles* (New York: Penguin Books, 1983), 44.
20. JJ to HSW, March 11, 1922, *I*, 182.
21. Stelio Crise, *And Trieste, Ah Trieste* (Milan: All'Insegna del Pesce d'Oro, 1971), 41.
22. Ibid.
23. Benco, "James Joyce in Trieste," 55.
24. Ettore Schmitz to JJ, June 10, 1924, *III*, 98.
25. Ibid.
26. SJ to JJ, February 26, 1922, *III*, 58.
27. Richard Ellmann, *Four Dubliners* (New York: George Braziller, 1987), 66.
28. SJ to JJ, February 26, 1922, *III*, 59.
29. Richard Ellmann, *James Joyce* (New York: Oxford University Press, 1982), 467.
30. Herbert Gorman, *James Joyce* (New York: Farrar & Rinehart, 1939), 265.
31. JJ to Alessandro Francini-Bruni, July 23, 1924, *III*, 101.
32. Jacques Mercanton, "The Hours of James Joyce," in Potts, *Portraits*, 243.
33. Dario de Tuoni, *Ricordo di Joyce a Trieste* (Milan: All'Insegna del Pesce d'Oro, 1966), 53.
34. JJ to Jacques Mercanton, March 14, 1940, *III*, 470.
35. SJ to JJ, August 7, 1924, *III*, 102.
36. SJ to JJ, February 26, 1922, *III*, 59.
37. JJ to SJ, March 20, 1922, *III*, 61.
38. SJ to JJ, August 7, 1924, *III*, 101.
39. Ibid., 103, 104, 105.
40. JJ to SJ, September 28, 1925, *III*, 127.
41. JJ to SJ, March 26, 1926, *III*, 139.
42. JJ to Ettore Schmitz, January 30, 1924, *III*, 86.
43. Ettore Schmitz to JJ, June 10, 1924, *III*, 98.

44. John Gatt-Rutter, *Italo Svevo: A Double Life* (New York: Oxford University Press, 1988), 319.

45. Livia Veneziani Svevo, *Memoir of Italo Svevo* (Marlboro, Vermont: Marlboro Press, 1990), 83.

46. Stelio Crise and Bruno Chersicla, "Dario de Tuoni," in *è tornato Joyce* (Milan: Nuova Rivista Europea, 1982).

47. Gatt-Rutter, *Italo Svevo*, 325.

48. Silvio Benco, "Italo Svevo," *Pegaso* 1 (January 1929): 57.

49. Veneziani Svevo, *Memoir*, 85.

50. Noel Riley Fitch, *Sylvia Beach* (New York: W. W. Norton & Company, 1983), 425.

51. Ellmann, *James Joyce*, 560.

52. Niny Rocco-Bergera, "Italo Svevo and Trieste," *Modern Fiction Studies* (Spring 1972): 113.

53. JJ to Valery Larbaud, [? October 7, 1928], *III*, 183.

54. Gatt-Rutter, *Italo Svevo*, 329.

55. Veneziani Svevo, *Memoir*, 112.

56. R. Rendi, "Italo Svevo Waited Long for Fame," *New York Times Book Review*, November 11, 1928, 8.

57. JJ to Ettore Schmitz, November 21, 1925, *III*, 132.

58. Ettore Schmitz to JJ, February 15, 1926, *III*, 136.

59. Francesca Avon, "Per fortuna c'era Stannie," *Il Piccolo*, February 2, 1982, III.

60. Gatt-Rutter, *Italo Svevo*, 340.

61. Nino Frank, "The Shadow That Had Lost Its Man," in Potts, *Portraits*, 82.

62. JJ to SJ, [March 16, 1928], *III*, 171.

63. Ettore Schmitz to JJ, March 27, 1928, *III*, 172.

64. JJ to Ettore Schmitz, April 6, 1928, *III*, 175.

65. Mary Colum and Padraic Colum, *Our Friend James Joyce* (Garden City, N.J.: Doubleday & Company, 1958), 112.

66. JJ to HSW, February 18, 1927, *SL*, 320.

67. Ettore Schmitz to JJ, September 30, 1926, *III*, 143.

68. JJ to SJ, November 5, 1926, *III*, 145.

69. JJ to SJ, December 15, 1926, *III*, 148.

70. JJ to SJ, January 8, 1927, *III*, 149.

71. JJ to SJ, postmark March 22, 1928, *III*, 172.

72. JJ to Livia Schmitz, September 24, 1928, *I*, 270.

73. James Joyce, *The Critical Writings of James Joyce*, ed. Ellsworth Mason and Richard Ellmann (Ithaca: Cornell University Press, 1989), 257.

74. Lucia Joyce to Livia Schmitz, January 25, 1931, *I*, 298.

75. JJ to Valery Larbaud, April 13, 1931.

76. JJ to SJ, April 14, 1931, *III*, 216.

77. JJ to SJ, May 12, 1931, *III*, 219.

78. JJ to SJ, March 29, 1932, *III*, 241.

79. Crise, *And Trieste*, 49.

80. JJ to SJ, July 18, 1931, *III*, 221.

81. SJ to Herbert Gorman, August 8, 1931, *III*, 225.

82. JJ to SJ, August 22, 1931, *III*, 227.

83. Crise, *And Trieste*, 48.

84. JJ to Livia Veneziani Svevo, [January 1, 1939], III, 435.

85. JJ to Livia Veneziani Svevo, April 4, 1939, *I*, 404.

86. JJ to Livia Veneziani Svevo, [May 1, 1939], *III*, 439.

87. James Joyce, *Finnegans Wake* (New York: Viking Press, 1957), 301.

88. Veneziani Svevo, *Memoir*, 32.

89. JJ to Silvio Benco, [? April 1937], Biblioteca Civica in Trieste.

90. JJ to Dario de Tuoni, February 20, 1940, *III*, 467.

91. Dario de Tuoni, "James Joyce," *La Fiera Letteraria*, February 26, 1961, 5.

92. SJ to JJ, April 12, 1936, *III*, 381.

93. SJ to JJ, April 24, 1936, *III*, 382.

94. SJ to JJ, May 11, 1936, *III*, 383.

95. Ellmann, *James Joyce*, 697.

96. SJ to JJ, November 15, 1936, *III*, 392.

97. Denis Mack Smith, *Mussolini's Roman Empire* (New York: Viking Press, 1976), 28.

98. JJ to Carola Giedion-Welcker, November 18, 1936, *III*, 393.

99. JJ to Carola Giedion-Welcker, [? May 18], 1937, *III*, 397.

100. JJ to SJ, January 4, 1941, *III*, 507.

CONCLUSION

1. Philippe Soupault, "James Joyce," in *Portraits of the Artist in Exile*, ed. Willard Potts (New York: Harcourt Brace Jovanovich, 1986), 110.

2. Pierluigi Sabatti, "Così cocolo, gioviale," *Il Piccolo*, February 2, 1982, III.

3. Jacques Mercanton, "The Hours of James Joyce," in Potts, *Portraits*, 242.

4. Alessandro Francini-Bruni, "Recollections of Joyce," in Potts, *Portraits*, 45.

5. James Joyce, *Ulysses* (New York: Random House, 1961), 782.

6. JJ to HSW, June 27, 1924, *I*, 215.

7. Padraic Colum, "A Portrait of James Joyce," *New Republic*, May 13, 1931, 347.

8. EP to JJ, [about September 7, 1915], *II*, 364.

9. Constantine Curran, *James Joyce Remembered* (New York: Oxford University Press, 1968), 73.

10. Italo Svevo, *James Joyce* (New York: New Directions, 1950), 11.

11. Richard Ellmann, "A Portrait of the Artist as Friend," *Kenyon Review* (Winter 1956): 67.

12. Philippe Soupault, "James Joyce," in Potts, *Portraits*, 110.

13. Umberto Saba, "Trieste," in *Scrittori triestini del Novecento*, ed. O. H. Bianchi et al. (Trieste: Edizioni Lint, 1968), 561.

Bibliography

JAMES JOYCE

Ackroyd, Peter. *T. S. Eliot: A Life*. New York: Simon and Schuster, 1984.

Anderson, Chester G. *James Joyce*. London: Thames & Hudson, 1967.

Anderson, Margaret. *The Little Review Anthology*. New York: Hermitage House, 1953.

———. *My Thirty Years' War*. New York: Horizon Press, 1969.

Barolini, Helen. "The Curious Case of Amalia Popper." *New York Review of Books*, November 20, 1969.

Barry, Alyce, ed. *Djuna Barnes/Interviews*. Washington, D. C.: Sun and Moon Press, 1985.

Beach, Sylvia. *Shakespeare and Company*. Lincoln: University of Nebraska Press, 1980.

Beckson, Karl. *Arthur Symons: A Life*. New York: Oxford University Press, 1987.

Beckson, Karl, and John M. Monro. "Letters from Arthur Symons to James Joyce: 1904–1932." *JJQ* 4 (1966/67).

Beja, Morris, Phillip Herring, Maurice Harmon, and David Norris, eds. *James Joyce: The Centennial Symposium*. Chicago: University of Illinois Press, 1986.

Benco, Aurelia Gruber. "Between Joyce and Benco." *JJQ* (Spring 1972).

Benco, Silvio. "Italo Svevo." *Pegaso* 1, January 1929.

———. "Un illustre scrittore inglese a Trieste." *Umana* 1 (July 6, 1918).

Berrone, Louis. *James Joyce in Padua*. New York: Random House, 1977.

Bianchini, Angela. "Vita con James Joyce." *Approdo* 6 (1960).

Bosinelli Bollettieri, Rosa Maria. "The Importance of Trieste in Joyce's Work." *JJQ* (Spring 1970).

Brancati, Vitaliano. "Recollections of Professor Joyce." *JJQ* (Fall 1981).

Brown, Edward J. *Mayakovsky*. New York: Paragon House, 1988.

Budgen, Frank. *James Joyce and the Making of* Ulysses. Bloomington: University of Indiana Press, 1960.

———. *Myselves When Young*. New York: Oxford University Press, 1970.

Byrne, J. F. *Silent Years*. New York: Farrar, Straus, and Young, 1953.

Colum, Mary. *Life and the Dream*. Garden City, N.J.: Doubleday & Company, 1947.

Colum, Mary, and Padraic Colum. *Our Friend James Joyce*. Garden City, N.J.: Doubleday & Company, 1958.

Colum, Padraic. "A Portrait of James Joyce." *New Republic*, May 13, 1931.

Comitato Per L'Anno Joyciano. *Il ritorno di Joyce*. Trieste: 1982.

Connolly, Cyril. *The Selected Essays of Cyril Connolly*. Edited by Peter Quennell. New York: Persea Books, 1984.

Costello, Peter. *James Joyce: The Years of Growth 1882–1915*. New York: Pantheon Books, 1992.

Crise, Stelio. *Epiphanies and Phadographs: Joyce e Trieste*. Milan: All'Insegna del Pesce d'Oro, 1967.

———. "Humus triestino dell'opera di James Joyce." *Umana* (November/December 1969).

———. "Joyce e Trieste." *Accademie e biblioteche d'Italia* 29 (1961).

Crise, Stelio, and Bruno Chersicla. *è tornato Joyce*. Milan: Nuova Rivista Europea, 1982.

Curci, Roberto. *Tutto è sciolto: L'amore triestino di Giacomo Joyce*. Trieste: Edizioni Lint, 1996.

Curran, Constantine. *James Joyce Remembered*. New York: Oxford University Press, 1968.

del Greco Lobner, Corinna. *James Joyce's Italian Connection*. Iowa City: University of Iowa Press, 1989.

———. *James Joyce's Italian Experience: Trovatore in Trieste*. Ann Arbor: University Microfilms International, 1981.

Delimata, Bozena Berta. "Reminiscences of a Joyce Niece." *JJQ* (Fall 1981).

de Tuoni, Dario. "James Joyce nella vecchia Trieste." *La Fiera Letteraria*, February 26, 1961.

———. "L'ultima casa di Joyce a Trieste." *La Fiera Letteraria*, no. 18, 1961.

———. *Ricordo di Joyce a Trieste*. Milan: All'Insegna del Pesce d'Oro, 1966.

Dillon, Eilís. "The Innocent Muse: An Interview with Maria Jolas." *JJQ* (Fall 1982).

Domian, Sergio. "I dieci anni triestini di James Joyce." *L'Interprete* 2 (1959).

Edel, Leon. *Stuff of Sleep and Dreams*. New York: Harper and Row, 1982.

Ellmann, Richard. *a long the riverrun*. New York: Alfred A. Knopf, 1989.

———. *The Consciousness of Joyce*. New York: Oxford University Press, 1977.

———. *Four Dubliners*. New York: George Braziller, 1987.

———. *James Joyce*. New York: Oxford University Press, 1982.

———. "James Joyce, Irish European." *Umana* (May/September 1971).

———. "Joyce and Yeats." *Kenyon Review* (Autumn 1950).

———. "A Portrait of the Artist as Friend." *Kenyon Review* (Winter 1956).

———. "Speaking of Books: Italo Svevo and Joyce." *New York Times Book Review*, January 21, 1968.

Fairhall, James. *James Joyce and the Question of History*. Cambridge: Cambridge University Press, 1993.

Fitch, Noel Riley. *Sylvia Beach and the Lost Generation*. New York: W. W. Norton & Company, 1983.

Furbank, P. N. *Italo Svevo: The Man and the Writer*. Berkeley: University of California Press, 1966.

Galli, Lina. "Livia Veneziani Svevo and James Joyce." *JJQ* (Spring 1972).

———. "Svevo and Irredentism." *Modern Fiction Studies* (Spring 1972).

Gatt-Rutter, John. *Italo Svevo: A Double Life*. New York: Oxford University Press, 1988.

Gillet, Louis. *Claybook for James Joyce*. Translated by Georges Markow-Totevy. New York: Abelard & Schuman, 1958.

Givens, Seon, ed. *James Joyce: Two Decades of Criticism*. New York: Vanguard Press, 1963.

Gogarty, Oliver St. John. *It Isn't This Time of Year at All!* Westport, Conn.: Greenwood Press, 1954.

———. "The Joyce I Knew." *Saturday Review of Literature*, January 25, 1941.

————. *Mourning Becomes Mrs. Spendlove*. New York: Creative Age Press, 1948.

————. "They Think They Know Joyce." *Saturday Review of Literature*, March 18, 1950.

Gorman, Herbert. *James Joyce*. New York: Farrar & Rinehart, 1939.

Gregory, Lady Augusta. *Seventy Years: 1852–1922*. New York: Macmillan Publishing Co., 1974.

Guidi, Augusto. "Gli anni triestini di Joyce." *Umana* (May/September 1971).

Hughes, Eileen Lanouette. "The Mystery Lady of 'Giacomo Joyce.' " *Life*, February 2, 1968.

Hutchins, Patricia. *James Joyce's World*. London: Methuen & Co., 1957.

Joyce, James. *Araby*. Translated into Italian by Amalia Popper. Empoli: Ibiskos Editrice, 1991.

————. *Chamber Music*. Edited by William York Tindall. New York: Columbia University Press, 1954.

————. *Collected Poems*. New York: Viking Press, 1944.

————. *The Critical Writings of James Joyce*. Edited by Ellsworth Mason and Richard Ellmann. Ithaca: Cornell University Press, 1989.

————. *Dubliners*. New York: Penguin Books, 1983.

————. *Exiles*. New York: Penguin Books, 1983.

————. *Finnegans Wake*. New York: Viking Press, 1957.

————. *Giacomo Joyce*. London: Faber & Faber, 1984.

————. *Letters of James Joyce*. Edited by Stuart Gilbert. Vol. 1. New York: Viking Press, 1966.

————. *Letters of James Joyce*. Edited by Richard Ellmann. Vols. 2 and 3. New York: Viking Press, 1967.

————. *Letters to Sylvia Beach 1921–1940*. Edited by Melissa Banta and Oscar A. Silverman. Indianapolis: Indiana University Press, 1987.

————. *Poesie e prose*. Edited by Franca Ruggieri. Milan: Arnoldo Mondadori, 1992.

————. *A Portrait of the Artist as a Young Man*. Edited by Chester G. Anderson. New York: Penguin Books, 1982.

————. *Selected Letters*. Edited by Richard Ellmann. New York: Viking Press, 1976.

————. *Stephen Hero*. New York: New Directions, 1963.

————. *Ulysses*. New York: Random House, 1961.

Joyce, Stanislaus. *The Complete Dublin Diary of Stanislaus Joyce*. Edited by George H. Healey. Ithaca: Cornell University Press, 1971.

————. *Joyce nel giardino di Svevo* (Joyce in Svevo's Garden). Edited by Carlo Giovanella. Trieste: MGS Press Editrice, 1995.

————. "Joyce and Svevo." *Stork*, September 1932.

————. *The Meeting of Svevo and Joyce*. Edited by Sergio Perosa. Trieste: Del Bianco, 1965.

————. *My Brother's Keeper*. New York: Viking Press, 1958.

————. "Ricordi di James Joyce." *Letteratura* (July/September 1941).

Kain, Richard M. "An Interview with Carola Giedion-Welcker and Maria Jolas." *JJQ* (Winter 1974).

Lebowitz, Naomi. *Italo Svevo*. New Brunswick, N.J.: Rutgers University Press, 1978.

Levin, Harry, ed. "Carteggio inedito: Italo Svevo-James Joyce." *Inventario* (Spring 1949).

————. *James Joyce*. New York: New Directions, 1960.

Lewis, Wyndham. *Blasting & Bombardiering*. Berkeley: University of California Press, 1967.

Lidderdale, Jane, and Mary Nicholson. *Dear Miss Weaver*. New York: Viking Press, 1970.

Linati, Carlo. "A Visit with Joyce." *JJQ* (Fall 1981).

Longenbach, James. *Stone Cottage: Pound, Yeats, and Modernism*. New York: Oxford

University Press, 1988.

MacCabe, Colin, ed. *James Joyce: New Perspectives.* Bloomington: Indiana University Press, 1982.

Maddox, Brenda. *Nora: The Real Life of Molly Bloom.* Boston: Houghton Mifflin Company, 1988.

Magalaner, Marvin, ed. *A James Joyce Miscellany.* Carbondale: Southern Illinois University Press, 1962.

Magalaner, Marvin, and Richard M. Kain. *Joyce: The Man, the Work, the Reputation.* Oxford: Plantin, 1990.

Mahaffey, Vicki. "Fascism and Silence: The Coded History of Amalia Popper." *JJQ* (Spring and Summer 1995).

Maier, Bruno. "Joyce, Trieste, e Svevo." *Rotary.* Rivista Mensile dei Rotary Club d'Italia (April 1982).

Manganiello, Dominic. *Joyce's Politics.* London: Routledge & Kegan Paul, 1980.

Mattioni, Stelio. "My Friend, James Joyce." *JJQ* (Spring 1972).

McAlmon, Robert, and Kay Boyle. *Being Geniuses Together.* London: Hogarth Press, 1984.

Melchiori, Giorgio. "Mr. Bloom in Venice." *JJQ* (Fall 1989).

Mikhail, E. H., ed. *James Joyce: Interviews and Recollections.* New York: St. Martin's Press, 1990.

Monroe, Harriet. *A Poet's Life.* New York: Macmillan, 1938.

Moore, Harry T. *The Priest of Love: A Life of D. H. Lawrence.* New York: Penguin, 1981.

Mottola, Alfonso. *Immagini triestine per Giacomo Joyce.* Supplement to *JJQ* (Spring 1991).

Nadel, Ira B. *Joyce and the Jews.* Iowa City: University of Iowa Press, 1989.

Nelson, James G. "James Joyce's First Publisher: Elkin Mathews and the Advent of *Chamber Music.*" *JJQ* (Fall 1985).

O'Brien, Edna. "Joyce and Nora." *Harper's,* September 1980.

O'Connor, Ulick. *All the Olympians: A Biographical Portrait of the Irish Literary Renaissance.* New York: Atheneum, 1984.

———. *Oliver St. John Gogarty.* London: Jonathan Cape, 1963.

O'Laoi, Padraic. *Nora Barnacle Joyce: A Portrait.* Galway: Kennys Bookshops and Art Galleries, 1982.

Pearl, Cyril. *Dublin in Bloomtime.* New York: Viking Press, 1969.

Pinguentini, Gianni. "James Joyce a Trieste nella casa di via Bramante." *La Porta Orientale* (April 1970).

———. *James Joyce in Italia.* Verona: Linotipia Veronese di Ghidini e Fiorini, 1963.

Poliaghi, Nora Franca. "James Joyce: An Occasion of Remembrance." *JJQ* (Spring 1972).

Potts, Willard. "Joyce and Carlo Linati." *JJQ* (Fall 1981).

———, ed. *Portraits of the Artist in Exile.* New York: Harcourt Brace Jovanovich, 1986.

Pound, Ezra. *Pound/Joyce: The Letters of Ezra Pound to James Joyce.* Edited by Forrest Read. New York: New Directions, 1967.

———. *Selected Letters 1907–1941.* Edited by D. D. Paige. New York: New Directions, 1971.

Power, Arthur. *Conversations with James Joyce.* Chicago: University of Chicago Press, 1982.

Prater, Donald. *A Ringing Glass: The Life of Rainer Maria Rilke.* New York: Oxford University Press, 1986.

Ramelli, Adriana. "Joyce e Trieste." *Lettere Venete* (April/September 1961).

Reid, B. L. *The Man from New York: John Quinn and His Friends.* New York: Oxford University Press, 1968.

Rendi, R. "Italo Svevo Waited Long for Fame." *New York Times Book Review,* November 11, 1928.

Reynolds, Mary T. "Joyce and Miss Weaver." *JJQ* (Summer 1982).

Risolo, Michele. "Mia moglie e Joyce." *Corriere della Sera*, February 26, 1969.

Rocco-Bergera, Niny, ed. *Atti del Third International James Joyce Symposium*. Trieste: Università degli Studi, Facoltà di Magistero, 1974.

———. "Italo Svevo and Trieste." *Modern Fiction Studies* (Spring 1972).

———. "James Joyce and Trieste." *JJQ* (Spring 1972).

———. "Joyce and Svevo: A Note." *Modern Fiction Studies* (Spring 1972).

———. Review of *Ricordo di Joyce a Trieste*, by Dario de Tuoni. *JJQ* (Summer 1969).

Rocco-Bergera, Niny, and Carlina Rebecchi-Piperata. *Itinerary of Joyce and Svevo through Artistic Trieste*. Trieste: Azienda Autonoma Soggiorno e Turismo, 1970.

Ryan, John, ed. *A Bash in the Tunnel*. Brighton: Clifton Books, 1970.

Scholes, Robert. *The Cornell Joyce Collection*. Ithaca: Cornell University Press, 1961.

Senn, Fritz, ed. *New Light of Joyce from the Dublin Symposium*. Bloomington: Indiana University Press, 1972.

Spoo, Robert. "Joyce's Attitudes toward History: Rome, 1906-07." *Journal of Modern Literature* (Spring 1988).

Staley, Thomas F. "James Joyce and Italo Svevo." *Italica* 40, no. 4 (1963).

———. "James Joyce in Trieste." *Georgia Review* (October 1962).

———, ed. *Joyce Studies Annual 1992*. Austin: University of Texas Press, 1992.

———. "The Search for Leopold Bloom: James Joyce and Italo Svevo." *JJQ* (Summer 1964).

Stock, Noel. *The Life of Ezra Pound*. New York: Pantheon Books, 1970.

Summerfield, Henry. *That Myriad-Minded Man: A Biography of G. W. Russell—A.E.* Totowa, N.J.: Rowman and Littlefield, 1975.

Svevo, Italo. *James Joyce*. Translated by Stanislaus Joyce. New York: New Directions, 1950.

———. *Saggi e pagine sparse*. Milan: Mondadori, 1954.

Svevo Fonda Savio, Letizia. "A Daughter's Tribute." *Modern Fiction Studies* (Spring 1972).

Svevo Fonda Savio, Letizia, and Antonio Fonda Savio. "James Joyce: Two Reminiscences." *JJQ* (Spring 1972).

Symons, Julian. *Makers of the New: The Revolution in Literature 1912–1939*. New York: Random House, 1987.

Tuohy, Frank. *Yeats*. New York: Macmillan Publishing Co., 1976.

Updike, John. "Questions Concerning Giacomo." Review of *Giacomo Joyce*, by James Joyce. *New Yorker*, April 6, 1968.

Veneziani Svevo, Livia. *Memoir of Italo Svevo*. Translated by Isabel Quigly. Marlboro, Vermont: The Marlboro Press, 1990.

———. "Ricordo di James Joyce." Trieste: Tip. Moderna, 1956.

Wilson, Edmund. *Letters on Literature and Politics 1912–1972*. Edited by Elena Wilson. New York: Farrar, Straus, Giroux, 1977.

Ybarra, T. R. *Verdi*. New York: Harcourt, Brace and Company, 1955.

TRIESTE

Alessi, Rino. *Trieste viva*. Rome: Gherardo Casini, 1954.

Antoni, Claudio. "A Note on Trieste in Joyce's Time." *JJQ* (Spring 1972).

Bartoli, Edgardo, and Nicoletta Brunner. *Nonna Trieste*. Trieste: S. D. Modiano, 1970.

Benco, Silvio. Il Piccolo *di Trieste*. Rome: Edizioni Fratelli Treves, 1931.

———. *Trieste e il suo diritto all'Italia*. Trieste: Cappelli, 1952.

Bianchi, O. H., M. Cecovini, M. Fraulini, B. Maier, B. Marin, and F. Todeschini, eds.

Scrittori triestini del Novecento. Trieste: Edizioni Lint, 1968.

Botteri, Guido. *Trieste 1868–1918.* Trieste: Edizioni Lint, 1968.

Cary, Joseph. *A Ghost in Trieste.* Chicago: University of Chicago Press, 1993.

Clough, Shepard B., and Salvatore Saladino. *A History of Modern Italy.* New York: Columbia University Press, 1968.

Coceani, Bruno, and Cesare Pagnini. *Trieste della "belle époque."* Trieste: Libreria "Universitas" Editrice, 1971.

Corsini, Gianfranco, and Giorgio Melchiori, eds. *Scritti italiani.* Milan: Mondadori, 1979.

Crise, Stelio. *And Trieste, Ah Trieste.* Milan: All'Insegna del Pesce d'Oro. 1971.

Dedijer, Vladimir. *The Road to Sarajevo.* New York: Simon and Schuster, 1966.

Dedijer, Vladimir, Ivan Bozic, Sima Cirkovic, and Milorad Ekmecic. *History of Yugoslavia.* New York: McGraw-Hill Book Co., 1974.

Favetta, Bianca Maria. *Il "Verdi": Mito di un teatro.* Trieste: n.p., 1971. Reprint. *La Porta Orientale* (May/June 1971).

Grindrod, Muriel. *Italy.* New York: Frederick A. Praeger, 1968.

Hearder, H., and D. P. Waley. *A Short History of Italy.* Cambridge: Cambridge University Press, 1963.

Hemingway, Ernest. *A Farewell to Arms.* New York: Charles Scribner's Sons, 1957.

Hofmann, Paul. *Cento città.* New York: Henry Holt and Company, 1988.

Jelavich, Charles and Barbara Jelavich. *The Establishment of the Balkan States.* Seattle: University of Washington Press, 1977.

Loseri, Laura Ruaro. *Guida di Trieste.* Trieste: Edizioni Lint, 1985.

———, ed. *Il civico museo del Risorgimento di Trieste.* Trieste: Civici Musei di Storia ed Arte, 1980.

Lyttelton, Adrian. *The Seizure of Power: Fascism in Italy 1919–1929.* Princeton University Press, 1987.

Marek, George R. *The Eagles Die.* New York: Harper and Row, 1974.

Maserati, Ennio. "Il socialismo triestino durante la grande guerra." *Trieste*, November/December 1964.

Morris, Jan. *Destinations.* New York: Oxford University Press, 1980.

Novak, Bogdan C. *Trieste, 1941–1954.* Chicago: University of Chicago Press, 1970.

Pagnini, Cesare. *I giornali di Trieste.* Milan: Centro Studi, 1959.

Pozzetto, Michele. *1912 pianta topografica della città di Trieste.* Reprint. Trieste: Linea Studio, 1988.

Rutteri, Silvio. *Trieste: Spunti dal suo passato.* Trieste: Edizioni Lint, 1968.

———. *Trieste: Storia ed arte tra vie e piazze.* Trieste: Edizioni Lint, 1981.

Schiffrer, Carlo. "Fascisti e militari nell'incendio del Balkan." *Trieste*, May/June 1963.

Seton-Watson, Christopher. *Italy from Liberalism to Fascism.* London: Methuen & Co., 1967.

Silvestri, Claudio. "La missione di Prezioso." *Trieste*, September/October 1960.

Slataper, Scipio. *Scritti politici.* Rome: Alberto Stock, 1925.

Smith, Denis Mack. *Italy.* Ann Arbor: University of Michigan Press, 1969.

———. *Mussolini's Roman Empire.* New York: Viking Press, 1976.

Stock, Mario. *Nel segno di Geremia.* Udine, Italy: Istituto per l'Enciclopedia del Friuli—Venezia Giulia, 1979.

———. *Trieste's Trade with America: The Beginnings.* Trieste: Edizioni Fachin, 1985.

Stuparich, Giani. *Sequenze per Trieste.* Trieste: Edizioni Dello Zibaldone, 1968.

———. *Trieste nei miei ricordi.* Milan: Edizioni Garzanti, 1948.

Tamaro, Attilio. *Storia di Trieste.* 2 vols. Trieste: Edizioni Lint, 1976.

Tapié, Victor L. *The Rise and Fall of the Habsburg Monarchy.* Translated by Stephen Hardman. New York: Praeger Publishers, 1971.

Trevelyan, Janet Penrose. *A Short History of the Italian People*. New York: Pitman Publishing Co., 1956.

Vaglio, Carla Marengo. "Trieste as a Linguistic Melting-Pot." *La Revue des Lettres Modernes* (*James Joyce*). 1994.

Valiani, Leo. *The End of Austria-Hungary*. New York: Alfred A. Knopf, 1972.

Valussi, Giorgio. *Le regioni d'Italia: Friuli—Venezia Giulia*. Vol. 5. Turin: Tipografia Sociale Torinese, 1961.

Zampaglione, Gerardo. *Italy*. New York: Frederick A. Praeger, 1956.

Index

About the Author

PETER HARTSHORN is an English Instructor at Showa Institute in Boston.

ISBN 0-313-30252-9

HARDCOVER BAR CODE